# Contents

## CHAPTER 2: SETTING NORMS FOR THE VIRTUAL MATH CLASSROOM 35

## CHAPTER 3: INCORPORATING MANIPULATIVES IN THE VIRTUAL MATH CLASSROOM 57

Visit www.theresawills.com for more resources.

# Preface

*Teaching mathematics at a distance is like raising a child.*

When I had my first child, I read and watched everything I could find about raising a baby. I had a lot to learn considering that I had never yet changed a diaper. I gathered all of the necessary equipment, such as crib, stroller, changing table, and clothes, and I collected the recommended *What to Expect* books and felt empowered with information. Then the unexpected happened. My baby, and every baby for that matter, did not fit the mold of the "average baby." Sure, the books contained lots of great information, but how could I possibly use it if my baby was different? My baby was hungry all the time, but the books said to feed every three hours. My baby loved to be in noisy rooms, but the books said babies should be in quiet places or listen to calming music. In addition to the inconsistencies in the books, it seemed like everyone I knew had advice. There was advice on the introduction of solid foods, sleep training, potty training, and even early academics. Everyone claimed that their advice was the best, and if I just followed the prescribed steps, it would resolve all my parenting questions. It didn't. This is how most teachers feel with online learning. Even after getting the equipment and books, their situations don't fit the mold.

Seventeen months after my first child was born, my second child entered the world. That's right, not only did I not have it figured out with my first, I was ready to have another go with a second. But hey, with two kids under two, I would at least remember what worked and what didn't, so I had an advantage. The only thing was, my kids couldn't be any more different. My son was an early riser, and his little sister was a night owl. My son was full of energy around other kids, my daughter took naps at play dates. My son tipped the scales at every doctor's checkup, and my daughter needed to have extra calories. The only thing that was consistent was that there was still abundant advice from other parents (and nonparents). Again, each piece of advice claimed to be the best, and if I just followed the prescribed steps, it would resolve all my parenting questions. It didn't. This is how many teachers feel about online learning at the start of another school year. What worked last year just doesn't work this year.

But, I got better. I was figuring it all out. And it wasn't because I *followed* anyone's advice, it was because I was *learning about* everyone's advice. I started to collect pieces of advice and keep them tucked away in nice little compartments of my growing parental brain. I stopped thinking of it as advice for my babies, and instead I thought of it as anecdotal stories. These were simply stories about another baby—the things that worked and didn't work for that child. I stopped trying to implement *their* way, because my baby was not *their* baby.

After collecting these stories, I learned the art of picking and choosing. When it was time to begin sleep training, I had heard about 20 different techniques and tricks. I had also learned that there would be no one-size-fits-all model. Instead, I picked a few things that I liked from different techniques and created the "Wills Method 1.0" technique. After implementing that for a bit, I altered my formula to create the "Wills Method 2.0." After some more practice, I altered it again and found a winner—it was the "Wills Method 3.0," and it consisted of elements of 12 different techniques, and even an invented technique. It was perfect for my baby . . . at least most nights.

Why is teaching mathematics at a distance like raising a child?

Teaching online is like raising a child because you will find that everyone has advice for you on what works and what doesn't work. But anyone who has worked in education knows that there is no one-size-fits-all technique. Teaching is a human and social endeavor and it is all about context and meeting all students' needs. What combination of ideas works best for my students will likely look a little different from what works for your students. The trick, however, is to stop considering it advice and begin thinking of it as anecdotal stories. Line the stories up on a bookshelf in your thoughts, and open them to get ideas, not prescribed recipes. There is no magic formula. Often, when people tell a story, they are generalizing their experiences over many instances. People generalize advice on potty training and on virtual manipulatives. When you are ready to implement the use of virtual manipulatives (or potty training), go back to their story, not their advice, and pick and choose what will work for you, your students, and your remote classroom.

Once you think you have the hang of this online teaching, you might have a second class (or second child) and learn that one model doesn't always translate to this new class. However, if you keep these stories at your fingertips, you will be able to pick and choose to create a recipe that works for this new class.

## What Will You Get Out of This Book?

This book showcases learner-centered guidance for high-quality mathematics learning that doesn't compromise pedagogy because of the change in venue. The goal of this book is to present you with ideas for practice and stories of teachers who have reimagined their online class while using familiar pedagogies from their face-to-face setting. These ideas will inspire you to consider how you will translate your mathematics class, whether you are working with a wide-eyed group of kindergartners or young adults who are ready to begin their careers in this new digital age. It will help you build that mental library and empower you to learn and choose and try, and learn and choose and try some more. This book contains many aspects of teaching mathematics, from how to build community to teaching problem solving, from whole-class lessons to partner activities, from homework to assessment, all while acknowledging real challenges and benefits of using technology to teach in a remote setting. There are many tips and suggestions that have worked for people in the past, including my own experiences teaching online for over 10 years, but this is not advice, it's not a formula.

When you come across something that feels like it fits for you and your situation, ask yourself why it fits. What are the structures, norms, and routines that allow it to fit nicely? When you find something that seems impractical, ask yourself why. What structures, norms, and routines would you need to have in place to make it more practical for you?

## How This Book Is Organized

Part I of this book covers the most critical points about *preparing* to teach remotely. This includes the purpose of technology and considerations of equity in terms of access to and use of technology, how your students interact with technology, and the role of technology in how you facilitate activities. It defines commonly used terms and applications as you consider your role as an educator in the remote classroom. Some of this may feel very generalized, but is important to consider if you're teaching *any* content online, just as you would if you were teaching face-to-face. This part of the book also shares a variety of online structures for presenting mathematics and how to select the appropriate structures for your mathematics goals. You will reflect on important questions that require you to consider your mathematics pedagogy and how to access these great teaching skills in online learning. You will learn how to set up classroom norms for safety and responsibility, and how to hold students accountable for appropriate behavior in the virtual environment. You will also learn about virtual manipulatives, how to find them, and how to give your students more agency in showing their thinking using these tools.

Part II of this book is all about the *implementation* of remote mathematics instruction. It shares a variety of practical strategies that you can implement in your virtual classroom regardless of whether you are new to online instruction or a seasoned veteran. You will become immersed in the stories of many teachers and how they translated their teaching to an online environment teaching mathematics, using current research and best practices around high-quality mathematics instruction to engage students in mathematical discourse, problem solving, and making mathematical connections. You will find comfort in the familiarity of the pedagogies such as rich tasks, whole-group math discourse, stations, games, and building communities of learners.

Part III tackles challenging aspects of teaching in the virtual classroom, such as homework and assessment and how to feel a sense of control even when students are completing assignments in a remote setting. As you read the stories of teachers who implement homework and assessments differently, you will hopefully feel inspired to consider the affordances of technology and how to harness all the advantages of the remote setting with honesty and integrity.

Just remember, there is no magical formula to remote teaching. You have to pick and choose the strategies and the approach that will work best for you. If you are just beginning your journey teaching remotely—or if you have begun to try and are looking to expand your practice—this book specifically identifies easy-to-implement routines, lesson structures, and group dynamics that you can use right away. If you are a seasoned online teacher, you will enjoy the strategies that build rich collaboration, interaction, and discussion among students as you release ownership and increase student agency. There is something here for everyone. And just like the teachers whose stories you will read in this book, when you are feeling confident about your online teaching pedagogy, remember to share *your* story with your colleagues and peers. We are all better together.

# Acknowledgments

Thank you to all the educators who have influenced this book.

Thank you to the incredible community of math educators at George Mason University. Margaret Hjalmarson, Courtney Baker, Jennifer Suh, and Toya Frank, thank you for believing in my vision of an online math class that didn't compromise pedagogy. Special thanks to Laura Bitto, Kimberly Morrow-Leong, and Deb Crawford, who were with me side by side, and slide by slide, in creating these routines.

Thank you, Vickie Inge, for the introduction to synchronous online instruction.

Thank you to Dennis McLoughlin and Molly Rawding for giving me confidence in making mistakes, and then showcasing those mistakes, unapologetically, to the world.

To my kids, Evan and Josephine, when the world shut down you were resilient and always supported me in writing this book and helping teachers, even when that meant less playtime. To my husband, Mike, for the coffee dates and daily walks where you listened to me talk about the development of the book.

Finally, a special acknowledgment to Corwin, Erin Null, Jessica Vidal, and Sara Johnson for encouraging me to write this book and get the message out.

## Publisher's Acknowledgments

Corwin gratefully acknowledges the contributions of the following contributors:

Natalie Crist
Coordinator of Elementary Mathematics
Baltimore County Public Schools
Baltimore, MD

Shelley Dickson
District Math Specialist
Fayette County Public Schools
Lexington, KY

Kevin Dykema
Eighth-Grade Math Teacher
Mattawan Middle School
Mattawan, MI

Anna Maria Graf
Supervisor of Curriculum & Instruction
Freehold, NJ

Kimberly Morrow-Leong
Adjunct Instructor
George Mason University
Fairfax, VA

Michael D. Steele
Professor of Mathematics Education
University of Wisconsin–Milwaukee
Milwaukee, WI

# About the Author

**Theresa Wills, PhD**, is an assistant professor of mathematics education in the School of Education at George Mason University, where she works with inservice mathematics specialists and preservice elementary and secondary teachers. Theresa has taught synchronous online classes and webinars since 2010 and researches teaching practices that are adaptable to the online environment. She is a former classroom teacher and math coach who still volunteers weekly in K–12 classrooms.

# INTRODUCTION

What is good mathematics instruction? My first year teaching, I thought it was about teaching all 150 standards, in a nicely structured, step-by-step way, so that my students were prepared for the next grade. Luckily, I had a math coach who asked me, "Is the goal of your lesson to teach arithmetic or mathematics?" That has always stuck with me. She coached me that year to view mathematics as the art of problem solving. It goes so far beyond correctly operating on numbers and arriving at a correct answer. It is an activity that involves thinking, reasoning, discussing, justifying, and proving. She coached me to understand that, through this problem-solving lens, I could teach those 150 standards, but in ways that were not so scaffolded, not so obvious, and not so boring. If you've picked up this book, you likely already know all of this. The danger, of course, is that in moving instruction to a remote setting, we have to be sure that our primary goal is to stay true to what mathematics is really about and not reduce it to teaching arithmetic.

# What Is Good Mathematics Instruction?

Before we can possibly consider what rich mathematics instruction looks like when done remotely or online, we first have to ensure a common understanding of what rich mathematics instruction is, period. At its core, it is about developing mathematicians—people who see patterns, are curious about those patterns, and wonder if there is order to those patterns. Mathematicians think flexibly and creatively to determine solutions to questions. When their solution is proven incorrect or only works for a subset of situations, they become engrossed in determining why and how and work tirelessly thinking about the problem for long periods of time. Frustrations come and go, but are short-lived, and we call those "productive struggle." There is nothing like the joy of working in the productive struggle zone and then discovering something new. It brings a sense of euphoria to the mathematician and gives them the motivation to continue their quest of finding patterns in their world, and making sense of those patterns.

How can we as educators empower every student to feel like a mathematician? What are the tenets of this rich instruction that we can carry from the face-to-face world into the realm of distance learning? There are a number of fundamental non-negotiables that research agrees encompass rich mathematics instruction, regardless of the venue in which it occurs. From the student mathematician's point of view, these non-negotiables include the five process standards—more recently articulated in eight numbered standards for mathematical practice (SFMPs)—that characterize "doing" mathematics, and from the educator's point of view, these non-negotiables include the eight Mathematical Teaching Practices (MTPs) (see Figure i.1 on the facing page).

Another non-negotiable in rich mathematics teaching is attention to access and equity. The National Council of Teachers of Mathematics (NCTM, 2014a) describes access and equity in mathematics education in their position statement as follows:

> Creating, supporting, and sustaining a culture of access and equity require being responsive to students' backgrounds, experiences, cultural perspectives, traditions, and knowledge when designing and implementing a mathematics program and assessing its effectiveness. Acknowledging and addressing factors that contribute to

*differential outcomes among groups of students are critical to ensuring that all students routinely have opportunities to experience high-quality mathematics instruction, learn challenging mathematics content, and receive the support necessary to be successful. Addressing equity and access includes both ensuring that all students attain mathematics proficiency and increasing the numbers of students from all racial, ethnic, linguistic, gender, and socioeconomic groups who attain the highest levels of mathematics achievement.*

Figure i.1

# Rich Mathematics Instruction as Defined by NCTM's Process and Practice Standards and the Eight Mathematical Teaching Practices

| NCTM PROCESS AND PRACTICE STANDARDS | MATHEMATICAL TEACHING PRACTICES |
|---|---|
| • **Problem Solving**<br><br>**SFMP 1.** Make sense of problems and persevere in solving them.<br><br>**SFMP 5.** Use appropriate tools strategically.<br><br>• **Reasoning and Proof**<br><br>**SFMP 2.** Reason abstractly and quantitatively.<br><br>**SFMP 3.** Construct viable arguments and critique the reasoning of others.<br><br>**SFMP 8.** Look for and express regularity in repeated reasoning.<br><br>• **Communications**<br><br>**SFMP 3.** Construct viable arguments and critique the reasoning of others.<br><br>• **Connections**<br><br>**SFMP 6.** Attend to precision.<br><br>**SFMP 7.** Look for and make use of structure.<br><br>• **Representations**<br><br>**SFMP 4.** Model with mathematics. | 1. Establish mathematics goals to focus learning.<br><br>2. Implement tasks that promote reasoning and problem solving.<br><br>3. Use and connect mathematical representations.<br><br>4. Facilitate meaningful mathematical discourse.<br><br>5. Pose purposeful questions.<br><br>6. Build procedural fluency from conceptual understanding.<br><br>7. Support productive struggle in learning mathematics.<br><br>8. Elicit and use evidence of student thinking. |

*Source:* Adapted from *Principles and standards for school mathematics* (NCTM, 2000), Common Core State Standards for Mathematics (National Governors Association Center for Best Practices and Council of Chief State School Officers, 2010), and *Principles to actions: Ensuring mathematical success for all* (NCTM, 2014).

The National Council of Supervisors of Mathematics (NCSM) and TODOS: Mathematics for All (2016) add to this statement that

> *a social justice stance interrogates and challenges*
> *the roles power, privilege, and oppression play*
> *in the current unjust system of mathematics*
> *education—and in society as a whole.*

With the transition to remote learning comes another lens for considering equity and access, and that is the technology that we use to deliver instruction. Therefore, it is critical that we consider the International Society for Technology in Education (ISTE, n.d.) essential condition: "Robust and reliable access to current and emerging technologies and digital resources, with connectivity for all students, including those with special needs, teachers, staff, and school leaders."

The guidance, suggestions, and activities in this book deliberately pay heed to and are in service of these fundamentals of good mathematics instruction.

## What Does Rich Mathematics Instruction Look Like?

Einstein is known for the following statement: "If I had an hour to solve a problem, I'd spend 55 minutes thinking about the problem and five minutes thinking about solutions." Polya (1945) gives us timeless advice from almost a century ago that good teachers don't tell students the mathematics, they ask it. But how is this possible when we have so many standards to teach in a year? By following the principles and practices shown in Figure i.1.

Let's look at an example from both the teacher's point of view and the student's point of view. Imagine that you are teaching a lesson on area. This example explores the area of a triangle, but as you read this, consider the learning progression of this big idea and how it applies to your grade-level content. In elementary school, students count the number of squares in a rectangular array, middle schoolers use formulas to find the area of 2-D figures, and calculus students calculate the area under a curve. In this example, Miss Cimorelli incorporates the math teaching practices in her lesson about the area of a triangle.

| | |
|---|---|
| **Establish mathematical goals to focus the lesson. (MTP 1)** | **Goal:** Students will explore relationships between triangles and rectangles in order to determine the formula for area of a triangle. |
| **Implement tasks that promote reasoning and problem solving. (MTP 2)** | She decided to introduce a rich task that will motivate students to think flexibly as they find relationships between rectangles and triangles. The task required students to consider different cake pans for a cake company to create a triangular cake.<br><br>This task is open-ended and allows for every student to access the task, regardless of background knowledge of the area of triangles and rectangles. For example, she knew from her preassessment that Kate has very little background knowledge on calculating area of shapes, but she is very skilled at visualizing geometric shapes. Zach is in many ways opposite in that he is quick to solve area problems using standard formulas, but rarely uses geometric models to explain his reasoning. |
| **Support productive struggle in learning mathematics. (MTP 7)** | Miss Cimorelli noticed that Zach is frustrated because he can only imagine the cakes cut in one direction, diagonally, and isn't motivated to find other ways. She asked Zach purposeful questions to encourage him to think with curiosity.<br><br>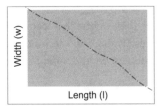 |
| **Pose purposeful questions. (MTP 5)** | Miss Cimorelli knew that Zach was interested in the solution, but he needed to learn how to justify his reasoning and to justify it in multiple ways. To do this, she used purposeful questioning to guide him, while not overscaffolding.<br><br>**Miss Cimorelli:** Zach, how did you find this example?<br><br>**Zach:** I knew the formula and this is how you make it half.<br><br>**Miss Cimorelli:** Are there other ways of making $\frac{1}{2}$?<br><br>**Zach:** Yeah, but I don't know how.<br><br>**Miss Cimorelli:** Since the bakers can use icing as glue, this lets us make as many cuts as we want. What other ways could you cut the rectangle and rearrange the pieces to make triangles? |

*(Continued)*

(Continued)

| | |
|---|---|
| | **Zach:** Ohhh, I guess there are lots of ways.<br><br>Zach begins another model:<br><br>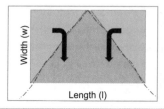 |
| **Use evidence of student thinking. (MTP 8)** | In preparing for the whole-class discussion, Miss Cimorelli selected three student samples. While there were additional representations available, she knew that by selecting only a few, she could facilitate a deeper conversation about the connections between these three representations.<br><br>**Zach's Thinking**    **Paige's Thinking**    **Han's Thinking**<br><br>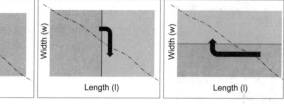 |
| **Facilitate meaningful mathematical discourse. (MTP 4)** | In the vignette that follows, Miss Cimorelli facilitated a whole-class discussion. She knew the importance of asking questions that support student understanding and sense-making. |
| **Use and connect mathematical representations. (MTP 3)** | Miss Cimorelli used questions that required students to compare the three models in order to connect the mathematical representations.<br><br>**Miss Cimorelli:** Zach, you mentioned that you knew the formula for area of a triangle. How did that help you to make the cuts on the cake?<br><br>**Zach:** Well, I knew one-half times length times width, so I just cut it in half and you can see that there are two triangles that are exactly the same. *(Zach flipped the other triangle so that it lies on top.)*<br><br>**Miss Cimorelli:** Paige, you found another way of looking at one-half. Can you explain your way to us?<br><br>**Paige:** I cut the rectangle in half first, then showed it was the same as Zach's by flipping the top triangle to cover the space in the lighter triangle. This shows that the area of half of my rectangle is the same as the area of Zach's triangle.<br><br>**Miss Cimorelli:** What do these two have in common? |

| | |
|---|---|
| | **DeMarco:** They are both talking about half of the rectangle is all you need to make that triangle. |
| | **Miss Cimorelli:** Who can rephrase DeMarco and tell us more? |
| | **Yessica:** He's right, they are both half, it just depends when you do the half part. In Zach's, he cut it in half at the beginning and made two same triangles, but Paige cut the rectangle in half and then showed that you can see the same triangle with just that much cake. |
| | **Miss Cimorelli:** Han, can you show us your design? |
| | **Han:** It's the same as Paige, I just cut it sideways. |
| | **Miss Cimorelli:** Han said it was the same as Paige. Who can tell us what is the same and what is different? |
| | **Melanie:** They both used less cake. It's like the cake pan can be half the size and then you move a little chunk of cake to make the triangle, but Zach's has two triangles so it's twice as much cake. |
| | **Miss Cimorelli:** Let's reconsider that formula $\frac{1}{2}(l \times w)$. What does that mean in each situation? |
| | **Zach:** So the length times width is how you find the area of a rectangle, and I just took half. |
| | **Melanie:** But Paige started with just half, half the length and Han started with half the width. So it's like $(\frac{1}{2} \times l) \times w$ or $l \times (\frac{1}{2} \times w)$. |
| | **Zach:** But those formulas are all the same. |
| | **Miss Cimorelli:** Indeed, the expressions are equal to one another, but the visuals help us to see how they are equal. For tonight's homework, you are going to draw visuals as you practice the formula. |
| **Build procedural fluency from conceptual understanding. (MTP 6)** | Miss Cimorelli assigned students additional practice using one of the three versions of the formula that they discussed in class. As students practiced using the formulas, they were practicing procedural fluency that is based not on a series of letters and numbers, but on the conceptual understanding of $\frac{1}{2}$ that they explored in class. |

Let's consider this same task from the student's point of view using the NCTM process standards.

| | |
|---|---|
| **Problem Solving** | Students were tasked with exploring a real-world situation—triangular cakes and the way that bakers could cut the cakes to create triangular pieces. They had many tools available, including paper, cake pans, rulers, scissors, and pencils. The problem was open-ended enough to support various ideas, giving each student an opportunity to problem-solve independently, in small groups, and in the whole group. |

*(Continued)*

(Continued)

| Reasoning and Proof | Students explored the conceptual understanding behind the abstract representation, or formula, of the area of a triangle and its relationship to $\frac{1}{2}$ of a rectangle with similar length and width measurements. Through exploration, students were able to reason through various examples to determine how the $\frac{1}{2}$ was preserved in the model and formula. |
|---|---|
| Communication | Students communicated in their small groups and whole groups as they explored the designs that peers presented. Since students had various background knowledge, they needed to communicate clearly how their visual model matched the abstract model, or formula, or how their visual model matched another student's visual model. |
| Connections | During the whole-group discussion, students found connections between the three visual representations and three ways of interpreting the abstract formula. They found similarities (all had $\frac{1}{2}$) and differences (the half was subdivided in different ways) between the three visual models in order to make the generalization that the area of a triangle is $\frac{1}{2}$ that of the rectangular cake pan. |
| Representations | Students were encouraged to create many representations. There were several ways that a rectangle could be cut into two equal triangles, and each representation could be compared to others in order to make generalizations about the abstract representation or formula. |

## INSTRUCTIONAL MOVES THAT SUPPORT RICH INSTRUCTION

Ensuring rich mathematics instruction doesn't just happen by magic. It is made up of a thousand smaller choices and micro moves that you make every day to make it a reality, such as the following:

- **Setting, practicing, and reinforcing clear norms:** Teaching mathematics begins with setting up a space to learn. Both physical spaces, such as desks or carpet spots, and social norms are needed in order to create a classroom environment that is inclusive, open to mistakes, and rich with student discourse, all while maintaining a structured and orderly environment. This setup is fundamental to classroom management, and these physical and social spaces need to be identified and practiced in the remote setting so that students are responsible and accountable for learning mathematics.

- **Connecting mathematical representations:** Teaching mathematics is so much more than showing students how to solve an equation; it is about visualizing, connecting, and modeling problems. An abundance of tools and manipulatives are available to students in face-to-face classrooms that support their conceptual understanding. As students model patterns with manipulatives, they are better able to transfer those models into numbers, and then into generalizations and rules. This crucial transition is needed in the remote classroom and can be accessed using virtual manipulatives as well as household items.

- **Offering daily structure:** Mathematics classrooms have various structures that purposefully engage students in short routines to multiday projects, low to high levels of cognitive demand, and new-to-review concepts. A skillful teacher balances the needs of their learners to include daily routines, whole-class tasks, small-group guided instruction, games, projects, assessments, and homework. These same structures are needed in the remote classroom. Through the use of multiple virtual modalities, students can speak and listen to each other, show and view representations, and even play games together.

- **Making student thinking visible:** When teachers use student work as evidence of understanding, it is required that the teacher first *see* the student's work. In the face-to-face classroom, this is seen when the teacher walks around the classroom and observes students building models, drawing pictures, talking with a partner, writing equations, and even making facial expressions. This observation is far more skilled than ensuring that students are on task; it incorporates many elements of formative assessment and is just as vital in the remote classroom. Many programs and applications bridge the physical distance between teacher and student and provide opportunities for students to upload video and images live, and in real time, so that teachers can watch the learning unfold in its raw, rough-draft form.

- **Practicing meaningful formative and summative assessment:** Teaching mathematics is a never-ending progression of concepts and ideas based on prior mathematical knowledge. Great teachers preassess this knowledge from each student and differentiate activities and lessons to guide students as they progress to new understanding. Along the way, the teacher must assess the students' understanding in order to determine the next set of activities and lessons. This constant assessment and planning is at the heart of great teaching, and it goes far beyond any multiple-choice test. This need for assessment is just as important in the remote classroom, but students have much more agency in how they complete the assessment. Gone are the days of solving simple equations with one-number answers because the technology gives students this access at their fingertips. Gone are the days of every student having the same test because of the immediate transfer speeds over social media. Assessments in the remote classroom use robust, problem-oriented situations that require students to apply basic number sense to rich situations.

# Translating Rich Instruction to a Virtual Setting

It can seem daunting to reimagine how the practices, routines, and activities that you have mastered in your face-to-face teaching might work in an online environment. First, we have to think about the transition process and the role technology plays, and then we can have a clearer sense of what rich online math instruction looks like.

## USING TECHNOLOGY TO TRANSLATE MATH TO DISTANCE LEARNING

The first step to reimagining instruction to a remote setting is to think through what technology does and doesn't allow us to do. I use the Substitution, Augmentation, Modification, Redefinition (SAMR) model (Puentedura, 2013) when considering how to reimagine a structure. The SAMR model is a framework that identifies *how* technology is used in comparison to *how* the assignment was accomplished without the technology. This framework uses a continuum from Substitution—meaning that the technology didn't bring anything new to the assignment, just a difference in the modality by which it is submitted or completed—to Redefinition—meaning that the assignment could not have been imagined without the tools offered by the technology. This is a useful framework when considering how to transition assignments from the face-to-face setting to the online setting. Each level of the model defines the level of technology integration (see Figure i.2).

Consider the activity of eliciting background knowledge through the Brain Dump strategy in a face-to-face class. The teacher begins by asking all students what they know about angles and triangles, for example. Students raise their hands and quickly respond with many ideas as the teacher writes them down on the whiteboard. Once the ideas are listed, the teacher then instructs students to work together in small groups to sort the ideas into various categories of their choosing in order to make a web diagram about what they know about triangles. At several times throughout the unit, the students will return to their web diagram and update it. At times, the updates will only need to include written additions, crossing out previous connections and revising them, or complete revisions on new paper. Finally, at the end of the unit, the groups present their web diagrams and engage in a whole-group conversation about how the web diagrams show their understanding of the unit. This activity leverages the advantages of prior knowledge, group work, visual representations, connections between mathematical ideas, whole-group discussion, and revisions. But how do you implement those in a remote classroom, and how can the SAMR model support you in reimagining this activity to be *better* than what is possible in the face-to-face class? Let's structure the transition.

Figure i.2

## Sample Activity Using the SAMR Model

| SUBSTITUTION | AUGMENTATION | MODIFICATION | REDEFINITION |
|---|---|---|---|
| Uses technology to simply substitute an activity or assignment without changing its function | Uses technology to substitute an activity or assignment but with some functional improvement | Uses technology to make the task better than it could have been accomplished without technology | Uses technology in a way that the task simply could not be accomplished without the technology |

*(Continued)*

(Continued)

| SUBSTITUTION | AUGMENTATION | MODIFICATION | REDEFINITION |
|---|---|---|---|
| Students raise their virtual hand and the teacher uses a document camera to record all the various ideas. Then the students are sent to breakout rooms to create their web diagram using the interactive whiteboard, which allows all students to use a virtual marker and create their diagram. | Students interact using the previous step, but instead of using an interactive whiteboard, they create their web diagram using interactive slides where they can use options like copy/ paste to make the web diagram process more efficient. Throughout the unit, students can simply move terms around the slide rather than creating a new slide. | The students do not raise a hand but rather type directly on the shared slide. The teacher gives enough time for students to all type a few ideas. Then the students are sent to breakout rooms with a duplicate of the previous slide as they create the web diagram on their own slide. Simultaneously, they can see the web diagrams of other groups as they evolve in real time. The teacher can also view these web diagrams on the shared slides even when in different breakout rooms.<br><br>Throughout the unit, students and teachers can view the history of the web diagram to determine how it changed over the course of the unit. | Students interact using the previous step but also elicit comments from around the world by uploading their web diagram to social media. Each time they revise their web diagram, they must attend to the comments posted by other users by either responding to the comments or using the comment in the revision. When the final web diagram is complete, they conduct a live YouTube video and use emojis and comments in real time to edit their presentation. |
| There is no functional change. The physical hands are virtual hands, the whiteboard is a virtual whiteboard, and the small groups still discuss and draw using microphones and a virtual whiteboard. | There is little functional change that leads to efficient revisions. Tools such as copy and paste, ability to move objects rather than rewriting them, and duplicate objects create an efficient experience while maintaining the same fundamental activity. | Technology is in the forefront, and this task relies on the technology in order to be implemented. Students are no longer waiting their turn to add to the brain dump, they are all simultaneously adding. Small groups are no longer working in isolation, they are | This task is completely redefined in the public space. Social media and live video presentations give students the opportunity to explain their product with a variety of perspectives, not just those of students and teachers at their school or in their community. |

| SUBSTITUTION | AUGMENTATION | MODIFICATION | REDEFINITION |
| --- | --- | --- | --- |
| | | able to view the updated progress of all other groups in the class. This task is completely modified to give more students a voice. | |

Let's look at a high school geometry example. Consider the proof that the sum of all angles in a triangle is 180 degrees. In a typical face-to-face classroom, students might cut out a triangle, rip off the corners, and realign them to show that they create a straight line, which equals 180 degrees. If the entire class of students completes this activity, the whole class might observe 20 to 30 examples, and even a few nonexamples due to human inaccuracies. This can lead them to developing a proof.

This same activity can be done online, and we can use the SAMR framework to consider *how* the technology is used. The **Substitution** level defines activities that use technology but have no functional change. For example, students can still do the paper-ripping activity, take a snapshot of the product, and upload it to a shared space so that all students can view the 20 to 30 triangle examples. This is classified as substitution because the transition to online learning has no functional change, just the modality by which it is presented.

The **Augmentation** level defines activities that go beyond the Substitution level to add functional change. For example, the ability to copy and paste an image of a triangle in order to create multiple perfectly congruent shapes (without human error) allows the exploration of the activity to become more exact. The copy/paste feature is a great improvement, but it doesn't ultimately change the task.

The **Modification** level defines activities that use technology for significant task redesign. For example, when students explore triangles using geometry software (Geogebra, Geometers sketchpad, or CAD), they can twist, turn, flip, invert, and modify the triangle into infinite possibilities while viewing the change of the angles and consistent sum. This technology gives them the opportunity to view every single possibility imaginable. This provides a significant task redesign.

The **Redefinition** level defines activities that simply cannot be implemented without technology. For example, after geometry students explore the relationship between triangles and the sum of angles, they create a presentation and present it live on YouTube, where other high school students from around the world watch, comment, and use emojis to respond in real time. The presenters use this information to answer questions in real time and clarify any misconceptions. This peer interaction with students around the world offers a unique task redesign that still focuses on the initial goals of the task: that students can explore the relationship between triangles and the sum of their angles and be able to use reasoning to create a proof.

## REIMAGINING RICH MATHEMATICS INSTRUCTION ONLINE

With the SAMR model in mind, let's briefly take a look at some initial concrete ways that rich mathematics instruction based on fundamental process or practice standards can look when conducted at a distance (see Figure i.3).

Figure i.3

## Sample Ideas for Reimagining Math Instruction at a Distance

| **Problem Solving**: Students should explore meaningful and relatable problems using a variety of strategies to solve and self-assess their understanding of mathematical ideas. ||
| --- | --- |
| **FAMILIAR USE IN A FACE-TO-FACE CLASSROOM** | **REIMAGINED USE IN AN ONLINE CLASSROOM** |
| • Work independently while recording their thinking on paper. | • Students can turn off sound and microphones to incorporate quiet independent work time. |
| • Problem-solve in small groups to develop strategies. Notebooks are usually used and shown to group members to convey ideas. | • Use interactive slides to share ideas to other groupmates. Students can copy/paste peers' ideas to modify while preserving original strategy. |
| • After the math task discussion, the student can self-assess their understanding of the problem, solutions, and strategies by comparing their notes to those presented. | • Students can, in the moment, self-assess their strategies as they view other groupmates or entirely different groups developing strategies on interactive slides. |

**Reasoning and Proof**: Students should explore the "why" to solutions, make conjectures, and use logical reasoning to determine if an argument is logical by creating examples and nonexamples.

| FAMILIAR USE IN A FACE-TO FACE-CLASSROOM | REIMAGINED USE IN AN ONLINE CLASSROOM |
| --- | --- |
| • Students share their reasoning with classmates through partner work and whole-group discussions. | • Students can efficiently make duplicate copies of mathematical ideas in order to display patterns that evolve into generalizations. |
| • Students can cooperate as a class to create multiple examples and nonexamples to determine generalizations that lead to proofs. | • Students can use mathematical software to explore infinite possibilities with the click of a button. |

**Communication**: Students should discuss mathematical ideas, strategies, examples, and nonexamples using both familiar and mathematical language as a way to examine their thinking.

| FAMILIAR USE IN A FACE-TO-FACE CLASSROOM | REIMAGINED USE IN AN ONLINE CLASSROOM |
| --- | --- |
| • Partner-share, small-group, and whole-group discussions are facilitated by talking, listening, pointing, visuals, and facial expressions. | • The teacher can facilitate breakout rooms with partners or small groups of students who discuss their ideas through multiple modalities: voice, video, chat, and interactive slides. |
| • Students take turns speaking. | • All students can have a voice simultaneously through interactive slides and chat box while one person is speaking. |

**Connections**: Students should explore connections between problems solved in the math classroom with prior experience and problems in their world. They should also explore how mathematical ideas are connected to one another through various notations, strategies, and representations.

| FAMILIAR USE IN A FACE-TO-FACE CLASSROOM | REIMAGINED USE IN AN ONLINE CLASSROOM |
| --- | --- |
| • Teachers prepare images or videos of real-world situations to build prior knowledge. | • Students provide images (copy/pasted into interactive slides) of prior knowledge and real-world experiences. |
| • Students take turns making connections orally during whole-group discussion. | • Students respond through multiple modalities to make connections and can copy/paste strategies next to one another. |

*(Continued)*

(Continued)

Representation: Students should explore problems that use and create mathematical models and representations and explore relationships as they move from one representation to another.

| FAMILIAR USE IN A FACE-TO-FACE CLASSROOM | REIMAGINED USE IN AN ONLINE CLASSROOM |
|---|---|
| • Handheld manipulatives such as pattern blocks, snap cubes, and counters | • Household manipulatives such as buttons, cereal, and blocks<br><br>• Virtual manipulatives<br><br>• Collaborative manipulatives used in interactive slides |
| • Drawings in notebooks | • Drawings in notebooks and uploaded onto interactive slides where other students can copy and edit the drawings |
| • Drawings on posters or chalkboard | • Snapshots of notebook drawings or video of notebook entry shared to the class |
| • Algorithms and procedures recorded step by step, handwritten in a notebook | • Algorithms and procedures annotated through a prerecorded video<br><br>• Algorithms and procedures recorded step by step, handwritten in a notebook, and uploaded via image snapshot<br><br>• Equation notation software used to digitize the steps |
| • Tables and graphs in calculators | • Collaborative data input and manipulation using interactive spreadsheets<br><br>• Screenshots of tables and graphs created in virtual manipulatives |

The goal of this book is to give you situations that require you to think about good mathematics teaching and learning and purposeful transitions to remote instruction. You will learn the purposeful moves that teachers consider when making the transition, and how they keep mathematics at the heart as they reflect and reimagine their remote instruction.

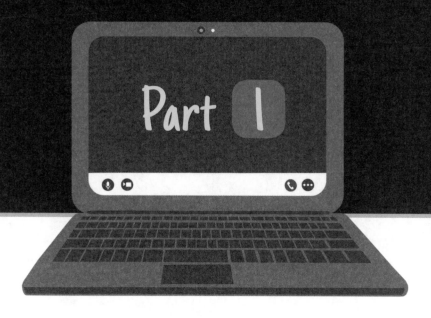

# GETTING READY

Just as with face-to-face teaching, a major component of teaching math online is planning. Preparedness comes in many forms. From the remote classroom structures and expectations and norms you set, to how you build relationships with your students and how they build relationships with each other, to how you actually plan and implement your math lessons, the investment of time you put in up front should be purposeful and efficient.

Part I of this book will orient you in your planning process as you move from the familiar face-to-face setting of the classroom to a distance learning setting, whether synchronous or asynchronous. The goal is to help you get ready to make this transition whether you start the year this way, or there is a midyear shift. Alternatively, you may be in a hybrid learning situation, in which case this book will guide you in the distance learning portion of your planning. Here you will find guidance on how to keep kids engaged, how to socially and emotionally care for them, and what kinds of mathematical tasks you can plan to make the most of the learning environment. You'll have an opportunity to consider how technology can help replicate or replace concrete learning, and how to anticipate and plan to respond to student thinking.

+ chapter

**1**

# SETTING THE STAGE FOR THE VIRTUAL MATH CLASSROOM

Welcome to the adventure of learning to teach mathematics remotely! Whether you are new to virtual instruction or a veteran, it is important to anticipate how your lessons will unfold differently in the online environment. This chapter will give you an overview of technologies and the tools out there. You will learn both the fundamental tools and how to anticipate student interaction, collaboration, and engagement. There are a plethora of tools available, and while subtle differences might exist, this chapter explores the fundamental purpose of the tool and how to leverage the affordances it offers you in online learning.

# Instructional Delivery

As we begin our journey together, it is important that we have a common definition of three terms to describe instructional delivery in an online learning environment that will be used throughout this book: synchronous, asynchronous, and blended.

**Synchronous:**
Online instruction when students learn live, in real time

**Synchronous:** This instructional format is live and in real time. Students are required to log in to the class session at an assigned time. You should use synchronous teaching when you want to

- Interact with students
- Observe body language
- Ask a question and listen to students' responses
- Facilitate a class discussion or small-group breakout groups
- Observe a student's problem solving as it develops
- Set the stage for independent learning/tasks

**Asynchronous:**
Offline instruction when students work anytime they choose

**Asynchronous:** This instructional format allows students to complete assignments anytime they choose. This is not to say that you can't have deadlines—even daily deadlines help students to develop organizational skills—but the important thing about the asynchronous format is that there is flexibility in when students do the work. You should use asynchronous teaching when you want to

- Assign prerecorded lessons for students to watch
- Incorporate independent projects
- Teach time management and organization techniques
- Assign an independent assessment or purposeful practice of skills or concepts

**Blended:** A mix of live online classes with offline independent work

**Blended:** This format utilizes the advantages of both synchronous and asynchronous instructional delivery. Some of the class sessions are live with interaction, and some of the sessions are independent. You should use blended teaching when you want to

- Record a lesson for students who could not attend class at the assigned time

- Assign a group project with independent components
- Have students complete a follow-up assignment after the synchronous class

# Equitable Learning Online

Teaching online contains another element for which students can gain or be restricted from access to learning. Students who have access to up-to-date technology, fast Internet, and immediate tech support will have fewer challenges than students in the opposite situation. As you consider the diversity of your students, make note of inequities that lead to inaccessible curriculum.

It is important to create a plan with your administrator and technology support teacher for how to address these inequities to give all students an equitable entrance to and experience with your online class. Special attention should be paid to the basic technological needs of underresourced populations. When students or school divisions do not have access to basic remote learning needs such as Internet connections and devices, it can significantly hamstring student learning experiences. With all the gadgets out there, it can feel overwhelming and financially impossible to supply each student with basic tools. I recommend three tools: Internet access, a computer with a webcam, and a headset with microphone.

## HARDWARE AND GADGETS

I frequently get asked this question from teachers, parents, and administrators: What devices and gadgets should I buy? For some, this list gets ordered and delivered without a second thought. However, for many others, this question is loaded with financial implications. For this reason, I recommend only one or two devices.

- **Chromebook:** This laptop-style computer meets all basic needs. Currently, it is the most affordable device, priced at under $100, and comes equipped with a webcam, microphone, automatic updates, and virus protection. It is web based, so while it cannot download programs and software, it can access websites and applications on the web. I prefer this to tablets, even for our youngest learners. It might take longer for kindergartners to learn the hand-eye coordination of a mouse, but there are so many more features that are accessible on a laptop than tablets. If touchscreens are necessary, chromebooks with touch screens are still less expensive than most PCs and Macs.

- **Headset with noise-cancelling microphone:** This does not need to be expensive to gain the benefits. A headset can help the student with productivity by focusing their attention on the assignment and not other audio distractions in the home. When shopping for this, search for key terms such as *background noise reduction, unidirectional, boom,* or *noise-cancelling microphone.* There should be a physically extended mic that reaches to your cheek. A noise-cancelling microphone is a game changer when collaborating online. It doesn't pick up the background noise of a TV, adults and siblings, or sounds of the city.

## INTERNET SPEED

There are many things that may increase or reduce a student's access to your online class, and Internet speed has the potential to be the biggest factor. But there are some things that you can do to level the playing field.

### Video Streaming and Bandwidth

Streaming video uses a lot of bandwidth. That means that if a student is working with a poor Internet connection or slow speed, they will not be able to access the class in the same way as students with high speeds. If you regularly stream video via your webcam, be sure to check in with students on the quality of the video. Poor connections often lead to choppy interactions and confusion about directions or participation.

In general, I don't stream my video over the webcam. My students hear my voice and interact with the online tools rather than watch my face. I only stream myself when I am showcasing the mathematics and even then, only when it is the very action that I want to display, such as stringing beads on a pipe cleaner to show groups of 10 or showing the length on a measuring tape. Consider the reason that you stream and whether the benefits outweigh the inequities in the delivery.

Video streaming is not limited to your webcam. It also includes videos that you share via the teleconferencing tool during synchronous instruction. If you planned to share a video that is linked to YouTube (or TeacherTube if your school division restricts access to YouTube), for example, you can share the link with your students instead of the streaming video. When you give the student the link, they can watch it on their own and pause when the video has finished buffering. This can be liberating to students who have varied signal strength because they get to access the video as intended, rather than a choppy, glitchy version. Once finished with the video, students return to the synchronous class setting and we move on with the lesson.

## Power and Internet Outage

There are many things that we want to teach our students about time management and submitting assignments on time, but we need to consider a few elements that are out of their control. One of these is power and Internet outages. We must acknowledge and be prepared for the fact that not all students live in situations where they have consistent and reliable access to Internet and power. Interruptions may be short-term in the case of weather- or natural-disaster-related events, or can be more severe in areas of income insecurity. My neighborhood has above-ground power and cable lines, and I often lose Internet and power during storms. When I teach online, I frequently make a backup plan for days with heavy wind or rain. My plan usually includes connecting to my cell phone as a hotspot (however this uses cell phone data, which may not be readily available for many students learning remotely) or simply moving to an asynchronous lesson for the class that day. To ensure equitable learning, be sure to consider what you know about your students' circumstances, be realistic about what students can and cannot do in the event of interruptions, and offer extensions on deadlines and other ways of communicating with you.

## Proactively Helping Students Prepare

As teachers, we have a great responsibility to not only teach students the academic content, but also help them learn how to interact with their world. Consider helping students (and families of young students, especially) to stay organized and ready for class with these proactive tips:

- [ ] Before the school year begins, check your Internet speed. It is possible that you are using an outdated modem and are not able to get the Internet speed that you are paying for. If you rent a modem, most Internet providers will swap it out at no charge.
- [ ] Charge your devices when not in use. This includes any wireless devices, laptops, tablets, mouse, headset, and so on.
- [ ] Set all tablets and computers to update programs and operating systems regularly.
- [ ] Maintain a virus protection program (not necessary with Chromebook).

Creating a checklist like this will help your students transition into being responsible adults in their digital world.

## THINGS WITHIN A STUDENT'S CONTROL

Chapter 2 discusses the importance of norms, rules, and routines to maintain classroom management. From an equity standpoint, it is also important to consider which norms are in a student's control and which are not.

For example, sometimes, when we try to teach students good study skills, we create norms such as be in a quiet place, which works great for some students. The reality is that some students are unable to be in a quiet place. The home may not have a dedicated quiet room, there may be many people living in the house who are home during the day, the student may be baby-sitting younger siblings, and perhaps the student can focus better if a cartoon is on in the background so that younger siblings are not a distraction. The existence of distractions and background noise may be outside of a student's control, but how they respond to these concerns can sometimes be within their control. Your job is to be aware of your students' ability to control their environment and set norms accordingly in order to help them and their classmates stay focused. Let's look at some practices that may help.

## Using the Microphone in Small Groups

In order to engage students in participation and discussion, I used to require all microphones to be on, both in whole class and in small groups when working with me or in breakout rooms. I used this norm in all my classes. I had good intent in that I wanted students to discuss ideas together, and the best way to discuss ideas is by having their microphones on all the time. Over time I learned that this is not always feasible for everyone. Sometimes there are conversations in the background that are disruptive or even embarrassing, construction that is noisy, and pets that are beyond a student's control. It can also lead to just more background noise and chatter than students are comfortable processing, as well as challenging echoes. So, I changed this norm to be, microphones "active" in small-group discussions. The difference between "on" and "active" is that rather than passively leaving them on, but maybe not contributing to the discussion, the expectation is that students speak often, but they have to turn their microphones on only when speaking . . . hence they are more *active*.

## Using the Camera

As a teacher, I love to see my students' faces and observe their body language and facial expressions. Both in the face-to-face classroom and online, these observations can inform my instruction. However, these observations in the online space are different from in a classroom, because they not only show the student, but also the home environment. Sometimes the home environment can be distracting both to other students in the class and to a student who may be embarrassed to show the home setting. As students move into adolescence, they are often more concerned about visual appearance, which may take away from the mathematics lesson. You might ask yourself, do I really need to see all my students at this moment, or only when they are showing me how they regrouped their manipulative in order to add? I recommend considering the purpose of video, and using it only when purposeful.

# THINGS OUTSIDE A STUDENT'S CONTROL

Just as with background noise, there will be many other things outside of a student's control when engaged in distance learning that we need to be attentive to, supportive of, and flexible about. These may be things they have less ability to manage or mitigate.

## Speech Differences

Speech is a major component to online learning. Because audio is such an important factor, it can magnify accents, dialects, and speech disorders/difficulties. This can result in some students participating less often than in a face-to-face class. There are many accessibility tools available both within the teleconferencing program (such as captioning) as well as programs or extensions (such as voice to text). In addition, if your students use voice to text applications, they might have an unfair advantage over students whose speech is not well recognized or even recognized at all by the program.

## Outdated Devices

School districts often survey families about technology available to students for distance learning. They don't always update the survey as often as needed to ensure that every student has a working and updated device. You should be prepared to confront outdated devices and have a plan for how to respond. Be sure that students know what to do if their device malfunctions during homework, in the middle of class, during a presentation, or while watching a video. Be sure students have easy access to your school or district's technology help number, so that they can get the dedicated IT support that they need and you can continue teaching.

## Additional Responsibilities

As teachers, we may think that our students are home and able to be fully attentive. However, just because a student is home doesn't mean that they are able to be 100 percent focused. If the parent(s) is working, your student might be a caretaker for other children in the household. In some cases, younger siblings are watching a video while the older child is interacting in your class. They can be distracted because the younger siblings are fighting or a toddler didn't go down for a nap during the synchronous class time. A proactive way of becoming aware of student responsibilities is to create a space for anonymous feedback (such as Google Forms). Be aware that your students might have other responsibilities and they don't have full control over their attendance or attentiveness during class.

## CLOSING THE GAP ON MATERIALS AND RESOURCES

There is a bright side to equitable mathematics in online learning, and this comes in equal access to resources and materials. Due to the plethora of free online manipulatives, free interactive graphing calculators, and free geometry software, students who may not have previously had financial access to these tools can gain access in the online world. Similarly, if supplies such as paper, books, and other materials were not easily available, there is an almost infinite amount of space online. If we consider these affordances and leverage them in our online class, we have the potential to level the playing field in terms of virtual manipulatives and models used to show thinking.

# Technology Tools

When teaching online, there are some common tools that you will use regardless of what platforms your school has adopted, or if you plan to teach in a synchronous, blended, or asynchronous model. These tools are necessary for organization, consistency, and efficiency.

## LEARNING MANAGEMENT SYSTEMS

The Learning Management System (LMS) is the platform for the class home page where students enter their online class. The LMS varies by school district but is usually a secure website that connects student logins with their registration at their school. Learning Management Systems are used in all instructional delivery formats: synchronous, asynchronous, and blended. There are usually choices within the LMS platform to support instruction, such as assignments, readings, recordings, videoconferencing tools, and grades. Currently, examples include Blackboard, Canvas, and Google Classroom.

## THIRD-PARTY WEBSITES AND TOOLS

Third-party websites and tools are the other websites, links, videos, and programs that you will use in your class, regardless of the instructional delivery format. They are used to connect students to outside resources that enhance your curriculum. Current examples include YouTube, Khan Academy, educational websites, virtual manipulatives, Desmos, Microsoft Word, and CAD programs. In addition, your curriculum text or school division resources may have virtual tools for teachers and students to access.

## INTERACTIVE SLIDES

Interactive slides are used in all instructional delivery methods and are characterized by a slide deck that both students and teachers interact with and can edit simultaneously. This is more than simply sharing a slideshow presentation in that all users interact with and modify the presentation. When using interactive slides, students can upload images of their drawings, insert screenshots of their virtual manipulatives, create models using shapes and arrows, and comment using text boxes. Current examples include Google Slides, Microsoft PowerPoint, Desmos, Jamboard, Peardeck, and Seesaw.

## VIDEOCONFERENCING TOOLS

Videoconferencing tools are specific to synchronous instruction formats because they connect students and teachers through live audio and/or video streaming. Current examples include Zoom, Blackboard Collaborate, Microsoft Teams, Google Meets, and Seesaw (K–3 only). There are several components to any videoconferencing tool:

- **Audio:** The ability to speak and listen to live audio
- **Chat box:** The ability to read and type in a live space
- **Video streaming:** The ability to watch or display people in front of their computers
- **Share applications:** The ability to view or watch programs from another person's computer

# Technology Implementation

Successful technology implementation requires more planning than you may be used to. However, there are many great advantages because of the abundance of technology tools, apps, and collaborative shareability. From virtual manipulatives to interactive whiteboards and video directions, the choices can seem endless. In addition to these technological tools, it is important not to discount traditional paper-and-pencil drawings, concrete manipulatives using everyday objects students have access to at home, and abstract notation, as students can upload pictures or videos of these into your virtual classroom space. As you sift through all of these resources, you must identify which technological tools are most appropriate to your lesson goals and how students will interact with those tools. When planning, consider the following questions:

- What technology tools will my students have access to?

- Will I provide the technology tools or have students search for them?

- Does the technology tool allow for different mathematical models (e.g., linear model, area model, set model)?

- Does the technology tool support students' thinking of the mathematical situation?

- How long will it take my students to learn the technology tool versus use the technology tool to show a mathematical strategy or representation?

- What mathematical ideas might the technology tool overlook?

- Will the technology tool be more or less efficient than using paper/pencil or handheld manipulatives?

- How do I practice using the technology tool myself?

- What low-tech tools (such as paper/pencil) are relevant, and how will my students share these in collaborative spaces?

Let's explore each of these questions in more detail.

**What technology tools will my students have access to?**

A simple web search for "virtual math manipulatives" will provide hundreds of results for interactive tools. Each of these tools has advantages and disadvantages, and you must consider the role of the tech tool as it relates to the mathematics task. This is similar to a face-to-face classroom as a teacher considers all the manipulatives available in the classroom and the advantages and disadvantages to using each manipulative for the math task. When anticipating student thinking, you should explore the potential tech tools and anticipate student usage and potential misconceptions. In addition, you should plan for unstructured exploration time as students become familiar with the tech tool before actually building its use into your lessons.

### Will I provide the technology tools or have students search for them?

In order for students to work efficiently, you may want to sift through the plethora of virtual manipulatives ahead of time and identify a few that are best used to meet the mathematical goal. This is especially true for young students. Importantly, as students get older and are more experienced in an online setting, you do not always have to be the provider of the tech tool. It is indeed a 21st century skill to learn to search and sort the tech tools themselves. This should only be practiced, however, after you have modeled several lessons with a variety of tech tools.

### Does the technology tool allow for different mathematical models (e.g., linear model, area model, set model)?

It can be tempting to select the same tech tool over and over because both you and the students become comfortable with it. NCTM's (2014b) *Principles to Action* calls on teachers to present students with multiple representations so that students can make connections between those models. Much like choosing only one problem-solving strategy or one visual representation, this can result in students being unable to connect to various models. For example, consider fractional representations. There are linear models, area models, and set models, and all are equally important to gain a full understanding of fractions in various situations. If you only select technology tools that use a linear model, student thought will become fixed within this model and students will not see connections to other representations.

### Does the technology tool support students' thinking of the mathematical situation?

Not all technology tools are best for all problems. As you'll read about in Chapter 8, it is important to select tools based on how you anticipate students will approach and solve a problem. A crucial part of your preparation is to do this anticipation by solving a problem yourself in multiple ways, and *then* deciding which technology tool is the best match to assist students in that thinking process. Having a mismatch can lead to unnecessary misconceptions. For example, in the following hopscotch problem, the teacher selected a geoboard tool without fully anticipating how her students would approach the problem. The tool could not create a visual model that matched with the problem scenario described. This led to confusing representations that did not connect to the problem, which had never happened when students used paper and pencil.

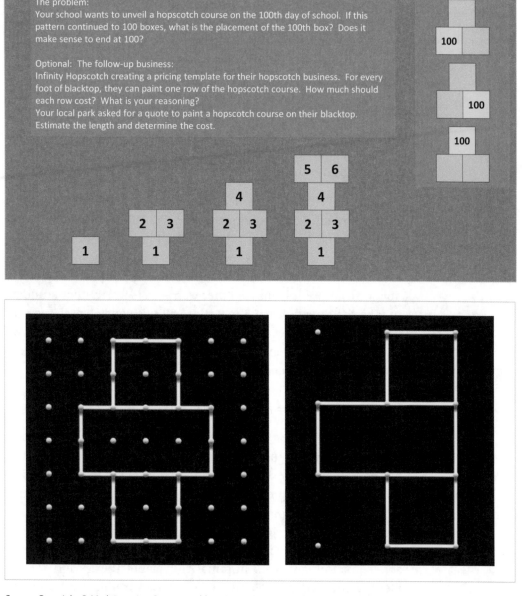

## How long will it take my students to learn the technology tool versus use the technology tool to show a mathematical strategy or representation?

Learning a technology tool has many advantages, and yet a clear disadvantage: it is time consuming. While it might take students time to learn the tech tool, you should consider this learning as it connects to digital literacy and digital citizenship.

Digital literacy and digital citizenship are not only school division goals, but also important life skills that our students need to practice in a structured environment before graduation. Digital literacy refers to the ability to navigate technology. Students need to learn how to save files, organize folders, use tools such as copy/paste, navigate the web, and identify reputable people and posts. Digital citizenship refers to a student's contributions to the digital world. Students should learn appropriate ways to chat, blog, and post to social media. They should learn how to identify harmful people and programs and safe practices online. They should be able to identify fact versus opinion and understand the foreverness of comments that they post online.

Educational curricula frequently embed STEM, and there is value in the way students explore these tools. Thinking like computer engineers also builds students' minds. Plus, once students learn the tool, they will use the tool with more efficiency in the future. Making the time investment at the beginning can pay off considerably with future lessons. In other words, it is worth it for students to take the time to learn a tool they will use consistently and that builds their skills beyond the task at hand. But it may not pay off to have students spend time learning a tool that they won't use in the future or that doesn't provide additional learning benefits.

## What mathematical ideas might the technology tool overlook?

Good mathematical tasks are used to help students uncover key mathematical ideas. Sometimes, the tech tool is too advanced to use with all developmental levels of students and can be a case where the tool is a distraction that gets in the way of good learning. For example, if you are teaching a lesson about graphing and correctly choosing the best graphical representation for a data set, some spreadsheets automatically label the $x$- and $y$-axis, identify the dependent and independent variable, and plot the

**Digital literacy:** The ability to navigate technology

**Digital citizenship:** A student's contributions to the digital world data. This may give too much away for students just learning about graphs and takes away a learning opportunity. You should consider if the technology tool replaces or enhances the exploration of the mathematics.

### Will the technology tool be more or less efficient than paper/pencil or handheld manipulatives?

Efficiency is an important consideration when implementing a math task in the synchronous online environment. If you expect to use student-elicited responses for the math discussion after 20 minutes of exploration time, you must provide experiences that can be explored, with appropriate tools, in that allotted time. This means there is still a place for paper-and-pencil representations in a virtual classroom, when more concrete tools will be more efficient. Students can use paper/pencil or mini whiteboards to collaborate with group members by using the video streaming feature on the teleconferencing tool or by taking a picture of their handwritten or drawn work and uploading it to the slides. They might also use physical manipulatives such as paper clips, cereal, pasta, beans, and more. Students can upload images of these traditional face-to-face representations to the interactive slides for the class to view.

### How do I practice using the technology tool myself?

Before you implement any technology tools, be sure to anticipate student responses and technological issues, and plan how you will respond. First, try the tool with a friend or colleague. Be sure to make a copy of your interactive slide so that you can have a clean version while you and your planning partner test out the copy. Consider asking friends who have access to different devices so that you see how the tool(s) play out with different operating systems and browsers. PCs, Macs, and Chromebooks all use a physical keyboard and mouse, which have benefits and drawbacks compared to tablet devices. Tablets and phones often use an app to interact with the slides. Be sure to download the app and open the presentation using it. Test out how the technology is different in each situation. Ensure that you know how to turn on features such as the hotspot, the camera, the videoconferencing tool, and the Learning Management System. Once you have a willing friend, ask them to make a mistake so that you are prepared for student mistakes. Consider your language and tone, and role-play the situation to give you practice using those words.

**What low-tech tools (such as paper/pencil) are relevant, and how will my students share these in collaborative spaces?**

With all the digital gadgets and apps available, it is easy to jump to a Google search of virtual tools to draw and write numbers, expressions, and multistep equations, but paper and pencil and other low-tech modalities still have their place. Teachers need to balance the cognitive demand of learning new technology with learning new mathematics content. This is seen in the classroom as teachers read aloud word problems to balance the literacy demands so that students can focus on the mathematics of the problem. Similarly, paper and pencil; homemade manipulatives (such as Lego®s, beans, and egg cartons); colorful sketches; Play-Doh shapes; and glued craft sticks all have a place in the remote classroom. There are a variety of ways that students can upload their low-tech tools using video and images, both during the creation process and for the final product. Many of these upload tools are embedded in the Learning Management System, teleconferencing tools, interactive slides, and third-party apps.

## ●●● REFLECT AND REIMAGINE

Whether this is your first remote class or you have experience teaching online, if you are transitioning from a face-to-face classroom, you will need to reimagine your course delivery. This chapter gave you considerations for technology and equity. As you consider the topics in this chapter, reflect on the tools:

- What LMS and teleconferencing tools will my students access? Will they have access to multiple tools?

- How might I use these tools to support collaboration and interaction between my students?

- What third-party tools, apps, and manipulatives can my students access?

- Are my students already familiar with the physical version of the tool? How can I build on that?

- What can I do in my classroom to create a more equitable environment for my students?

+ chapter

2

# SETTING NORMS FOR THE VIRTUAL MATH CLASSROOM

When you think about the beginning of the school year, you can't help but recall the time spent helping students learn the routines, procedures, and rules of the classroom and school. For our youngest learners, this consumes a significant portion of class time. As students get older and are more familiar with the structure of school in general, not as much time is typically spent. But regardless of the students' age and grade level, norms and rules are an important structure for all K–12 classrooms. This is true no matter whether instruction is happening face-to-face or online. Here are some fundamental reasons why they are important:

- They keep students safe.
- They reduce distractions and increase productivity.

- They help to maintain a good flow of your lesson.
- They give students agency during small-group work or in breakout rooms.
- They help foster kindness and community.
- They provide students with predictable structures for regular classroom routines.

Classroom expectations and norms also provide a roadmap for learning the expectations and norms of the world beyond the physical or virtual school doors. When students practice how to be safe and respectful to others, they are preparing to be safe and respectful adults as well as thoughtful digital citizens. And this kind of practice is not solely needed for the physical classroom. Practicing online norms is just as important.

Whatever you choose as your norms and rules, remember to use asset-based language. This positive language can be essential in getting students to think about responsibility rather than a list of restrictions. This also gives you the positive language to redirect students back to the productive behavior. Figure 2.1 offers some examples.

Figure 2.1

## Sample Expectations Using Asset-Based Versus Restrictive Language

| EXPECTATIONS USING ASSET-BASED LANGUAGE | EXPECTATIONS USING RESTRICTIVE LANGUAGE |
| --- | --- |
| Use kind and respectful language. | Don't be mean and disrespectful. |
| Reduce or eliminate background noise. | Don't play music or have loud noises in the background. |
| Raise your virtual hand when you want to speak. | Don't yell out when you want to speak. |
| Be a cyber hero when someone needs help. | No cyberbullying. |
| Missteaks happen; use Ctrl-Z to undo. | Don't delete anything. |
| Use your away message when away from your keyboard. | Do not leave during class time. |

When setting up rules and norms for your online math classroom, it is important to consider the following categories:

- Safety
- Kindness and Community
- Student Agency
- Focus and Productivity
- Lesson Workflow
- Small-Group Instruction and Breakout Meetings
- Patience and Productive Struggle
- Materials and Manipulatives Management

Let's look at each of these in more detail.

# Safety

As educators, we consider safety in face-to-face classrooms, and we must also consider it for online classes as well. Online safety relates to a student's physical and mental well-being as well as making good choices as both a responsible collaborator and a participant.

## BE A CYBER HERO WHEN SOMEONE NEEDS HELP

It is important to begin your online course with a discussion about cyberbullying and how to be a cyber hero. Be sure to empower students to speak up and support their peers, especially in difficult situations. Cyberbullying can reach beyond unkind words and include images and words that jeopardize student safety and security.

Further, students need a way of notifying you when they feel unsafe or disrespected, or are witnessing bullying. There are a variety of ways that students can do this. In most teleconferencing tools, students may send a private chat message that immediately notifies the teacher. The added benefit of this instant and private chat is that the offending students do not receive this notification. There are also anonymous ways of sending a notification, such as using a questionnaire, form, poll, or anonymous email. Consider the benefits of immediate notifications and anonymous notifications and set norms that allow students to send feedback. Younger students will need to establish and practice a safety protocol with a teacher and trusted adult. This protocol should include the differences between unkind and unsafe language, pictures, and video, and it should include a sample script that is practiced in both the classroom and the home. As with each norm, be sure to discuss and practice them often with your students. Figure 2.2 presents a sample that I have used to support students in early elementary.

## Figure 2.2

## Sample Cyberbullying Discussion Support

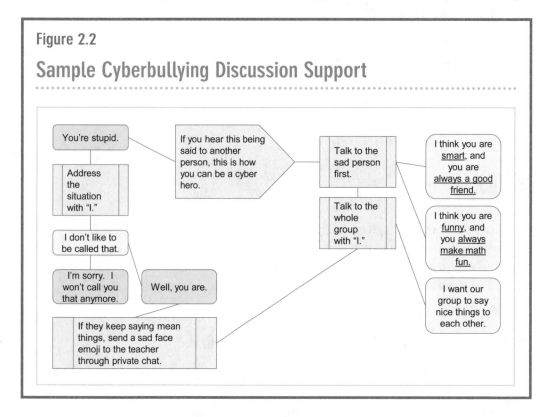

## ONLY USE APPROVED WEBSITES

Before sending students to third-party websites, ensure that they are safe and approved for use following your school or district's Internet policy. For example, don't make the mistake of assuming that the benefit of using a virtual manipulative is worth the risk, just because the risk doesn't appear obvious. There can be hidden risks with regard to exposing private student information, downloading computer viruses and malware, exposing students to material or ads that are content- or age-inappropriate, and accessing unsecure sites that allow other websites to intercept information for unintended purposes. Some incredibly useful websites require parental permission. Anticipate how you plan to use these websites and give yourself enough planning time to seek the necessary permissions.

## DO NOT DRIVE DURING INSTRUCTION

This directive is meant for high school students who have their driver's license and, while it might seem like common sense, all important norms and rules must be both stated and repeated. By repeating the importance of safe driving, students are reminded that you care about their safety and the safety of others. When you hear or see through video a student participating while driving (unfortunately it does happen even when stating the norm), be prepared to calmly state that they are to immediately stop participation, and when they arrive at their destination safely, to log back in. Be sure that they know their safety is more important to you than your class. You can include additional safe driving discussions such as texting while driving and general distractions.

# Kindness and Community

Online classes can include a rich community of learners, but only through purposeful planning and implementation of community-building strategies. In addition, students need modeling and practice with both the language and tone of kind communication online.

## PATIENCE AND ENCOURAGEMENT

Students desire patience and encouragement whether it involves longer wait time, support with a new tech skill, or persisting to solve a problem. This might sound different at various grade levels, but the need to practice and model proper language and tone are constant. I like to give my students a list of encouraging phrases to say, and I model this list frequently.

- Give yourself grace as you try the new tech tool.
- I'm happy to help, but I can also be patient while you try.
- Keep trying, I want to know your idea.
- This is challenging for me too, let's keep working on it together.
- We can try a different way together.

## REMEMBER THAT MISSTEAKS HAPPEN—
## USE CTRL-Z

Beginning each day with a reminder that mistakes happen is a great way to value learning. When you showcase your mistakes, and teach students how to fix them, you are modeling that you are a part of the "everyone." Students are always watching how you model addressing mistakes. To ensure that you have a demeanor that is calm and patient, it is important that you anticipate mistakes and prepare a script of the language that you will use to address the mistake. I model this at the beginning of each new school year or semester by misspelling the word *mistake*. In the first few classes, some students pick up on it and use their microphone to tell me about the mistake. Others use the chat box, and still others simply change the spelling on the slide. In each situation, I am eager to model my language and tone.

Here is an example of how our conversation could play out.

## Dr. Wills: MISSTEAKS Happen

**Jarome:** Dr. Wills, the word "mistakes" is misspelled. It should be M-I-S-T-A-K-E-S.

**Dr. Wills:** Jarome, thanks for noticing and letting me know using a kind tone. Would you fix the error on the slide for me? Did everyone else hear how Jarome let me know about my mistake?

**Kayla:** He was really nice about it.

**Rodney:** He told you before he fixed it.

**Talia:** Yeah, and he explained the right way to spell it.

**Dr. Wills:** Sometimes, our peers will make mistakes like delete our picture. How would that make you feel?

**Talia:** Really upset, especially if I worked a long time on it.

**Jess:** It depends if it is gone forever. If they do an undo then it's no big deal.

**Dr. Wills:** Jess, that is exactly what we are going to do today. We are going to learn how to undo our mistakes in a couple different ways. We are also going to practice how to let your peer know that they made a mistake using calm and patient language and tone.

## UPDATE YOUR PROFILE PICTURE

Can you remember a time you entered someone's home, and their walls were covered with beautiful pictures of their family? There might be silly pictures, pet photos, and additional loved ones. It is in our human nature to enjoy seeing new pictures and also ask questions and make connections to those pictures. You can use this to your advantage in online learning by creating a classroom norm where students are encouraged to update their profile picture regularly. Encourage them to include loved ones, hobbies, pets, or other things they are proud of. When you do this, you are inviting students to share their individuality and that you value their uniqueness. Don't forget to take a minute or two to comment on photos, either in small groups or by writing a chat message to the student.

# Student Agency

Agency is about giving students a voice and a choice in their learning. Agency is a natural desire for all humans. It is why we become interested in a hobby, and how we choose to learn more. In many cases, it's what separates learning for fun and learning for a test. When we learn for fun, we choose our source for information, such as online tutorials, paid subscriptions, discussion boards, blogs, and neighbors with similar experiences. Sometimes we might immerse ourselves in the activity for hours on end, and often lose sleep in the name of excitement and motivation. This is an example of full agency.

**Student agency:** The opportunity for students to have voice and choice in their learning

The opposite can be seen in many classrooms around the world as students learn for a test. Students are told what to learn, how to learn it, and when to learn it, and they are given little to no choice. When these circumstances occur in classrooms, students begin to see themselves as passive learners who need the teacher's direct guidance and knowledge in order to do anything or solve any problem. They become *dependent* learners rather than *independent* learners.

But things are changing. In today's mathematics instruction, teachers are giving students more voice and agency by implementing things like math discussion routines and using meaningful open-ended questions and investigations. In building this agency, it is through managing the classroom effectively, setting norms, frontloading rules and expectations, and developing meaningful consequences that we can ensure safety and rich learning. Online learning has a unique ability to harness student passions, provide choices for learning new information, and create specialized norms to give students more agency in their education.

## STUDENT AGENCY THROUGH DISCUSSION

In mathematics, one of the easiest ways to build student agency in the remote classroom is through discussion and math talk. Math Practice Standard 3 (National Governors Association Center for Best Practices and Council of Chief State School Officers, 2010) states that students must be able to construct viable arguments and critique the reasoning of others. It is through the implementation of this standard in our instruction that students have the opportunity to practice agency. Consider this scenario:

> How can you find the solution to 83 − 15?
>
> Explain your thinking.

Using Number Talks (Parrish, 2014) structures, students explore and explain several different types of strategies. To solve this problem, students not only get a choice in the method that they use to solve the problem, they also get a voice in how they explain their thinking. Here are some sentence frames that can be used with students to build their agency during discussion:

- I agree/disagree with _____ because . . .
- I didn't understand what you said. Can you explain it again/a different way?
- Can you explain your thinking?
- How/Why did you choose that strategy?
- I thought about the problem differently. I chose to . . .
- What I heard _____ say was . . .
- Can I share a different way to solve the problem?

## STUDENT AGENCY THROUGH CHOICE

Another way to build student agency is through the use of choice. We often don't realize how few actual choices students get to make for themselves during a typical school day. When students are given the opportunity to exercise choice, they are more engaged, feel empowered in their own learning, and become more independent. Here are some simple ways to build choice into your remote classroom:

- Give students a Must Do and May Do list of activities to complete.

- Allow students to create their own word problem with a scenario/topic they select.

- Allow students to select the manipulative that makes the most sense to them in the moment.

- Allow students to choose their partners.

- Ask open-ended questions and allow students to relate their prior knowledge to mathematical experiences.

- Allow students to create their own answer in a multiple-choice scenario by providing three answers and a blank box.

## STUDENT AGENCY THROUGH SMALL GROUPS

As schools move toward online instruction, they often impose restrictions on pedagogical decisions based on fear. Often one of these restrictions is the use of small groups in breakout rooms. The fear is that without direct adult supervision, students will not stay on task or will uncover unique or inappropriate ways of using the school's technology platforms. They flex their creative and childlike tendencies as they test our rules and consequences. But, much as in the face-to-face classroom, students have always tested our boundaries, and they do it to determine social norms. It is up to us to define the line and use the same classroom management procedures in our remote classrooms.

The benefits of breakout rooms can potentially far outweigh the fears. When students are given the opportunity to work in small groups, they learn how to communicate with others, express themselves, advocate for their own ideas, and build their problem-solving skills. They also have the opportunity to practice important peer discussion and feedback techniques that can empower them even beyond the classroom.

Much like small groups in a face-to-face classroom setting, there are routines that must be practiced and gradual release that teachers must implement to ensure that students can work independently, are self-starters, and can stay focused for predictable amounts of time. The structure shown later in Figure 2.3 demonstrates how you might begin breakout rooms, but it is important to consider your unique class makeup as you decide the rubric for moving to the next phase.

## STUDENT AGENCY REQUIRES TIME AND PLANNING

In order to be successful in building student agency in your online math classroom, you have to be willing to invest time in building students' skill sets to be successful. For example, using new technology tools that can enhance students' opportunities for small-group discussion and demonstrate their thinking may feel overwhelming at first for both you and your students. But it's important to remember that it may take longer than one day or even one week for everyone to learn how to use the tools effectively—and that's okay. Once the technology skills are learned and the proper routines and procedures are put in place, lessons and activities will be much easier to implement in the future.

In addition to time, you also have to invest in the planning and organization of routines and procedures in order to set students up for success. When students enter our classroom, either face-to-face or online, we can restrict their agency in the name of classroom management—it is much easier to be the "disseminator of knowledge" than the "facilitator of student learning"—or we can give students the tools to be safe and learn effectively in a responsible environment. As you consider how you build agency with your online students, it is important to anticipate the challenges of the situation but not to eliminate them altogether. Agency is not only a part of learning, it is the part of learning that brings passion, motivation, and engagement. The most important thing about student agency is the connection to rules, norms, clear consequences, and practice.

# Focus and Productivity

There are so many distractions that can interrupt a student's learning process. These can be distractions in the home environment, such as siblings, housework being completed around them, or loud yard work happening outside. The distractions can also be related to the technology itself, including visual, audio, and Internet speed. Sometimes these distractions affect only the specific student or their group, while others can halt productivity for the entire class. Be sure to discuss distractions with your students, while being mindful that not all students are able to remove these distractions, and determine how you will support those students.

## TURN OFF STREAMING DEVICES

If students are struggling with Internet speed, it can be helpful to turn off additional streaming devices or shut down other unused applications on devices in the house, if possible. While not all residents of the household can halt their productivity for the student's class, some streaming, such as the student watching a YouTube video on another device, does not use Internet bandwidth efficiently. Consider a lesson, similar to turning off light switches to save electricity, that teaches students about Internet bandwidth.

## REMEMBER, WE ARE RECORDING

There are many programs that allow you to record live, synchronous class instruction and make the recording available to students. This is especially helpful when a student is unable to eliminate major distractions, they experience unusually poor Internet connection, there is a power outage, or they are simply sick. The ability to review a recording can help the student feel caught up or can provide support to students who want to watch a lesson again to build their comprehension. It is your duty to always tell students if and when you are recording a session. This can easily be achieved at the very beginning of class. In addition, if you make the recordings available to students, be sure to give them information about how and where to access those recordings along with rules about privacy. Recordings should never be shared publicly or on social media by teachers or students. Finally, students should be taught how to use the recordings. Recordings are not like reading a book from chapter to chapter. Sometimes it is better to fast-forward to moments of importance or rewind, pause, or rewatch while applying a procedure. For emergent or multilingual learners, captioning in English and/or home languages can support the reading of spoken words. All of these skills need to be taught directly to students so that they can access recordings efficiently and effectively.

## REDUCE OR ELIMINATE BACKGROUND NOISE

It can be incredibly distracting to try to have a conversation with someone who has a lot of background noise. These noises can include someone cooking, a dog barking, TV in the background, or even the regular ding of a cell phone. By having a discussion with students about the need to reduce or eliminate background noise if possible, you can frontload the importance of this norm and have students become aware of their surroundings. In the event that the background noise cannot be eliminated (such as a renovation in the upstairs apartment), you should allow students the option of turning off their mic unless they are speaking.

## MUTE YOUR MIC IN LARGE GROUPS

Most activities do not require all 20+ students to verbally respond simultaneously. Unless you are doing a whole-group activity, such as choral counting or reading, you should consider requesting that students mute their microphone in whole groups. In addition to removing the distractions of 20+ microphones, you can value student privacy by eliminating the need to intrude in the audio space of their home.

# Lesson Workflow

As a classroom teacher in a face-to-face setting, you have experience in how to pace your lesson workflow appropriately and have strategies to pause instruction during interruptions, such as a visitor knocking at your classroom door or the front office calling for someone to go home early for a doctor's appointment. The practice of anticipating interruptions and developing strategies to maintain lesson workflow is also important in the remote classroom.

## USE A VIRTUAL PARKING LOT

Some of the most elegant and beautiful problem solving can be stunted with an off-task question, such as "When is our math project due?" Suddenly, students are no longer interested in making mathematical connections and instead are concerned with project anxiety. It can be difficult to get students back on track. One way to reduce this is through a virtual parking lot. There are many "virtual sticky note" apps or websites that could be used for this, such as Jam Board or Padlet. I prefer to include a slide at the end of my Google Slides lesson presentation because then I remember to answer all of the questions before the end of class.

Regardless of the platform that you use for this strategy, students will utilize the parking lot if they know that you value it and actually respond to their questions. As an added benefit, both you and other students can respond to the questions in the virtual parking lot at any time, which means that you can use instructional downtime to write responses, which makes a more efficient class closure.

## BE PREPARED FOR CLASS

Like adults, students have a variety of responsibilities outside of school. Sometimes it is daily after-school clubs and activities, or it might be babysitting, working a job, or helping around the house. For younger students, parent responsibilities will vary and parental support and guidance may not be available regularly. If you assign an asynchronous reading or assignment, and your expectation is that it should be read or completed before a live (synchronous) class on a specific day, it is important that you state that clearly and describe the importance of the norm. This helps students understand the importance of being a responsible member of the class or small group. Also, giving students notification of the section of the reading that is most important can motivate them to not only read the relevant section, but also become interested in continuing reading the rest of the piece. The important thing to remember is that this norm is often not an intuitive skill for students. Especially in a virtual classroom where most, if not all, of the work is done at home, students must learn how to organize their time appropriately so that they are present for live instruction and also can balance their schedules to accommodate time for the asynchronous/independent tasks or assignments that must be completed.

## RAISE YOUR HAND TO SPEAK

When you hold a conversation in the classroom, there are norms and procedures for whose turn it is. And although they may look a little bit different, these same norms need to be established in an online class. Some teleconferencing tools give students the option to raise their hand virtually. It might even give students a number in the "queue." As in a face-to-face class, students need to understand that just because they are the first to raise their hand, that doesn't mean that you pick them to speak each time or immediately. Sometimes you give wait time, then when you see who has their hand raised, you select particular students to respond.

## SHARE NEW IDEAS USING THE MIC

Another way of keeping your lesson timing on track is to purposefully consider what is said over audio and what is typed in the chat box. A successful class will use both audio and chat box so that students can experience participation using multiple modalities. I use the norm of sharing new ideas over the mic in my classrooms. This means that when I ask a question, such as "When you subtract, do you always put the bigger number first?," I invite students to raise their hand and then respond in order of the queue. If their idea has already been shared, then they lower their hand and agree to use the chat box to respond. In cases of our youngest learners or for students with limited English proficiency, an established emoji can show that they connected with the shared idea. In addition, I will ask students who post new ideas in the chat box to expand on those ideas using their microphones. This way, the airspace is filled with new ideas to consider while the chat box is a way of checking for understanding and relating to the idea.

## PREPARE FOR LATE STUDENT ARRIVAL

It is important to implement norms and routines to minimize teacher direction and maximize independent student agency. For example, by making your breakout room plan available for the day's lesson, the late student knows where to read or listen to the directions. Then, the student can move to their assignment slide and breakout group, introduce themselves, and engage with the group immediately, without missing a beat. Figure 2.3 shows a sample breakout room plan, including the directions and the group assignments.

# Small-Group Instruction and Breakout Sessions

Small-group instruction is a staple of face-to-face mathematics classrooms. These small groups give students practice with

## Figure 2.3

## Sample Breakout Room Plan

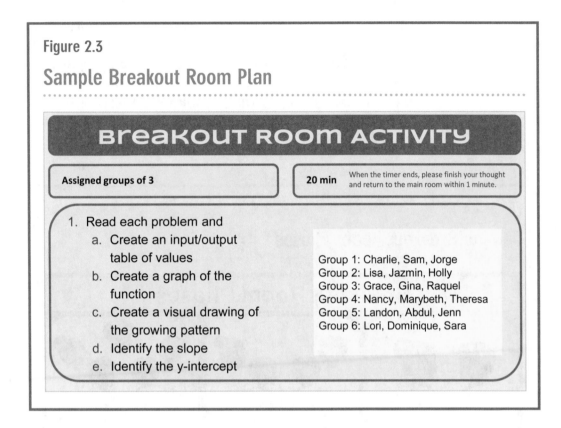

# BreakOUT ROOM ACTIVITY

| Assigned groups of 3 | 20 min | When the timer ends, please finish your thought and return to the main room within 1 minute. |

1. Read each problem and
   a. Create an input/output table of values
   b. Create a graph of the function
   c. Create a visual drawing of the growing pattern
   d. Identify the slope
   e. Identify the y-intercept

Group 1: Charlie, Sam, Jorge
Group 2: Lisa, Jazmin, Holly
Group 3: Grace, Gina, Raquel
Group 4: Nancy, Marybeth, Theresa
Group 5: Landon, Abdul, Jenn
Group 6: Lori, Dominique, Sara

cooperative social skills along with tailored mathematics practice in purposefully designed groups. Group design is often based on daily content goals, social skills, self-starting independence, persistence in problem solving, and representations. Each of these design criteria can be used in heterogeneous and homogeneous groupings. For example, when all students in the group have similar background knowledge and specific math learning goals, they can learn one mini-lesson together. When students have varied background knowledge and mathematical experiences, they can bring diverse perspectives, conceptions, and representations to the small group. However, when creating small groups based on a mathematical learning goal, ensure that those groups are based off of one particular goal, and change regularly. NCTM (2018, 2020a, 2020b) recommends that K–12 mathematics "dismantle inequitable structures, including ability grouping and tracking, and challenge spaces of marginality and privilege" (Huinker et al., 2020).

When students enter breakout rooms or participate in small-group instruction, we want them to be responsible, independent, and collaborative. Establishing the norms for this kind of instructional setting requires plenty of practice, but the benefits include active learning, engagement, increased ideas and representations, and authentic student voice. Small groups are an essential part of collaborative learning in a face-to-face classroom and they need to remain essential (as breakout rooms) in the online environment too.

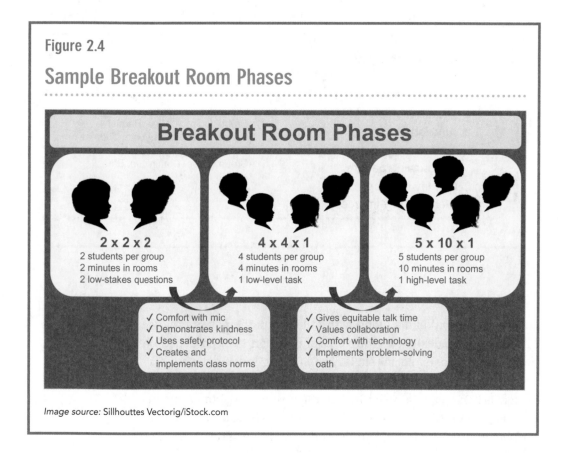

**Figure 2.4**

## Sample Breakout Room Phases

*Image source:* Sillhouttes Vectorig/iStock.com

## LEAVE YOUR MIC ACTIVE

Before any typing begins, all mics are turned on and students say hello. I encourage students to keep their microphones on at all times during small-group time, but if circumstances at home do not allow for that because of heightened background noise, it is okay for a student to mute themselves as long as they turn their mic on when they are speaking and still speak often.

When all mics are active, the conversation is more casual and more incomplete thoughts are shared. These incomplete thoughts are the very element of discussion that is often missing from online learning, but is essential in face-to-face classes and to building rapport among the students.

The first few times students participate in a breakout room, it is important to keep the groups small (e.g., two to three students), make the time limit short (e.g., two minutes), and give them a "get to know you" script to follow. Students always start with, "Hello, my name is _____." Then there is a second part to the script that helps students get to know each other better. Examples are as follows:

- My favorite dessert is _____ because _____.
- One thing I am really good at is _____.
- The food I dislike the most is ____ because _____.
- If I could be any animal in the world I would be a ____ because ____.
- My favorite toy is _____ because _____.

## TALK BEFORE TYPING

It can be tempting for students to begin typing on their group's recording space, especially if they are excited to share a mathematical idea. However, this can result in inequitable collaboration in both speaking and written form. For that reason, I typically remind students to talk before typing.

## DECIDE ON ROLES AND RESPONSIBILITIES

Roles can help maintain equitable participation and keep the group on time. These roles can highlight unique characteristics about students. Some students are especially skilled at typing, or ensuring that everyone gets a chance to speak or is comfortable with technology. I like to use the following roles:

- **Time Keeper:** Gives clear directions on keeping the group on pace
- **Secretary:** Types on group slides
- **Image Finder:** Uses keywords to find images to add to the group slide
- **Communicator:** Uses the chat to let the teacher know when teacher help is needed

- **Math Mayor:** Ensures equitable talk time
- **Tech Tutor:** Is knowledgeable about the technology used in the activity

## ANNOUNCE WHEN AFK (AWAY FROM KEYBOARD)

Have you ever been assigned to a group during a professional development training only to find out that everyone needed to use the restroom except you right at the start of work time? It is no fun to be in a group by yourself, and this can feel the same in an online class. It is important to realize that students might need to step away from their computer. To make a more productive group time, I structure breaks throughout the lesson and use a visual cue, such as a dedicated slide, to inform students of the upcoming break. However, there are times that students need to step away and it is important to establish the norm that students use an away message when they are away from the keyboard (AFK). Then, when it is time to create breakout rooms, you know which students have stepped away and can use that in your planning.

# Materials and Manipulative Management

Once teachers identify the tools that they will use in the classroom, they will need to manage those tools, consider pitfalls, and plan for tech mishaps.

## MAKE A COPY BEFORE MODIFYING

One of the greatest affordances of online instruction in the mathematics class is the ability to modify different mathematical representations on an interactive slide. However, because students can edit interactive slides simultaneously, it is important to maintain a copy of the original representation. This allows both the student who created the original and the student who made the modification to showcase their thinking in the recording space. As a general practice, teachers can make copies of the class presentation throughout the learning time so that they can recover unintended deletions and ensure that slides are clutter free and accessible to all. Figure 2.5 shows an original slide and a copied slide with student modifications.

## Figure 2.5

## Sample Original and Modified Slide

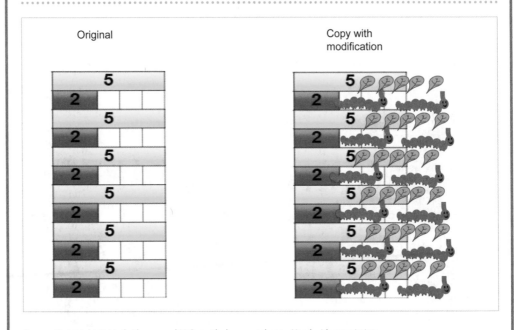

Original

Copy with modification

## ALLOW FOR FLEXIBLE COLLABORATION

Because all students can edit interactive slides simultaneously, you may find that some students grab and drag the same shape or text box at the same time. This can frustrate students if they are not aware of this technological phenomenon. I use a calm voice early and often to remind students that "if someone else is writing in the same space as you, simply click to a new place and begin typing." I remind them that they are showing their ability to be a flexible collaborator, and I celebrate those students during class.

## KEEP MATERIALS OFF THE SLIDE

In some activities, I like to keep a choice of virtual manipulatives, images, or shapes to the side of the slide. These are still accessible to students even if they are not placing them directly on the slide because they are in edit mode. (Note that items off the slide are not available in present mode.) In Figure 2.6, students use the base-ten blocks on the sides of their slide to drag and drop onto the slide. Their solutions are on the slide, and tools are off the side.

## Figure 2.6

## Materials Off the Slide Example

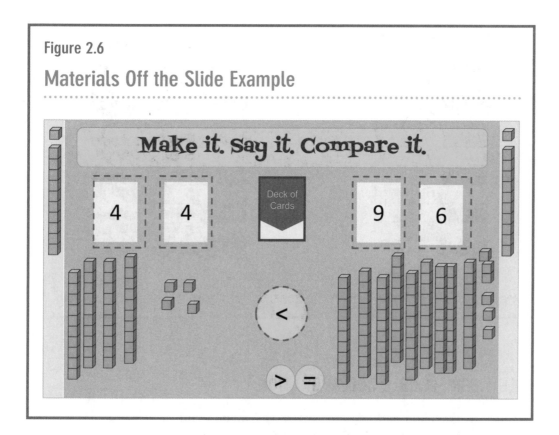

## ••• REFLECT AND REIMAGINE

Reimagining norms, rules, and student agency requires creative and purposeful thinking in a remote classroom. You might find that some of these norms are non-negotiable, and are required for learning and safety. You might also find that some of these norms are developed over time. Consider these norms related to safety, focus and productivity, student agency, lesson workflow, small-group instruction, kindness and community, and materials and manipulatives as you anticipate how students will interact and collaborate in your remote class. As you decide your norms, determine which should be modeled at the beginning of the year or semester, and which require mastery before introducing. As with all norms, they require proper time to model and practice. As you reimagine your remote classroom, it can be useful to think about a "perfect world" situation, and make that world your goal.

- What norms will I need to ensure are present before I can get to a "perfect" classroom?

- When and how often will I practice these norms with my students?

- How will I know when my students are ready for my perfect class?

- How will I use gradual release to transition students from dependent learners to independent learners?

For more practice, tutorials, and templates, visit www.theresawills.com.

+ chapter

3

# INCORPORATING MANIPULATIVES IN THE VIRTUAL MATH CLASSROOM

One of the most important ways students learn new mathematical concepts—regardless of their complexity—is through the use of tools, whether they be objects, pictures, or drawings. The tools help students to visualize, in their own mind, the relationship between the object and the mathematics concept (Suh, 2007). Even when teaching online, it is important that students have access to tools that build their conceptual understanding. This is especially important for elementary students so that they have a strong foundational understanding of the key mathematical concepts, but also for students in middle school, high school, and beyond.

# Planning for Virtual Manipulatives

**Manipulatives:** Any physical or virtual objects or materials that students can move around in order to help them learn mathematical concepts

Virtual manipulatives describe any virtual tool that you change, stack, connect, group, drag, spin, or otherwise move to model mathematical ideas. Some of these tools are direct replacements of physical manipulatives from the classroom such as spinners, dice, cards, snap cubes, and pattern blocks.

## FINDING VIRTUAL MANIPULATIVES

Begin your search with familiar manipulatives that you have used in a face-to-face classroom. For example, a web search for base-ten blocks will result in dozens of applications, web-based tools, and downloadable programs that all use base-ten blocks. Once you become comfortable searching for manipulatives that you are familiar with, you can make broader searches for other manipulatives, such as two-colored counters, linking cubes, fraction bars, or algebra tiles. It can also be helpful to use synonyms for virtual manipulatives such as *interactive, modify, online, web-based, drag and drop, activity,* and *game.*

Your students might be assigned identical school computers, or they might use a variety of personal devices such as a PC, Mac, Chromebook, iPad, Kindle, or even a cell phone. It can be daunting, expensive, and impractical to ensure that the virtual manipulative is available on all devices. I recommend beginning with a choice of three different websites that all offer base-ten blocks. Much as you would give your students general exploration time before using physical base-ten blocks in a face-to-face classroom, you should do this online as well and learn who can and cannot access different apps. Maintaining a list of student devices can also be useful.

## SELECTING VIRTUAL MANIPULATIVES

There are advantages to both the teacher selecting the manipulative and the student selecting the manipulative to use in solving a problem. When the teacher selects the manipulative, there is less time spent on web searches, ensuring that it is appropriate to use for the particular problem and that it can be used on a variety of devices. However, when students locate the manipulative, it can enhance their digital citizenship skills and increase the rigor of the problem-solving activity. Students would need to consider the type of manipulative that they want to use, summarize the name or application in the web search, and finally learn the manipulative as they apply it to the problem. In either case, purposeful planning will result in a more predictable classroom implementation.

When teaching younger students to use virtual manipulatives, you should have some that they use on a regular basis, but do not limit them to only those tools. The skill of being able to search for something on the web is important for young children too. Many five-year-olds use the microphone on tablets to search for their favorite shows on Kids YouTube. This real-world example is evidence that young kids are ready to search and evaluate information for their needs, but this digital literacy and application to academics does not happen overnight. Sometimes offering early finishers the challenge of searching for another tool (perhaps name some but don't link them) is a great way to maintain engagement and infuse digital literacy.

# Evaluating for Instructional Purpose

You will soon find that some virtual manipulatives are better than others, and that the definition of better depends on the mathematical goal. When evaluating a manipulative for instructional purposes, it is important to consider how students will use it, how it is related to the mathematical goal, and how it is used to build conceptual or procedural understanding. A good virtual manipulative is one that is user-friendly, is accessible, is related to the mathematical goal, and supports connections to conceptual and procedural understanding.

## USER-FRIENDLINESS AND ACCESSIBILITY

Student usability and accessibility is important to consider as you balance the time it takes to learn and manipulate the virtual tool. Determine if it is intuitive and invites students to interact without extensive knowledge of the tool. Assess the dexterity needs and hand–eye coordination and compare that with the developmental levels of your students. You might even ask some students to try them out. With proper planning, you can ensure that your choice results in smooth implementation.

One facet of user-friendliness is to consider if and how students will collaborate while using the virtual manipulatives. Some manipulatives, especially third-party manipulatives, require students to interact independently and then insert a screenshot of their finished model to the group recording space. Other manipulatives can be manipulated together in the small group. Consider how you want your students to discuss and connect each other's models while collaborating.

## APPLICATION TO MATHEMATICAL GOALS AND STUDENT LEARNING

Finding the right virtual manipulative requires the right application to the mathematical goal. I personally have a few favorite tools that I use in almost every problem-solving situation, but not everyone sees how to use them in different problems. It is important to try out the manipulative with the problems that you assigned to ensure that the manipulative helps students to understand the mathematics goal of the lesson.

The purpose of a virtual manipulative is to build conceptual and procedural understanding, but beware of apps that do too much of the thinking or manipulating for the student, thus robbing them of the chance to reason. Look for virtual manipulatives that help you scaffold the learning without removing the problem solving. For example, if you are teaching a lesson on geometry and the fundamental lesson defines squares as a subset of rectangles, then you don't want the app to simply draw a square. Rather, tools such as Geogebra will require students to code the square to maintain right angles and congruent sides. Similarly, if students are learning about regrouping and trading tens and ones using base-ten blocks, the app should allow for students to determine when to group and break apart and not do it automatically, so that the students can apply their conceptual understanding.

# Integrating Physical and Virtual Tools

There are a variety of tools available to support student understanding by manipulating objects as they generalize the mathematics. When teaching in an online math class, it can be tempting to only consider virtual tools and manipulatives, but attention should also be spent on the physical objects that students can still use and access from around the house. Just about anything can become a manipulative, such as cereal, spaghetti, beans, paper clips, buttons, and bottle caps. Another physical tool is traditional paper and pencil for recording algorithms and drawings. There is still a place for these tools, and they should still be included in the online class. Teachers can establish norms that make these tools visible to the rest of the class so that they can be integrated in whole-group discussions. Figure 3.1 provides some examples of mathematical concepts and common physical manipulatives that can be used to support student learning and are easily found at home.

## Figure 3.1
## Common Manipulatives Around the House

| Place Value | • Pennies, dimes, and dollars<br>• Cereal and spaghetti<br>• LEGO bricks<br>• Paper clips<br>• Beads and string |
|---|---|
| Computation and Operations | • Buttons<br>• Beans<br>• Beads<br>• Bottle caps |
| Building Arrays | • Cheez-it® crackers<br>• LEGO bricks |
| Fractions | • Egg cartons<br>• Muffin trays<br>• Toys with different attributes (Shopkins, small dolls, marbles, Nerf cartridges, and blocks or LEGO bricks of various shapes and colors) |
| Measurement | • Rice, sand, and water to fill containers<br>• String<br>• Measuring tape<br>• Measuring cups<br>• Paper clips, cubes, or other equal-sized objects (nonstandard measurement) |
| Probability | • Dice<br>• Paper clip spinners<br>• Coins<br>• Game pieces<br>• Cards |

## USING PHYSICAL MANIPULATIVES AND DRAWINGS

Whether it is you or the student who is modeling their physical manipulative, sometimes it is the very action or movement that you want to showcase during the discussion. If this is the case, it is critical that the class watch the action in real time. This can be viewed through live streaming a demonstration by the teacher or other students on all videoconferencing programs. The student can direct the camera downward to show the movement and you can facilitate the discussion while other students observe the demonstration. Students can also be empowered by learning how to take a screenshot and posting their model in a shared slide.

Other times, even in an online setting, you may want students to use paper and pencil to draw and record problem situations and their reasoning. Sometimes these drawings are better than what is accessible in the digital space and can be incorporated in the class discussion similarly to how you would use them in a face-to-face classroom. Students can upload images of their work using a phone, tablet, scanner, or computer camera and then display the images for the class to view.

### MathType Tools

Because mathematics uses a variety of symbols, placements, and notations, it is important that students learn the customs for representing algorithms. Many MathType tools make fractions, exponents, and even integrals visible in the digital space. However, some students may struggle with the labor-intensive nature of creating a digital representation. It is important to consider the balance of uploading a snapshot of student work and the use of MathType tools.

Let's take a look at how Mrs. Radke's second graders explored regrouping in order to add 37 + 28. Mrs. Radke used Google Slides to facilitate her whole-group discussion and allowed students to share their contributions to the discussion by adding their own slides. Some students used physical manipulatives and others used paper and pencil. Mrs. Radke valued both types of tools and included both in her whole-group discussion.

## Mrs. Radke: Manipulatives

Mrs. Radke's second-grade students were modeling 37 + 28 using manipulatives and drawings. Logan used spaghetti and Cheerios™ as his physical manipulative. He counted out 37 Cheerios and threaded groups of 10 Cheerios at a time onto a string of spaghetti until he made three strings of 10 with 7 Cheerios remaining. He repeated this manipulation for 28, creating two strings and 8 remaining Cheerios. Finally, Logan regrouped the 15 loose

Cheerios to make one more string and was left with 5 remaining Cheerios. Since it was the action of threading the Cheerios onto the spaghetti that modeled the regrouping, it was critical that Logan share this movement. Logan did so by enabling the video streaming feature on the class videoconferencing tool and completed the movement for the class to view live and in real time.

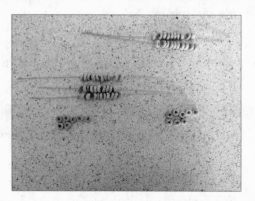

Toby decided to use a drawing to show his thinking. He drew 37 tally marks and circled three groups of 10 and then 28 tally marks and circled two groups of 10. Finally, using a winding line, he grouped the 7 tally marks from the 37 with 3 tally marks from the 28 to show the regrouping. Because the winding line was so clear in the completed image, uploading the picture and sharing it with the class was the ideal way to make his thinking visible.

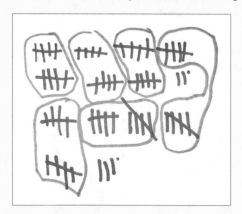

## USING VIRTUAL TOOLS

Web-based manipulatives offer both static and dynamic interactions with the tools. In a static situation, students display a still image, which offers a snapshot into their thinking. Students can travel to another website and interact with the virtual manipulative and then take a screenshot of their work and display it to the class. Remember to empower students to learn the skill of taking a screenshot. This can be taught, and even young kids deserve access to this powerful skill.

In addition to web-based manipulatives, students can use the simple shape features of the interactive slides in slide-sharing platforms such as Google Slides. These tools mimic the hands-on manipulation in a math class.

Let's revisit Mrs. Radke's second-grade class. During this part of the lesson, students showed how they used virtual manipulatives to show 37 + 28.

## Mrs. Radke: Virtual Tools

Farhat used virtual base-ten blocks to showcase how she completed the addition. She interacted with the drag-and-drop program to drag 3 rods and 7 unit pieces to the work space, along with 2 rods and 8 units. The web-based program used animation to automatically regroup the remaining 15 unit pieces into a new rod with 5 pieces left. Then, Farhat copied her screen and uploaded it to the class presentation. While the static display shows Farhat's thinking, it only shows the end result of her thinking. It does not show her thinking as she engaged with the animation of the regrouping. Mrs. Radke saw this image appear on Farhat's slide and questioned her about her thinking. Farhat then shared her screen so that Mrs. Radke could see her moving the base-ten pieces in real time. This dynamic situation was then shown to the entire class by using a screen share feature as students made connections to physical models and Farhat's virtual animation.

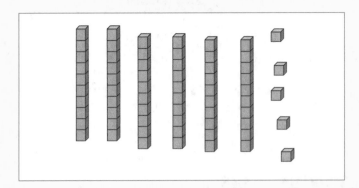

Justice copied and pasted 37 small circles from the tools in Google Slides and colored them blue. Then she created 28 small circles and colored them black. She rearranged the circles and grouped them using a rectangle. Her color-coding representation was visually clear, and Mrs. Radke used both the static visual and dynamic visual in her class. First, she asked students to look at the static model and identify the color coding, and why one rectangle contained two colors. After a minute of student wait time, she asked Justice to share her screen and move the circles around so that the other students could see the action of creating the circles and regrouping them using rectangles. Finally, because of the ability to easily and efficiently create a duplicate slide, Mrs. Radke asked her class to use Justice's circles and rectangles to complete a new problem: 19 + 13. Students quickly duplicated Justice's slide and worked independently to delete extra circles and regroup using the rectangle. Mrs. Radke asked students to identify their slide with their student number and she used these exit tickets as a formative assessment before planning for the next day's lesson.

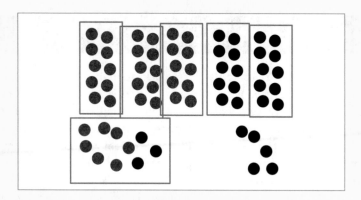

## ALLOWING FOR REPRESENTATIONS

Physical manipulatives are used in the classroom to give students a tool in which to model their mathematical thinking. In the physical classroom, space and the number of manipulatives are limited. If students were to model a very large number using square tiles, for example, they would run out of desk space and eventually square tiles. This is a beautiful moment in that students need to generalize the patterns that they created with the manipulative in order to transfer this model into a rule.

The online environment allows students to have infinite "desk space" as they can simply add more slides, zoom in and out, and change the size of the object or image on their slide. They can also use copy-and-paste features to create an infinite amount of manipulatives. It is important to consider the infinite possibilities online and how they will support students to use the tools to make generalizations. However, there needs to be a careful balance when allowing for infinite use of manipulatives. There is a clear affordance of student creativity and generalization of the use of the manipulative, but it could also result in some students being unable to progress to abstract representations such as numbers, symbols, and numerical algorithms.

Let's take a look at how the concept of infinite representations was carefully applied to regrouping in Ms. Rossi's fourth-grade class as they were exploring place value and adding through the ten thousands place.

## Ms. Rossi: Multiple Representations

Ms. Rossi's students were asked to visualize using base-ten blocks to model 12,499 + 13,622. Typically, in a face-to-face class, Ms. Rossi would use base-ten blocks in a purposeful learning progression—giving students time to explore double-digit addition, then triple-digit addition, and so on—so that they could identify patterns and make generalizations that applied to addition of any place value. That way, students could solve this problem without the use of base-ten materials, but yet still be able to visualize the base-ten blocks in their regrouping. Unlike the classroom, however, the digital world has almost infinite space to make copies. This

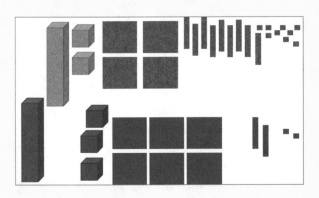

allowed a group of students to use base-ten blocks to add numbers that were previously inconceivable to model in the face-to-face classroom. A typical face-to-face classroom does not have that many hundreds squares and thousands cubes, and ten-thousands are nonexistent. In this example, the students simply copied and pasted as many images as they needed. Teachers should consider the benefits and drawbacks of both. Since students will have access to duplicate copying, and technology is only becoming more abundant, it is safe to say that they will always have access to this ability. However, the drawbacks are that if students don't conceptualize the overall idea of place value and regrouping, they will lack the number sense to estimate larger quantities.

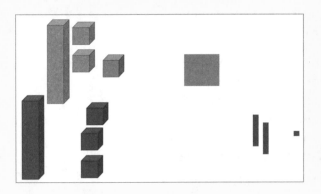

## BALANCING MANIPULATIVE USE

Just as in a regular classroom, it can be tempting to go directly to the kinds of manipulatives that you prefer, but consider the purpose of using manipulatives: students manipulate objects to notice patterns and connect them to other situations in order to create generalizations and build conceptual understanding. Therefore, it is important to consider the mathematical goal and the developmental progression of concrete materials before selecting manipulatives. In the previous examples, both Mrs. Radke and Ms. Rossi were aware of their teaching biases. Mrs. Radke prefers to showcase organized manipulatives, but recognizes that this organization is often revised after the initial manipulation. She acknowledged her bias and still presented Logan's Cheerio and spaghetti model even though it looked disorganized. She knew that the action of the regrouping was more important than the broken piece of spaghetti or the smashed Cheerio. Ms. Rossi prefers numerical algorithms that students upload using paper and pencil and a camera, but she knows the importance of students connecting their algorithm to concrete and conceptual understanding, so she purposefully incorporated the base-ten block model. In both cases, the teachers presented better lessons because they confronted their biases about manipulatives head-on. Their students benefited because they were viewing the problem with multiple representations while making generalizations in order to make connections to the mathematical goal.

## ••• REFLECT AND REIMAGINE

Both new and seasoned online teachers can consider the affordances and drawbacks of using various tools in the virtual setting. If you are new to remote teaching, you will want to use manipulatives that both you and your students are familiar with from a face-to-face class. This will bridge the mathematical connection while giving you room to work on the technological components as students learn to share their thinking in the visible online space. If you are a veteran, consider the ways that you have used manipulatives in your remote classes in the past and empower students to both find and implement

*(Continued)*

(Continued)

manipulatives that you did not anticipate for the problem as they build their digital literacy.

- Have you been purposeful in the selection of the manipulative?
- How did you evaluate the manipulative?
- Did you allow student choice?
- How did you offer tools that are easily accessible while balancing the needs of students who like the extra technology challenge?
- How did you leverage student voice in showcasing the manipulative rather than teaching it yourself?

For more practice, tutorials, and templates, visit www.theresawills.com.

# + chapter

# 4

# SELECTING ACTIVITIES FOR THE VIRTUAL MATH CLASSROOM

When first moving to an online class, it can be challenging to reimagine your typical in-class activities or lesson structures in such a way that they provide the same collaboration, interaction, and rigor. However, just because lessons happen remotely does not mean they should be reduced to a daily lecture-and-practice format. This chapter provides a variety of activities or lesson structures commonly found in the mathematics classroom and showcases how they can be modified to fit into an online setting (see Figure 4.1 for an overview). It also shares how real K–12 teachers have transitioned their face-to-face activities to an online format to support their own remote teaching. These teachers implement both synchronous and asynchronous formats, along with whole-group, small-group, and independent activities. As you read this chapter, consider the routines that you use in your face-to-face

## Figure 4.1

## Remote Learning Strategies at a Glance

| STRATEGY | COMPLEXITY LEVEL | DELIVERY METHOD | STUDENT TECHNOLOGY MODALITIES USED | INTERACTIVE SLIDE FEATURES | ADVANTAGES |
|---|---|---|---|---|---|
| Student-Led Math Show-and-Tell | Basic | Synchronous Asynchronous Blended | Camera Third-party video applications Chat box | Insert images and text boxes | This strategy helps students connect math to the real world. |
| Number Routines | Basic | Synchronous Asynchronous Blended | Microphone Chat box Raise hand | Drag and drop Color code text boxes | Students can practice strategies to build procedural fluency. |
| Math Congress | Basic/ intermediate | Synchronous | Microphone Chat box | n/a | Students can debate mathematical noticings and wonderings through questions. |
| Rich Tasks | Intermediate | Synchronous Blended | Assignment dropbox Microphone Chat box Breakout rooms | Insert images and text boxes | Students can investigate a high-level cognitive thinking situation with multiple representations and connections. |
| Small-Group Guided Instruction | Intermediate | Synchronous Blended | Video streaming Microphone Chat box | Varied | The teacher can teach mini-lessons to a small group of students with similar learning goals. |
| Games | Advanced | Synchronous | Microphone Breakout rooms | Drag and drop Insert images and text boxes | Students can practice procedures and identify strategies that lead to generalizations. |

classroom—or in your virtual classroom if you are already teaching remotely—and ask yourself how students collaborate and interact. Think about the pedagogical practices you want to continue in your remote class. Figure 4.1 provides a list of the activities provided in this chapter as well as information to help you make informed choices about which ones you may want to try in your own instruction. While the grade levels in the examples vary, as you read, consider how you can apply the same kind of activity within the grade you teach.

# Student-Led Math Show-and-Tell

**Purpose:** To showcase real-world application of a mathematical concept

**Digital Tools Needed:**

- Live teaching platform
- Slide-sharing program (e.g., Google Slides)
- Digital photo device
- Interactive video recording program (e.g., Flipgrid)

**Student Technology Skills:**

- Participate in live chat
- Take and upload photos
- Create slide design
- Record video

**Difficulty Level:** Basic

**Teaching Method:**

☑ Synchronous

☑ Asynchronous

☑ Blended

**Process:**

1. After being introduced to a mathematical concept, have students find real-world examples of the concept.

2. Instruct students to take photos of those real-world examples or gather them from online sources.

3. Explain to students that they will create their own slide or video recording with their selected examples. This can be done independently or in small groups outside of live teaching.

4. During live teaching, have each student or small group share their examples and make connections by typing in the chat box. (Note: Young students and/or students with limited English proficiency will need additional time and instruction on keyboarding skills to effectively use the chat box. However, emojis are a great way of showing connections and students really enjoy them. Consider the following norms:

   - 🙂 **Happy face:** I connect with that
   - 😍 **Heart eyes face:** I love that idea
   - 🤔 **Thinking face:** I'm not sure I agree with that
   - 🤯 **Mind blown face:** a-ha moment

*Image source:* Iefym Turkin/iStock.com

Take a look at how Ms. Rawding used the Show-and-Tell strategy in her third-grade classroom.

Ms. Rawding has been teaching online for only a week but learned to modify her Math Show-and-Tell lesson about 3-D shapes for her online class. She teaches a synchronous class for students who can log on during the live class time, and she also provides a recording and similar activity for students who attend asynchronously.

## Ms. Rawding: Student-Led Math Show-and-Tell

In previous years, when Ms. Rawding taught in a face-to-face setting, her students brought in examples of various 3-D solids. They presented their items to the class using a show-and-tell structure. This year, instead of students bringing in the examples of a cube, rectangular prism, cylinder, or sphere to her online class, she asked them to find examples in their homes and upload photos to an interactive slide.

In the live class, students took turns showing their images, identifying the name of the 3-D solid and explaining why it was important. During the show-and-tell, students used the chat box to make connections through text and emojis. In this example, Marie was able to showcase her individuality, achievements, and hobbies all while using the academic vocabulary of cube, rectangular prism, cylinder, and sphere.

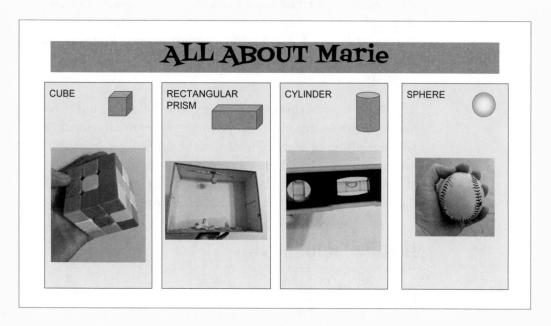

| **Marie:** | I picked a Rubik's Cube for a cube because I am learning how to do it. Now I can get a whole side the same color, but I can't get all the sides yet. |

**Marie:** I picked a Rubik's Cube for a cube because I am learning how to do it. Now I can get a whole side the same color, but I can't get all the sides yet.

**Noelle (via chat):** That's so cool.

**Hawthorn (via chat):** Lol. I peel off the stickers.

**Marie:** For the rectangular prism I took a picture of my diorama of the Apachi. I won an award for the best history diorama last year in second grade.

**James (via chat):** I remember that.

**Marie:** The cylinder is actually a level, but you have to look at the yellow part. I'm really good at helping my family when we need to fix something in the house and this is a tool that I know how to use. The baseball is my sphere. I've played t-ball, coaches pitch, and now I play machine pitch.

**Jordan (via chat):** Me too. What color is your team?

**Taylor (via chat):** Me too.

In the asynchronous classes, students recorded a short video of each object, identifying the name of the 3-D solid and explaining why they chose it. The next day, after all videos were posted, students engaged further by completing a video response to one or multiple peers' videos.

When implementing the Math Show-and-Tell, Ms. Rawding was sure to give students a place to showcase their personality alongside the mathematics content. She engaged other students through chat and video response. Best of all, since the students' work was digitized, Ms. Rawding used those images in lessons to check for understanding and make connections to individual students. By the end of the unit, Ms. Rawding's third graders knew the mathematical content of 3-D shapes, and a lot more about their peers' interests and hobbies.

This vignette showcased the strategy in third grade, but it can be applied across all grade levels whenever we want students to classify something or identify a real-world application in math. Secondary students could identify conic sections around them or the steepness of the slope of different roofs. Elementary suggestions include 2-D shapes, types of triangles, or arrays.

## Number Routines

**Purpose:** To quickly practice number sense on a regular or daily basis; can also be used as an entrance ticket or method to take attendance

**Digital Tools Needed:**

- Live teaching platform
- Slide-sharing program (e.g., Google Slides)

**Student Technology Skills:**

- Participate in live chat (optional)
- Drag and drop

**Difficulty Level:** Basic

**Teaching Method:**

- ☑ Synchronous
- ☑ Asynchronous
- ☑ Blended

**Process:**

1. Create a slide with a number line on it and movable text boxes, one per student.
2. Label the number line using numbers appropriate to the mathematical objective. An example follows.

| TD **3.51** | AD **3.511** | EW **3.520** | RT **3.519** | AM **3.543** | RA **3.530** | TW **3.53** | MZ **3.510** | AS **3.515** |
| PS **3.534** | JS **3.540** | CB **3.525** | TF **3.52** | MH **3.549** | JS **3.535** | LP **3.502** | KL **3.529** | EN **3.54** |

$$\longleftrightarrow$$

3.5                                                                                                      3.55

3. Type a number in each text box and assign each student a box by putting their initials in the corner.

4. As students enter the live classroom, instruct them to find their box and place it on the correct spot on the number line.

5. Once all boxes have been placed, allow students to change the color of any box they think may be in the wrong place. All users (students and teachers) observe all moving boxes simultaneously.

6. Lead a discussion about any of the colored boxes to determine whether they are placed correctly. If not, decide as a class where they belong instead.

7. With any remaining time, discuss placement of any other important numbers on the number line.

> **Alternative**
>
> Allow students to write a number of their choice in their box.

> **Chat**
>
> If appropriate, also allow students to use the chat feature to comment on the placement of the boxes.

Take a look at how Mr. Jones used the Number Routines strategy in his seventh-grade classroom. Mr. Jones was suddenly placed as an online teacher in the middle of the school year. He wanted to continue the use of quick, daily, number sense practice in his math class. His favorite was the Clothesline Math routine (Shore, 2018) in which he welcomed students as they entered the classroom and gave them a rational number on an index card. Students placed their belongings on their desk and walked up to the clothesline. They reviewed the numbers already placed on the clothesline and determined where their number fit in order from least to greatest. Then, they clipped their index card on the clothesline accordingly. As class began, Mr. Jones would ask a few students to justify their placement, and discussed various strategies for determining that placement. Mr. Jones had to reimagine this routine in his online class, but in doing so was able to re-create this activity with the same rigor, interaction, and discussion.

## Mr. Jones: Number Routines

When implementing the Number Routines strategy in his synchronous online class, Mr. Jones created an interactive slide with enough text boxes for all of his students. He gave students choice by allowing them to type in their own number and encouraged them to be creative and original. Students interacted with the slide by dragging their number down onto the number line. Once the numbers were placed, Mr. Jones asked the class to color code a text box blue if anyone thought it should be ordered differently. He used those blue text boxes first and engaged students in discussion.

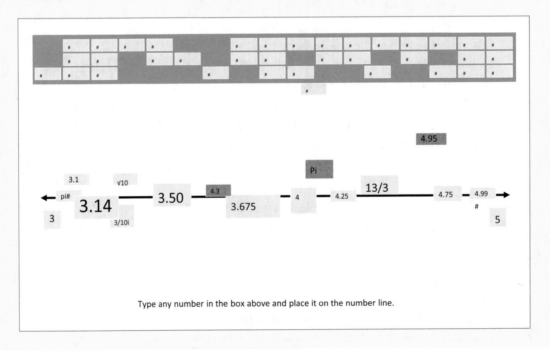

Type any number in the box above and place it on the number line.

| Mr. Jones: | I notice that four and three tenths is blue. Who would like to share with us why they shaded it blue? |
|---|---|
| Nora: | I made it blue because it doesn't go there. |
| Mr. Jones: | Why do you think that, Nora? |
| Nora: | Because the halfway point between 3 and 5 is 4 and that is not even at the halfway mark. It needs to go a little to the right of the halfway mark. |
| Mr. Jones: | Great reasoning looking for a halfway point. Who else sees another reason to move it? |
| Jules: | Uh, that's mine, and when I put it there, there weren't many numbers, so it made sense then, but now it should go to the right just past 4.25, or maybe $\frac{13}{3}$, I don't know what that is. |
| Mr. Jones: | It sounds like Jules agrees on the movement, but how far should they move it? How could we figure out $\frac{13}{3}$? |
| Megan: | 3 goes into 13 four times with 1 remainder so it's 4.1. |
| Mr. Jones: | Ah, so by dividing, you can turn it into a decimal? |
| Aki (via chat): | I think it's 4.3333333333333333333333333333333. |
| Mr. Jones: | Aki, it seems like you found a different answer, how did you find it? |
| Aki: | Same as Megan but a remainder of 1 is really $\frac{1}{3}$. |
| Megan (via chat): | Ooops, I remember that now. |
| Mr. Jones: | Speaking of fractions, I see *pi* is in blue. Who knows the ratio for *pi*? |
| Precious: | It's 3.14 and it works for every circle. |
| Mr. Jones: | You got it, but 3.14 is an approximation. Did you know that a slightly more accurate representation of *pi* can be written as $\frac{22}{7}$? |
| Precious (via chat): | Oh, right. |
| Mr. Jones: | Let's practice. Take a minute to divide $\frac{22}{7}$ and when you are ready, raise your hand. |

*<Mr. Jones waits 1 minute and many virtual hands are raised.>*

| Mr. Jones: | Go ahead, Darius. |
|---|---|
| Darius: | $\frac{22}{7}$ is going to be 3.14 because 7, 14, 21, that's the three and a little more is .14. |
| Mr. Jones: | Darius, you may move the blue box. We didn't get to the last blue box today, but take a minute and think about where it should go and your reasoning. |

When implementing the Number Routines strategy, Mr. Jones was sure to give every student a place to record a number. By asking students to type their own number, he opened the routine to give his students more access and creativity. During the discussion, he was sure to highlight students' strategies such as using the halfway point and division of fractions. He engaged students through the interactive slides, chat box, color coding of the boxes, and audio. He didn't single out students for incorrect placement; instead, he allowed the whole class to review the number line and give suggestions for new placements. By doing this, he transitioned ownership of the number line to the whole class, and they worked cooperatively to ensure its accuracy.

This vignette showcased the strategy in seventh grade, but it can be applied across all grade levels. In elementary grades, for example, this strategy can support ordering whole numbers, unit fractions, and decimals. Teachers of younger students may include the numbers already on the boxes so that students need only drag and drop, but as even the youngest students become digitally literate, consider gradual release and have them type the numbers in the boxes.

## Math Congress

**Purpose:** To debate mathematics using noticings, wonderings, and conjectures to develop questions for further exploration

**Digital Tools Needed:**
- Live teaching platform
- Slide-sharing program (e.g., Google Slides)

**Student Technology Skills:**
- Participate in live chat

**Difficulty Level:** Basic/intermediate

**Teaching Method:**
- ☑ Synchronous
- ☐ Asynchronous
- ☐ Blended

**Procedure:**

1. Pose the situation to students.
2. Ask students to notice and question in the chat box.
3. Ask students to elaborate on their chats.
4. Once students have identified a hypothesis, implement an investigation either independently or in small groups.

Take a look at how Mr. Hawk used Math Congress in his high school geometry class. Mr. Hawk conducts daily live synchronous classes. He enjoys using Math Congress (Fosnot & Dolk, 2002) before teaching specific theorems and proofs because it encourages students to look at geometry with curiosity and uncertainty as they discover patterns and try to justify rules. When he taught in the face-to-face classroom, he would have students physically move their desks into a horseshoe shape around the whiteboard. Then he would facilitate the discussion as students took ownership and debated ideas and developed generalizations. In his online class, he uses the chat box and audio to give students voice as they elaborate on their collective ideas. In this story, his students were exploring triangles inscribed in a circle with one length equal to the diameter. He held a Math Congress to first notice and wonder and then make the case for a potential rule or proof.

> **Facilitation Tips**
>
> It is not necessary to give enough wait time for all students to type, but create a norm that typing can continue even during the conversation. This helps to keep all students engaged.
>
> As a facilitator, you can control which students share over the audio, so select students who describe math related to the objective.

## Mr. Hawk: Math Congress

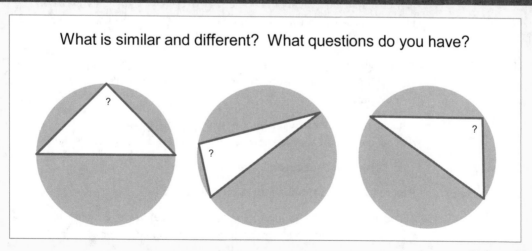

What is similar and different? What questions do you have?

*(Continued)*

(Continued)

| | |
|---|---|
| **Mr. Hawk:** | In the chat box, type what you see that is similar and different in these three images. Also, type questions that you want answered. |
| **Carlos (via chat):** | They are all triangles. |
| **Joan (via chat):** | They are inside of circles. |
| **Ichiro (via chat):** | They are different types of triangles. |
| **Mr. Hawk:** | Ichiro, can you explain a bit more about what you mean by different types of triangles? |
| **Kate (via chat):** | The question mark is always the biggest angle. |
| **Ichiro:** | The first triangle is isosceles, the second is obtuse, and the third is scalene. |
| **Sophie (via chat):** | The second is scalene too. |
| **Mr. Hawk:** | Ah, I see you are using geometry terms to classify the triangles. Sophie said that the second one is scalene too. Sophie, why do you think it is scalene? |
| **Kwame (via chat):** | I see scalene in the middle one too. |
| **David (via chat):** | Yeah, it is scalene, but it is also obtuse. |
| **Kwame (via chat):** | I don't think it can be both. |
| **Sophie:** | Well, scalene means that the sides are all different lengths, and there is a short, a medium, and a long. |
| **Nelson (via chat):** | I think they are all right triangles. |
| **David (via chat):** | I think the middle one is a scalene obtuse triangle because it has a really small pointy angle. |
| **Mr. Hawk:** | Nicely stated, Sophie. Scalene does mean different side lengths. David and Nelson are typing a lot about another way of classifying triangles. David and Nelson, please turn on your microphones and tell us how you are thinking about the triangles. |
| **Nelson:** | You can classify by sides and angles. I just put a piece of paper up to my computer and all the question marks fit into the corner, so they are all right angles. |
| **David:** | It might look like that, but all obtuse triangles have an angle that is really tiny and pointy, that is how you know that the middle one is obtuse, not right. |
| **Sophie (via chat):** | I just did the paper trick, and I agree with Nelson. |
| **Tina (via chat):** | Paper trick worked for me. They are all right triangles. |
| **Mr. Hawk:** | This is a great debate. You are going to go into small working groups to explore this more, and when we return, be sure to have evidence of your claims. |

Mr. Hawk implemented the Math Congress to elicit student ideas and questions worthy of investigation. He began by encouraging students to simply type their initial thoughts. He then directed the discussion based on these noticings and facilitated a respectful place for students to make claims and disagree. This disagreement was the very essence of the follow-up investigation. He used both the chat box and audio so that students could grapple with their idea and summarize it into words before speaking. This technique also helped build confidence in using the microphone. Since his students were used to both typing and listening, he could maintain engaged students as they disagreed in a mathematical debate that left students questioning and eager to construct additional geometric figures as they aimed to create reason and proof.

> ## Encouraging Participation
>
> It is important to use multiple modalities to engage all students in participation and to ensure that there are not a select few voices that are dominating. Consider using chat box, audio, hands up, and a shared slide where students can add text, images, memes, animated gifs, and more to convey their thoughts.

This vignette showcased the strategy in high school geometry, but it can be applied across other grade levels as well. Whenever students notice patterns within numbers, operations, geometric design, skip counting, and growth, they are using logical reasoning to make generalizations that can be explored further in order to reason and prove their generalizations using the Math Congress strategy.

# Rich Tasks

**Purpose:** To launch and investigate a rich mathematical task that values reasoning, high-level cognitive thinking, diverse student representations, and rich discourse

### Digital Tools Needed:

- Live teaching platform
- Slide-sharing program (e.g., Google Slides)
- Assignment dropbox

### Student Technology Skills:

- Upload assignments
- Create slide design

**Difficulty Level:** Intermediate

**Teaching Method:**

☑ Synchronous

☐ Asynchronous

☑ Blended

**Process:**

1. Assign as homework or prework a problem that will leverage prior learning to help you launch the rich task during the asynchronous class.

2. Assign a due date for the homework or prework with enough time to review student responses and create purposeful grouping before the next synchronous class.

3. Review several student solutions to the prework problem as a launch for the rich task.

4. During the synchronous class, group students to solve the rich task together. Provide a space such as Google Slides for displaying student work.

> ## Creating Groups
>
> Creating heterogeneous groups based on a variety of observations will increase the variety of strategies and solutions in group work.

Ms. Saunders, a high school math teacher, began online learning at the beginning of summer school. She was assigned a blended class that met synchronously three days a week on Mondays, Wednesdays, and Fridays. Students were required to complete independent asynchronous assignments the other two days each week. Ms. Saunders used the blended model to her advantage by giving students structured activities that related the asynchronous and synchronous lessons. This week, Ms. Saunders introduced students to various sine functions while focusing on the visual attributes of the graph such as amplitude, frequency, and phase. She assigned a launch to a rich task (Wolf, 2015) that required students to analyze three images of a single musical note sound wave.

> ## Rich Tasks
>
> Chapter 8 also includes a deeper discussion of rich tasks.

## Ms. Saunders: Rich Tasks

The students in Ms. Saunders's class were assigned a problem during their asynchronous class on Tuesday and were required to submit their solutions by the end of the day so that Ms. Saunders could review the solutions before their live class.

**Asynchronous Launch:** Look at the following graphs.

1. What patterns do you notice?

2. How do these patterns help you to predict and make generalizations?

3. Describe your pattern using numbers.

4. Research music note waves and bring two new ideas to class on Wednesday.

Task:  Look at the following graphs.
  1) What patterns do you notice?
  2) How do these patterns help you to predict and make
     generalizations?
  3) Describe your pattern using numbers.

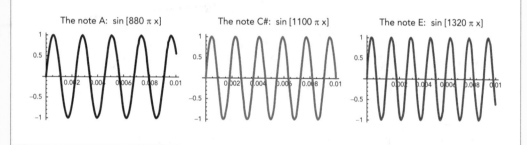

The note A:  sin [880 π x]     The note C#:  sin [1100 π x]     The note E:  sin [1320 π x]

On Wednesday morning, Ms. Saunders reviewed the student responses and created heterogeneous groups so that each group contained students who made different observations. Then, she selected two pieces of student work for the class opener.

| Student 1: | Student 2: |
|---|---|
| 1) They all go up first then down and then up and down many more times. | 1) The wave is more squished the later it is in the alphabet. |
| 2) Every musical note will go up and down. | 2) I predict that G will be the most squished. |
| 3) The waves go as high as y = 1 and as low as y = -1. | 3) When x = 0, they all cross through the origin. |

(Continued)

(Continued)

| | |
|---|---|
| **Ms. Saunders:** | Today, we are going to review two responses in your homework. These two responses give us a list of rules. To better understand the rules, let's discuss the opposites. Who can tell me the opposite of some of these rules? |
| **Thad:** | If they go down first and then back up it is the opposite of up then down. |
| **Ms. Saunders:** | Excellent way of noticing the direction of the waves. |
| **Gena:** | The opposite of going up and down is a heart beat. It goes up, down, flat, up, down, flat. |
| **Ms. Saunders:** | Yes, and nice connection to the real world. |
| **Sara (via chat):** | What if the waves went past 1 and −1? |
| **Nadim (via chat):** | The opposite of squished is pulled out. |
| **Ms. Saunders:** | Nadim, can you explain "pulled out"? |
| **Nadim:** | Like if you pulled a spring, the spaces in between would get wider. |
| **Ms. Saunders:** | If you pulled it, would the max height and min height change? |
| **Nadim:** | It might, but maybe not. |
| **Ms. Saunders:** | Today, you will apply the patterns that you saw to the task. |

*<Ms. Saunders places students in heterogeneous groups and they work on the task for 40 minutes.>*

Rich Task:
Using the three single note waves below, predict the graph for two octaves by sketching each note. Use numbers and patterns to make predictions and generalize your reasoning.

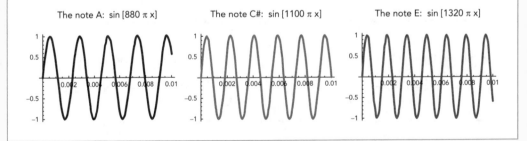

The note A: sin [880 π x]     The note C#: sin [1100 π x]     The note E: sin [1320 π x]

When Ms. Saunders implemented the Rich Task, she considered how she would use her blended sessions to maximize student participation, engagement, and rigor. She wanted students to think independently about the problem to identify diverse patterns and predictions as well as a variety of research on music notes. That way, each student in the group would have both prior knowledge and a unique contribution to the team. By requiring a due date on homework submissions, she was able to review them in order to make the heterogeneous groups, and those students complemented each other as they solved this Rich Task. These heterogeneous groupings provided the diversity of strategies that highlighted the important mathematical concepts of sine waves.

This vignette showcased the strategy in high school, but Rich Tasks can be applied across all grade levels. Rich tasks are used across standards and grade levels beginning at kindergarten. The tasks focus on generalizations and often have multiple correct solutions. Special considerations should be made for teaching young students how to take photos of their work, take screenshots of virtual tools, and practice with virtual manipulatives.

# Small-Group Guided Instruction

**Purpose:** To teach a targeted lesson to a small group of students with similar learning goals

**Digital Tools Needed:**

- Live teaching platform

**Student Technology Skills:**

- Turn on and off microphone and webcam

**Difficulty Level:** Intermediate

**Teaching Method:**

- ☑ Synchronous
- ☐ Asynchronous
- ☑ Blended

**Procedure:**

1. Create small groups of students based on similar mathematical learning goals.

2. Identify learning targets for each group and individualized student needs.

3. Conduct small-group instruction through the use of webcams.

Ms. Hertenberger, a second-grade teacher who transitioned her face-to-face class to an online class midyear, knew the importance of teaching small groups of students (sometimes called Guided Math) (Carpenter et al., 2014). In the beginning, she wasn't sure how to implement small groups when all 25 of her students logged in during the assigned synchronous class time. So she began by hosting office hours in which a small group of five to seven students attended a 30-minute synchronous session, once a week, for Small-Group Guided Instruction in math. During that time, she was able to give the students targeted math support without the responsibilities of 20 other students.

## Ms. Hertenberger: Small-Group Guided Instruction

The objective of this unit was to add two-digit numbers using models and drawings. Each day, Ms. Hertenberger engaged her whole class in a synchronous lesson about this objective, but then differentiated for individual student needs during the guided group instruction time. During this time, she used a physical whiteboard and simply streamed video to the small group. Her students streamed video back to show their work using their webcam. Through these small groups she was able to give extra support to students who were developing a conceptual understanding of two-digit numbers on Monday and progress through extending students' thinking of two-digit numbers to three-digit numbers by the end of the week.

| GROUP 1 | GROUP 2 | GROUP 3 | GROUP 4 | GROUP 5 |
|---------|---------|---------|---------|---------|
| Monday | Tuesday | Wednesday | Thursday | Friday |
| Use base-ten blocks to create two- and three-digit numbers, then record the number with a focus on digit order. | Use base-ten blocks to create and add two-digit numbers. | Use drawings and models to add two-digit numbers. | Use base-ten blocks and drawings to add three-digit numbers. | Use base-ten blocks and drawings to add three-digit numbers. |

By implementing a whole-class and Small-Group Guided Instruction routine, Ms. Hertenberger was able to engage all of her students in grade-level mathematics while supporting and extending that whole-group lesson to small groups of students to meet their unique needs.

This vignette showcased the strategy in second grade, but it can be applied across other grades as well. Regardless of the math topic, students often need targeted instruction that focuses on one specific concept or objective. When the teacher works in small groups of students, the formative feedback is often more observable. Consider topics such as fractions, multiplication, division, proportions, developing a function from an $x$-$y$ table, or operations with negative numbers. These topics often need reteaching or targeted intervention to determine misconceptions.

# Games

**Purpose:** To practice arithmetic or identify mathematical strategies and generalizations

**Digital Tools Needed:**
- Live teaching platform
- Slide-sharing program (e.g., Google Slides)

**Student Technology Skills:**
- Turn on and off microphone

**Difficulty Level:** Intermediate

**Teaching Method:**
- ☑ Synchronous
- ☐ Asynchronous
- ☐ Blended

**Procedure:**

1. Establish the necessary norms and procedures you want to have in place before students begin playing games independently. See Figure 4.2 for sample game norms and procedures.

2. Prepare the game in interactive slides. This can include creating the game yourself or providing a link to a game/interactive activity online.

3. Ensure that students understand the rules of the game and place them in breakout rooms with their assigned slide.

Figure 4.2

## Sample Game Norms and Procedures

| CLASSROOM MANAGEMENT NORM | RATIONALE |
|---|---|
| Everyone turns on their microphone in breakout rooms. | In order to collaborate, students need to hear each other, and the informal excitement and questions foster collaboration. |
| Try 3 Before Me | The phrase "try 3 before me" fosters independence during small group instruction. When students have a question, they should try to find the answer in three places before asking the teacher. Have clear directions or video in a predicate place, and consider allowing a group to enter another breakout room to ask questions about the game. |
| Use phrases like "How did you know to do that?" instead of "That's cheating." | In order to ensure kind behavior, students need to know that they can use and explain strategies. Thoughts of cheating are often a result of creating a strategy based on mathematics. |
| Share strategies and generalizations when you see them. | Even though students are playing against each other in small groups, the groups should share their collective strategies and generalizations in the whole-group discussion, so encourage them to work together to collect as many as possible. |
| Get help right away if someone is unkind or unsafe. | Students need to know how to behave and the consequences of misbehavior. Online platforms allow for private messages to the teacher so students can get immediate help in unkind or unsafe situations. |
| When a partner is disconnected, join another group. | Games are no fun if you are playing by yourself. In order to keep students independent and engaged, they need to know what to do and where to go if their partners become disconnected or leave their computer. |

Ms. Good is new to online teaching, but she has a plethora of math games and the classroom management skills to implement regular game days in her fourth-grade class. Ms. Good used games to discuss play strategy that is rooted in mathematical generalizations. When Ms. Good switched to online teaching, she considered games a non-negotiable part of her lessons. She was determined to not only implement games, but also continue the student-to-student collaboration that was essential in discussing the strategies that built major mathematical generalizations.

## Ms. Good: Games

Ms. Good began teaching her fourth-grade students how to be respectful and independent using The Product Game (https://www.nctm.org/Classroom-Resources/Illuminations/Interactives/Product-Game). Students opened the web applet and played the game against the computer, then typed their generalizations in the chat box. However, she was disappointed in the lack of real-time, peer-to-peer interaction. She described it as going out to dinner and everyone texting on their phone instead of engaging in conversation with one another. Later that week, she used the same game, but this time she used interactive slides and breakout rooms.

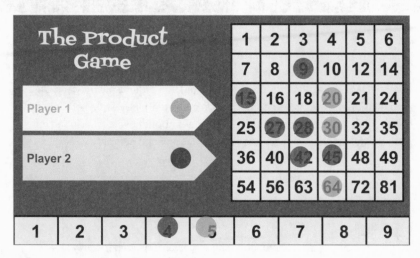

Source: www.theresawills.com/templates

Each pair of students was assigned a game board and a private room in which to chat over audio. She required a classroom management norm that students must have their microphones on while in the breakout room so that they could engage in casual conversation and communicate noticings while playing the game. As she rotated through the breakout rooms, she heard a chorus of conversation, both playful banter about missed opportunities and thoughtful generalizations about strategy related to mathematics. She noted these conversations and interwove them at the end of the class by calling on those students to share their strategies and generalizations.

Ms. Good already had some impressive norms and procedures to ensure collaboration, respectful behavior, and discussion about strategies in her face-to-face instruction. She also developed the online norms (from Figure 4.2) with her students and practiced them regularly.

This vignette showcased the strategy in fourth grade, but it can be applied in other grades as well. For example, secondary students can use generalizations to create strategy. Consider the games that your students already play in the face-to-face setting. Determine the mathematical purpose of the game and ensure that your digital version meets the same purpose.

## ●●● **REFLECT** AND **REIMAGINE**

When transitioning your face-to-face class to an online environment, it is important to reflect on your classroom norms, preferences, activities, and purpose. Know thyself and begin with your strengths. As you reimagine your remote class, reflect on a favorite activity that you did in a face-to-face class and consider how to transition it to an online setting. Revisit these questions as you read other chapters and develop ideas about how to transition your activity while maintaining the essential pedagogy and content.

- What is your favorite activity in the face-to-face classroom?
- What are students doing during this activity?
- How do students interact with the content?
- Are students collaborating together or working independently?
- How was the activity structured?
- How did the activity foster creativity?
- What norms, rules, and procedures did you address and practice to make this activity successful?

For more practice, tutorials, and templates, visit www.theresawills.com.

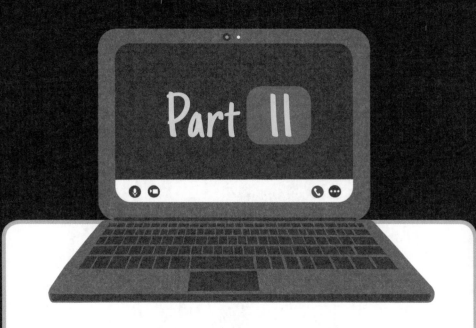

# FACILITATING INSTRUCTION

Part II of this book immerses you in classroom situations where you will get a glimpse of how a teacher uses pedagogical practices that leverage the advantages of technology to increase student engagement, interaction, and voice in the remote classroom. You will discover how to see student thinking as it develops in real time, even when you're not standing right in front of your students. You will see how to smoothly infuse classroom community-building moments into your lessons. You will learn how to implement math routines and rich tasks to make the mathematics come alive in your online class. This part of the book will give you stories that will inspire you to try your favorite math lessons online and feel confident in the procedures and norms to make those lessons successful.

+ chapter

5

# STRATEGIES TO BUILD STRONG MATH COMMUNITIES

With the incredible amount of digital information available today, one might assume that 21st century children could learn all the academic content they need to know from TV shows and online videos. But teachers are way more powerful than simply content deliverers. Teachers use a variety of formative and summative techniques to gauge every child's learning, differentiate on the fly, support their confidence and enjoyment of mathematics, insert humor and compassion, ask purposeful questions, and grow problem solvers. Teachers play a pivotal role in the lives of children that cannot be replaced by "Googling it." One of the most important roles of a teacher is to build a strong classroom community. This includes one-on-one relationships with students and peer-to-peer relationships, but the way that a teacher shows caring

## Figure 5.1

## Building Classroom Community Strategies at a Glance

| STRATEGY | COMPLEXITY LEVEL | DELIVERY METHOD | STUDENT TECHNOLOGY MODALITIES USED | INTERACTIVE SLIDE FEATURES | ADVANTAGES |
|---|---|---|---|---|---|
| Morning Meeting | Basic/ intermediate | Synchronous<br><br>Blended | Microphone<br><br>Video streaming<br><br>Raise hand<br><br>Chat box | Insert images and text boxes | Every student has the opportunity to share by either text or voice. |
| Icebreakers and Attendance Routines | Basic | Synchronous<br><br>Asynchronous<br><br>Blended | Microphone<br><br>Chat box | Drag and drop | This attendance routine is efficient since it launches the lesson and all students participate. |
| Microphone Love | Intermediate | Synchronous | Breakout rooms<br><br>Raise hand<br><br>Microphone | Drag and drop | This strategy builds confidence in using the microphone. |
| Breakout Rooms | Advanced | Synchronous | Breakout rooms<br><br>Microphone | Type text | This strategy builds confidence in using the microphone and keyboarding. |
| Well-Being Check-in | Basic | Synchronous<br><br>Asynchronous<br><br>Blended | Microphone | Drag and drop | This strategy provides teachers with insight on the social-emotional state of students. |

relationships is often different in an online setting (Borup et al., 2013). This is a lesson you surely know from your face-to-face teaching experiences, and teaching at a distance is no different. What is different in a virtual setting is *how* you build these relationships. Consider these questions:

- How do you get to know your students (if you don't already)?
- How do they get to know each other?
- Even if you have an established relationship with them, how do you translate that into an environment where they are learning from home, perhaps reluctantly?
- How do you keep that relationship alive and vibrant throughout your distance learning journey together?

This chapter is meant to answer these questions and offer some quick and productive routines and strategies (see Figure 5.1)—many of which involve mathematics—that will get your students talking, laughing, and embracing your inclusive classroom community.

## Using Your Morning Meeting

Morning Meeting (Davis & Kriete, 2014) is a community-building routine seen in many face-to-face elementary classrooms. It usually begins with students coming together on a rug or open space and welcoming their peers. It often includes routines such as identifying the learning objectives, checking the weather, and sharing out some student celebrations.

This routine provides the foundation for future student-to-student collaboration. It gives students a place to learn about each other's hobbies, interests, and stories. When students know more about each other, and identify commonalities, it creates a bond that translates to kind and inclusive interactions during mathematical discussions and investigations.

Morning Meeting can be adapted for use in the remote classroom using an open space for successes and celebrations and implementing a norm that every student may add to the slide in any modality that they choose, such as text or a photo.

Let's look at how Ms. Eaglen, a third-grade teacher, uses Successes and Celebrations in her Morning Meeting to build community.

## Ms. Eaglen: Successes and Celebrations

As Ms. Eaglen officially began her class one morning, she directed all of her students to a blank interactive Successes and Celebrations slide on the screen and asked students to enter something they wanted to celebrate or share from the weekend. Ten new text boxes emerged as students' ideas appeared simultaneously on the interactive screen. On this particular morning, one of Ms. Eaglen's students, Max, posted a picture of his new dog. Ms. Eaglen scanned all of the responses and asked a few students to elaborate through conversation using the microphone:

**Successes and Celebrations (please include your name; photos encouraged)**

My new dog! -Max

I finished Magic Treehouse #6. -Jonah

I made a castle with Legos with my dad. -Keisha

We did scooters and chalk in the streets. -PJ

I made sandcastles at the lake and caught a fish. -Johnna

Family movie night! -Sadie

I had a sleepover at my nana's house. She make me pancakes for breakfast. -Joel

I played Minecraft. -Logan

Played with my friends. -Bodie

| | |
|---|---|
| **Ms. Eaglen:** | Hi Max, is that a picture of your new dog? |
| **Max:** | Yeah, he's a beagle and his name is Gauge. |
| **Ms. Eaglen:** | He looks so happy. |
| **Max:** | He is. He barks a lot, but he loves to play. |
| **Emmett:** | I have a beagle too, and she barks a lot. |
| **Ms. Eaglen:** | Emmett, what is your beagle's name? |
| **Emmett:** | Lady. *<barking noises>* |
| **Ms. Eaglen:** | Is that Lady talking to us now? |
| **Emmett:** | Yes, let me go sit with her so she will quiet down. *<Emmett's screen shakes as he walks into another room and snuggles his dog.>* |

| Ms. Eaglen: | Johnna, did you have fun at the lake this weekend? |
| Johnna: | Yes, I even caught a fish. But we didn't eat it, we threw it back in to find his family. |
| Ms. Eaglen: | I've been fishing too, but I usually don't catch anything. |
| Rona (via chat): | I like fishing if someone else does the worms. |
| Ms. Eaglen: | Sadie, what movie did you watch during family movie night? |
| Sadie: | *Willy Wonka*, and I really wish I could go to that chocolate castle. |
| Keisha (via chat): | I love that movie. |
| Quincy (via chat): | Willy Wonka is so cool. |
| Ms. Eaglen: | It sounds like there is a *Willy Wonka* fan club. Raise your hand if you've seen this movie. |

*<8 of the 20 hands are raised in the virtual classroom.>*

| Ms. Eaglen: | Did you know that it was a book before a movie? How many of you want to check it out from the library and read it? |
| Keisha (via chat): | No way, so cool! :D |
| Rona (via chat): | I do I do I do |
| Ms. Eaglen: | Maybe we could even talk about *Willy Wonka's Chocolate Factory* in math this week. |

Several students typed excitedly in the chat box and shared their enthusiasm as Ms. Eaglen made a mental note to use this context for problem solving in her upcoming math lessons.

Ms. Eaglen may only need to dedicate five minutes of her Morning Meeting time to an interaction like this, but it reaps huge benefits, as there are several layers of purposeful planning and thoughtful instruction that Ms. Eaglen implements. Here are the intentional practices that Mrs. Eaglen strategically used to support her students:

- Ms. Eaglen used an unstructured interactive slide and that gave Max the space to upload a picture of his new dog. She knew that students needed a space for structure and nonstructure, and planned for both during her lesson.

- Sadie is nervous about using her microphone, so Ms. Eaglen wrote Sadie a private chat to let her know that she would call on her. Since it was about a personal experience, the stakes were low, which gave Sadie more success practicing using the microphone.

- Keisha loves to talk and type and share many experiences. By using both the chat box and the audio space, Ms. Eaglen gave all of her students a place to have a voice, even if they weren't called on to speak aloud.

- Ms. Eaglen preread all of the student responses as she selected students to elaborate. Since Johnna rarely posts, she purposefully selected Johnna to share her fun at the lake.

With purposeful implementation of Successes and Celebrations, and by asking students to elaborate on experiences, Ms. Eaglen built a culture of collaboration by showcasing all students using multiple modalities and connecting their experiences to each other.

This vignette showcased the strategy in third grade, but it can be applied across all grade levels as well. In order to relate mathematics to students' lived experiences, you can use Morning Meeting time to have students share out examples of when they find something in their home or community. When the options are open, students will begin to showcase their cultures and uniquenesses in your class. For example, when teaching about the foci of an ellipse, students often learn about the environmental advantages to using solar cookers. This reflective dome-shaped cooker uses the sun's energy to focus the reflections directly at the mathematical focus. During Morning Meeting, students can share similar dome items from their home and estimate the foci. As students share the cooking devices, diverse populations can showcase unique cookware, introducing their culture with pride. Examples might include the wok (Chinese), cataplana (Portuguese), dolsot (Korean), handi (Indian), kazan (Russian), palayok (Filipino), and tajine (Moroccan). Regardless of your mathematical topic, this routine is student-led and builds upon student experiences.

## Using Icebreakers and Attendance Routines

Classroom community and mathematics can be integrated into every part of the teaching, even during attendance taking. Attendance routines (Cameron, 2020) may seem simple on the surface, but the benefits are much deeper. For example, by asking students a multiple-choice question, you can identify which students are present, discuss mathematics, and also learn students' opinion based on the question. These opinions often lead to conversation, giggles, and enhanced peer-to-peer connections.

A variety of icebreakers could be used to build classroom community. When using them for attendance, it is important to keep them clean and simple so that they are useful for this purpose. I prefer Four Corners, Would You Rather?, What's Your Favorite, or Continuums. In each of these examples, students simply type their name in a specific location on a slide or type their name and very short response.

Let's take a look at how Mrs. Terry uses an icebreaker to serve three purposes: it accounts for attendance, it builds community, and it launches the math lesson about polygons. She begins by displaying an image to her fifth graders.

## Mrs. Terry: Icebreakers

**Mrs. Terry:**  What is wrong with this pizza?

*<Several microphones turn on and giggles fill the audio space as students try to explain the unequal size of the slices.>*

*<Simultaneously, six students type emojis in the chat box.>*

**Mrs. Terry:**  Ah, but there is something right about the pizza. Look at the shape of the slices, do you see it?

**Caitlyn:**  Well, they are cut up into triangles, but they are just really bad triangles.

*<Simultaneously in the chat box, four other students describe the triangles.>*

**Sanjay (via chat):**  It is a good amount of cheese and the pepperoni are not stacked.

**Mrs. Terry:**  Great noticings. It seems like we have some strong opinions. Have you ever had square pizza? What do you think is the best way to cut pizza?

*(Continued)*

(Continued)

*<Mrs. Terry directs students to the icebreaker slide that contains a Would You Rather?-style question and many blank text boxes. Students are familiar with the routine and know to insert their name into one of those text boxes. Mrs. Terry changes the color of several boxes to cue students that she will call on them to elaborate on their choice.>*

# THE BEST WAY TO CUT A PIZZA IS . . .

| START WITH A CIRCLE AND CUT TRIANGLES | | or | START WITH A RECTANGLE AND CUT SQUARES | |
|---|---|---|---|---|
| Sophia | Emma | | Taylor | Levi |
| Mia | Isabella | | Noah | Demarco |
| Caitlyn | Tania | | Kelli | Ethan |
| Jacob | | | Drew | |
| | Julian | | | |
| Daniel | | | TJ | |
| | | | | |
| | | | Dominique | |
| | | | | |
| Olivia | | | | Matthew |

| **Mrs. Terry:** | Caitlyn, you were the first to notice the triangles, and you also said that you would rather cut triangles. Can you tell us why? |
|---|---|
| **Caitlyn:** | Because it has a small point that you can bite right into. |
| **Mrs. Terry:** | That certainly makes it easier to eat. Taylor, why did you choose squares? |
| **Taylor:** | Because you can get the middle pieces with no crust. |
| **Lin (via chat):** | That's why I like square, but I love the crust, especially cheese-stuffed crust. |

*<Dominique drags her text box to the other side to change her answer.>*

| **Mrs. Terry:** | Dominique, can you tell us why you changed your answer? |
|---|---|
| **Dominique:** | Kelli reminded me that you get more stuffed crust with square. |

In this quick activity, you saw Mrs. Terry take attendance, build a community of kids who love discussing pizza, and launch the lesson on polygons. Rather than a roll call or monitoring students as they log on, Mrs. Terry simply keeps a copy of the icebreaker. As a way of building relationships with students who are reluctant to participate, Mrs. Terry gives them notice that she will call on them by changing the color of their text box. Finally, as Mrs. Terry dives into the lesson on polygons, she has already provided students with examples and nonexamples of shapes that can be classified as polygons and nonpolygons, and she can use those experiences to support her students who are still learning English.

This vignette showcased the strategy in fifth grade, but it can be applied in other grade levels as well. For example, Would You Rather? questions are especially relevant when learning system of equations, as the situational preference often changes at the solution to the system. For example, would you rather get a dollar each day or a payment plan that begins with a penny and then doubles every day (day 2 = 2 cents, day 3 = 4 cents, day 4 = 8 cents, etc.)? Once students place their names (taking attendance) they can defend their thinking, which will launch into the lesson.

## Learning to Love the Microphone

Using the microphone can be a challenge when teaching online. Some students are hesitant, and once they find the courage to speak, sometimes they are interrupted by another student. This can result in both students turning off their mics and becoming hesitant to use them again.

Similar to a face-to-face class, you can use small groups or even partners to motivate students to speak more often and build their confidence in using the microphone. The intimate nature of smaller groups, along with low-stakes topics, can help to relieve nerves about speaking. In addition, students in partner groups cannot hide as in a larger group. If there are specific topics to discuss, there are only two voices, which will spur more conversation.

Ms. Evans, a first-year kindergarten teacher who began online teaching at the start of summer school, uses two routines to get kids to talk: a pair-share routine (adapted from her face-to-face student teaching experience) and a rephrasing routine in which a student rephrases another student's explanation.

# Ms. Evans: Love the Microphone

Ms. Evans asked, "How many red fish and how many blue fish are in the fish bowl?" She waited for students to raise their virtual hands. She decided to call on Katrina, whose hand was raised.

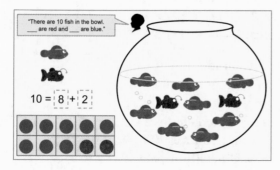

Image sources: Fish: SEREBRENNIKOV/iStock.com;
Silhoutte: Vectorig/iStock.com

| | |
|---|---|
| **Ms. Evans:** | How many red fish and how many blue fish are in the fish bowl? |
| *<Katrina raises her virtual hand.>* | |
| **Ms. Evans:** | Yes, Katrina? |
| **Katrina:** | Ten. |
| **Ms. Evans:** | Can you explain what you mean by 10? |
| **Katrina:** | Ten fish. |

Ms. Evans could sense that Katrina understood that there need to be 10 fish, but she also sensed confusion. She noticed that there were no other hands raised, which prompted her to give an example and give students a peer to discuss additional examples.

**Ms. Evans:** Katrina is right, there are 10 fish. In this example, 8 fish are red and 2 fish are blue. I'm going to place you with a partner in a breakout room to see if your group can find a different way to show 10 fish in the bowl. Be sure to turn on your microphone in the breakout room.

*<Ms. Evans creates 10 breakout rooms and evenly distributes her 20 students in pairs. She then navigates between breakout rooms and listens to student discussions. After several minutes, she returns the class to the main room.>*

**Ms. Evans:** How many red fish and how many blue fish are in the fish bowl? You can tell us your thinking or showcase your partner's thinking.

*<Seven hands are raised instantly.>*

**Mohammed:** James said it was five and five.

**Ms. Evans:** Well done, James, 5 plus 5 equals 10. How about you, Kathryn?

**Kathryn:** I know that 1 plus 9 equals 10, so only 1 red fish.

**Ms. Evans:** Yes, Kathryn, 1 red fish and how many blue fish?

**Kathryn:** Nine.

*<Ms. Evans continues to call on several students, and the conversation includes the voices of many different children.>*

Ms. Evans showed two important ways to increase students' confidence using the microphone. First, Ms. Evans used a strategy from her face-to-face class called a pair-share. She knew that when students talk with one other person, they can't hide and are more likely to participate. She also knew that since only one student was ready to answer, that they needed time to problem solve with another student. Finally, during the whole-group talk time, she welcomed students to showcase a peer's work. This reduced the risk of being wrong in class, which builds confidence in using the microphone.

This vignette showcased the strategy in kindergarten, but it can be applied across other grade levels as well. Students and adults often struggle with accepting the sound of their voice over the microphone. If students, especially adolescents, are building confidence in the microphone, lower the cognitive demand so that they can respond freely without the fear of being wrong. Use norms such as pair-share and move those pairs into quad-shares to continue low-stakes conversations that increase confidence. If you have students learning English, include sentence starters, link them to verbal translations, and model the use of the sentence starter before sending students to breakout rooms.

## Read-Alouds

Google Translate can be used to read directions and sentence starters in both English and home languages.

## Using Breakout Rooms

Breakout rooms are an engaging way for students to get to know each other and have more voice in a more intimate setting as they discuss topics in smaller groups. Throughout the year, you can build moments for students to share more about themselves in ways that are even connected to the mathematics they are learning. When students connect to one another through low-stakes opinion questions, they build relationships, making online learning less isolating. It also gives them an opportunity to share something about themselves. Furthermore, taking turns answering questions in small groups sets the stage for listening norms, such as listening to all group members and all students participate using the microphone.

In this example, Mrs. Sanchez launched one of her second-grade mathematics lessons using a relationship-building starter and an estimation routine.

Mrs. Sanchez posted an image of a fruit bowl piled high with shiny red apples. She asked her students to type their estimate of how many apples were in the bowl on the interactive slide and then move to a breakout room to explain their reasoning with three other students. Before students explained their mathematical reasoning, however, they read two questions and the accompanying sentence starters:

---

What is your favorite fruit, and when did you eat it last?

My favorite fruit is _____. I last ate it _____.

What was your estimate, and why did you choose that number?

My estimate is _____ apples. I chose _____ because _____.

---

When using these discussion starters, students first connected on a personal level and then discussed the mathematics.

This vignette showcased the strategy in second grade, but it can be applied in other grades as well. There are many current events that students observe in the news and on social media that are important to them. In order to build responsible citizens, the community-building question could be about a global or local issue. For example, when considering environmental issues with older students, the sentence stems could read as follows:

- One way that I want to make a difference to protect the environment is _____ because _____.

- My estimate of $CO_2$ in ten years is _____ parts per million because _____.

## Well-Being Check-in

Teachers have an incredible responsibility for not only teaching content to their students, but also teaching and supporting their students through their social-emotional well-being. Online learning can appear especially challenging to the observant teacher who is always watching for the excited grin or glassy eyes before tears emerge. You can implement an emotional check-in during your lessons in order to get a pulse on your students' emotions.

One way to do this is by using a template of student images and emojis to engage students in selecting the emoji that describes their current emotion. This practice can be enhanced by using it at the beginning and the end of a lesson. That way, if you need to reach out to a particular student, you can gauge who needs the extra phone call or email. Since you cannot use the same body language observational strategies in online classes, it is important to plan strategies that support the social-emotional state of your students.

Let's take a look at how Ms. Bolyard implements a well-being check-in in her kindergarten class.

## Ms. Bolyard: Well-Being Check-in

**Ms. Bolyard:** Good morning, class. I'm excited for today's class, so I'm thinking about the excited emoji. How are you feeling today? Move an emoji down to your photo to tell us how you are feeling. Remember that I like you no matter what. You are allowed to feel happy, sad, silly, mad, or any other emotion, and I will always like you.

*<Students move emojis on their image.>*

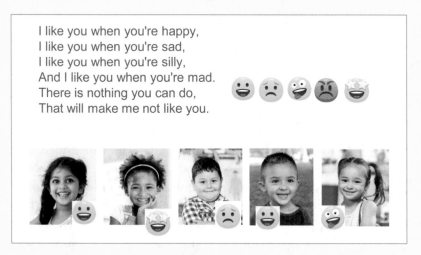

I like you when you're happy,
I like you when you're sad,
I like you when you're silly,
And I like you when you're mad.
There is nothing you can do,
That will make me not like you.

*Image sources:* DragonImages/iStock.com; nilimage/iStock.com; SDI Productions/iStock.com; ajr_images/iStock.com; Iefym Turkin/iStock.com nilimage/iStock.com

*(Continued)*

(Continued)

**Ms. Bolyard:** Janelle, I can see that you are excited today too. What are you excited about?

**Janelle:** I love seeing my friends on the computer.

**Ms. Bolyard:** I love seeing you all on my computer too. If you were feeling sad or mad, I invite you to share more with the class if you want.

**Aiko:** I'm mad because my computer wasn't working and made me late.

**Ms. Bolyard:** Thank you for sharing. I also get frustrated when my computer doesn't work. I will be extra patient with you today.

## Students in Crisis

Much like you anticipate mathematical solutions to problems, you should anticipate what to do when a student is in crisis. This strategy may bring out an opportunity for students to ultimately share sensitive information, because when a student is in crisis, they will tell the person that they trust, and that likely could be you, the teacher. Prepare yourself with knowledge and resources, and role-play the situations so that you can be the best you can be for that student. Proactively seek out the school guidance counselor and school psychologist and determine steps to take in the event a student needs immediate support.

Ms. Bolyard made sure to relate to the students and their emotions and she was also careful not to single out any of her students who were not happy. Instead, she invited them into the conversation and gave them room to express their emotions. When a student does not discuss why they are sad, Ms. Bolyard will pay close attention to them during the class and follow up with a phone call to their family at the end of class.

This vignette showcased the strategy in kindergarten, but it can be applied across all grade levels as well. Special considerations should be made for adolescents to choose their picture that is presented to the class. Rather than use the school image, ask your students to bring an image that they are proud of. It can include a sports photo, a dazzling selfie, a caricature, or a bitmoji. Adolescents can be especially self-conscious about their appearance, and allowing them to showcase their appearance in a way that they are proud of is a way of showing respect for their bodies and the images they choose to share online.

As you reimagine your remote classroom, consider how you will build community using quick routines to uncover student interests, peer collaboration, celebrations, and a lot of laughter. Implement a variety of strategies and approaches, and note potential benefits and drawbacks of each as you develop a list of the approaches that work best for you and your students. Ask yourself the following questions:

- How much time do I want to invest building a community of learners?

- How can I use multiple modalities (images, animated gifs, text, voice, and emojis) to build a community of learners?

- When do I want to use community-building activities to take the place of attendance or launch a math lesson?

- How do my community-building activities encourage students to become comfortable with the microphone?

- When do I want my students to engage in an informal conversation versus a formal conversation with academic terms?

- What immediate and long-term social-emotional supports are available at my school for students? Am I prepared to support students who share an emotional crisis?

For more practice, tutorials, and templates, visit www.theresawills.com.

+ chapter

6

# STRATEGIES TO PROMOTE STUDENT THINKING

## Making Student Thinking Visible

The National Council of Teachers of Mathematics (NCTM) lists "Elicit and use evidence of student work" as one of their eight Effective Mathematics Teaching Practices (NCTM, 2014b). Teachers know that in order to do this, they need to first make student thinking visible using a variety of activities that promote engagement, understanding, and independence (Ritchhart et al., 2011). In the face-to-face classroom, this is accomplished through manipulatives, drawings, words, and opinions shown on paper, on posters, or during presentations or mathematical discussions. This is more than students simply showing their work, because showing your thinking does not have a clear route, algorithm, or procedure. Showing your thinking is organic. Students can show their thinking online, and in fact, doing so online has the opportunity to increase motivation and engagement.

Figure 6.1

## Own-a-Space Strategies at a Glance

| STRATEGY | COMPLEXITY LEVEL | DELIVERY METHOD | STUDENT TECHNOLOGY MODALITIES USED | INTERACTIVE SLIDE FEATURES | ADVANTAGES |
|---|---|---|---|---|---|
| Visual Polling | Basic | Synchronous | Optional: microphone and chat box for further discussion | Drag and drop | The teacher has an efficient and anonymous visual of all student preferences. |
| Class Notebook | Basic | Synchronous | Optional: microphone and chat box for further discussion | Typing text | The teacher has an efficient, semi-anonymous collection of entire class responses. |
| Whole-Class Exit Tickets | Basic | Synchronous | Optional: microphone and chat box for further discussion | Typing text | All students respond and elaborate with various rationales. |
| Respond and Code | Basic | Synchronous | Optional: microphone and chat box for further discussion | Typing text<br>Fill bucket tool | The teacher has an efficient, semi-anonymous or public visual that shows whole-class categorizations. |
| Multiple-Choice Corners | Basic | Synchronous | Optional: microphone and chat box for further discussion | Drag and drop | The teacher has an efficient and anonymous visual of all student choices. |

| STRATEGY | COMPLEXITY LEVEL | DELIVERY METHOD | STUDENT TECHNOLOGY MODALITIES USED | INTERACTIVE SLIDE FEATURES | ADVANTAGES |
|---|---|---|---|---|---|
| Defend Your Choice | Intermediate | Synchronous | Optional: microphone and chat box for further discussion | Typing text | All students provide a rationale for their original choice in a semi-anonymous or public space. |
| Tweet Board | Intermediate | Synchronous | Optional: microphone and chat box for further discussion | Insert text box, shapes, and/or images<br><br>Edit text | The teacher has access to every student's prior knowledge through an unstructured, semi-anonymous brain dump. |
| Tweet Board Sort | Intermediate | Synchronous | Breakout rooms<br><br>Microphone<br><br>Chat box | Drag and drop<br><br>Insert text box, shapes, and/or images<br><br>Edit text | Students collaborate in smaller groups to determine categories and themes and then classify. |
| Dump and Develop | Advanced | Synchronous | Breakout rooms<br><br>Microphone<br><br>Chat box | Typing text | Students have access to more perspectives because they can read other groups' ideas as they further develop their group ideas. |
| Mine, Yours, Ours | Advanced | Synchronous | Breakout rooms<br><br>Microphone<br><br>Chat box | Insert text box, shapes, images, graphs, tables, equations, and so on. | Students build upon each others' work while beginning in their comfort zone and expanding to challenging responses. |
| Blank Slides | Advanced | Synchronous<br><br>Asynchronous<br><br>Blended | Optional: microphone and chat box for further discussion | Insert text box, shapes, images, graphs, tables, equations, and so on. | All students have choice in the modality in which they present. |

The most important part of making student thinking visible is to prepare a place for students to write, upload photos, and interact. Students need this explicit space for many of the same reasons they need carpet squares in primary grades and lockers in secondary grades. When they own a space, they will use it. These spaces can look different, and students can interact and collaborate in them differently. The "own-a-space" strategies in Figure 6.1 offer students a place to type, display, or develop their thinking. It is important to consider how you want your students to interact when you choose an own-a-space strategy.

Having students take turns and respond orally can take a long time and doesn't deliver the in-the-moment response you seek, the strategies that follow give you ways to view student thinking simultaneously, in real time.

## Visual Polling

Visual Polling is a simple, efficient, and completely anonymous way of asking for students' opinions. Interaction is simple and efficient because of the drag-and-drop feature, and since there is enough room for every student to participate, every student can share their thinking and make their voice heard. This is fundamentally different from polling in face-to-face settings. Often, due to social tendencies, students are always looking around the class to see how their friends are responding, and this in turn alters their response. Because Visual Polling is anonymous, students are more likely to record an honest answer.

Visual Polling is also a great strategy to use with young learners, since the questions can be written using familiar vocabulary, high-frequency words, or even images.

Consider using Visual Polling for quick checks, for mathematical dispositions toward a homework assignment, in statistics lessons, or in tasks with multiple correct answers.

Let's take a look at how Ms. Garcia, a seventh-grade math teacher who is new to online learning, used Visual Polling near the end of her unit on real-world percentages.

# Ms. Garcia: Visual Polling

Ms. Garcia suspected that she needed to conduct a few reteaching lessons, but she wanted to poll the students to determine if they felt the same needs. She asked them to move a blue smiley next to the objective if they could teach it to someone else, a gray face if they feel like they just need a bit more practice, and a white frown if they want a reteaching mini-lesson. Ms. Garcia was able to use the results of the Visual Poll to efficiently and purposefully group students into learning stations so that students could practice, extend, or relearn the targeted lesson. It was also evident that a whole-group lesson on solving word problems on percentages would be helpful to her students.

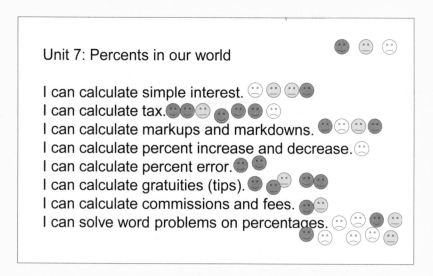

This vignette showcased the strategy in seventh grade, but it can be applied across all grade levels and with any academic standard. Special considerations should be made for kindergarten students as they are still mastering hand–eye coordination and the drag-and-drop abilities. While it may take a bit of practice for these younger learners, the purpose of this strategy is to efficiently and visually display the dispositions of all students in the class in a completely anonymous way, and it is transferable to any grade level.

# Class Notebook

This strategy is simple to create, efficient to implement, and semi-anonymous. It is done by creating a shared slide or contribution space where students can respond to a question, prompt, idea, or specific topic. The Class Notebook slide does not use any special tools or drag-and-drop abilities; students simply click and type during a synchronous learning session, often in a bulleted list or with short, discrete sentences.

By creating the bullet points initially, students have an easier time clicking without writing over each other. It is typically semi-anonymous because the student's name will appear as they are typing, but then will disappear when they complete their statement. Another option is to use numbered lists where students have a specific class number. This maintains the semi-anonymous features while giving the teacher individualized student data. This strategy is different from face-to-face check-ins because all students can view and respond to the collective class thinking in real time. Students who are unsure or hesitant to begin can read other responses as they grow their confidence and summarize their thinking.

Consider using Class Notebook whenever you want real-time responses from the entire class, such as a solution to a problem, a connection to another algorithm, opinions about selecting a procedure, or summarization of a lesson.

Here is an example of Class Notebook from Ms. Hubert, a seventh-grade math teacher.

## Ms. Hubert: Class Notebook

Ms. Hubert used Class Notebook at the end of her proportions lesson to check for conceptual understanding. During the lesson, students showed a variety of strategies and procedures, but the lesson focused on connecting multiple procedures rather than selecting only one procedure to solve all problems. She used the Class Notebook to see if her students made connections or if they were still gravitating toward one procedure. Her slide contained only bullet points, and students interacted by clicking on any bullet point and typing their response. Ms. Hubert used these data to plan her next lesson.

| When would you use a proportion to solve a problem? | |
|---|---|
| • When things are equal<br>• When two things are proportionate.<br>• When you know the ratios<br>• To cross multiply<br>•<br>•<br>• When 2 things are equal but different sizes.<br>• To find a bigger number<br>• Finding the unknown<br>• | • If you can set it up as 2 fractions<br>• When two things are related<br>• You would cross multiply<br>• When two things are equal<br>•<br>• Find the missing part of two fractions<br>•<br>•<br>• |

This vignette showcased the strategy in seventh grade, but it can be applied to other grades as well. Special considerations should be made for early literacy stages of students, and additional wait time may be needed for keyboarding skills. While it may take a bit of practice for younger learners, the purpose of this strategy is to display student-elicited thoughts efficiently and visually, and it is transferable to any grade level. Some other questions to consider are the following:

- Why are graphs important?
- What do you know about fractions?
- When would you use a table to solve a problem?

## Whole-Class Exit Tickets

This simple strategy gives each student an individual space to express their thinking. Students can record in an anonymous or assigned space, giving you additional data about your students. Because all students are typing simultaneously, you can view their thoughts and connections in real time. This is similar to an exit ticket in a face-to-face class where teachers ask students to respond to a quick and informative question and submit the response as they exit the classroom. The advantage of using this strategy in an online format is that no student sits quietly if they are unsure what to write. Instead, if they are unsure, they can read other responses and develop their own thinking.

Consider using whole-class exit tickets whenever you want to observe the content, representation, and speed of student responses while giving every student a voice.

Here is an example of how Mr. Beck used Whole-Class Exit Tickets in his fourth-grade class to determine if students can generalize their knowledge of common numerators to compare fractions that are too large to model.

## Mr. Beck: Whole-Class Exit Ticket

At the end of his lesson on common numerators, Mr. Beck asked his students to demonstrate their thinking about the following question: How do you know that $\frac{1}{99}$ is larger than $\frac{1}{100}$? Students clicked in their assigned box and simultaneously recorded their ideas using multiple representations: words, numbers, pictures, and drawings. He gave enough room for students to express their ideas by creating larger text boxes over three different slides. As their responses emerged, he was able to evaluate both the content and speed at which students submitted their ideas. Finally, he used their words to describe strategies on a class anchor slide that updated throughout the unit.

### How do you know that 1/99 is larger than 1/100?

| | | |
|---|---|---|
| When you have a common top number then you have to think about the bottom number. Smaller numbers are bigger. | If you made a common denominator, 1/99 is bigger | 100 is bigger than 99, so 1/99 is bigger than 1/100 |
| I would rather have a slice of pizza when it is shared with 99 people than 100 people. But they are almost the same size. | I think of 1/9 and 1/10 and I get more if I only have to share with 9 friends instead of 10 | 1/100 is closer to zero. |
| Because 100 is bigger than 99 | If you have less slices of pizza then the slices are bigger | 99 is less than 100 |

This vignette showcased the strategy in fourth grade, but it can be applied across all grades. Additional structure can be used for accountability such as adding a student number or name to each cell. Here are some additional questions that could be investigated:

- Is an equilateral triangle a subset of an isoceles triangle? Use definitions of both to defend your reasoning.

- When have you seen the fraction $\frac{1}{2}$ in your life? Respond in words or images.

- When would you need to double or halve something while maintaining the same ratio?

# Respond and Code

This whole-class strategy showcases student identity and commonalities among students. It does not require students to conform to predetermined labels, but rather allows them to express their opinion however they wish. In this strategy, a question is posed at the top of the slide. Students respond with their answer to the question in their own box labeled with their name. Young students or students with limited English proficiency can drag and drop images, emojis, or icons to respond to the question. By creating a space for every student, the teacher shows that they value every student's contribution. After all students have responded, the teacher provides a color-coding system unique to the responses. Students then go back to their box and change it to the appropriate color. This helps to facilitate discussion, easy identification, and grouping of the responses.

Consider using Respond and Code whenever you elicit student words with the intent to classify them into categories. This can be used in various math strands with multiple categories such as decimals, fractions and percents, or polygons and non-polygons.

Let's take a look at how Ms. Rodriguez used Respond and Code with her second graders during a graphing and statistics lesson.

# Ms. Rodriguez: Respond and Code

Ms. Rodriguez asked students to type their name and favorite sport in the text box. Then, after they all responded, she asked them to change the color of their text box such that:

White: Hockey

Black: Football

Light blue: Soccer

Dark blue: Basketball

She used the visual to ask students follow-up questions such as, "How many students like basketball?" and "How many more students like football than basketball?" Next, students used the data to make a bar graph. Finally, the students created questions that could be answered using the bar graph. Ms. Rodriguez later used this Respond and Code strategy to create homogeneous groups of students based on their favorite sport as they completed a group statistics project about their sport outside of live instruction time.

## What is your favorite sport?

| | | |
|---|---|---|
| Anthony - Hockey | Ann - Soccer | Jody - Soccer |
| Abdul - Hockey | Christa - Football | Jose - Soccer |
| Jeanette - Football | Amy - Basketball | Nicole - Soccer |
| Sara - Football | Elizabeth - Soccer | Donna - Hockey |
| Martha - Soccer | Jim - Football | Deshawn - Basketball |
| Amy - Soccer | Katy - Soccer | Chelsea - Basketball |

This vignette showcased the strategy in second grade, but it can be applied across other grades as well using any investigation question in preparation for graphing. This strategy can also be used across grade levels when students are problem solving. They can use the respond time to describe the way that they solved the problem (e.g., make a drawing, use substitution, use elimination, create a table, or use a combination of procedures). Then the class can classify them in order to determine what are efficient, easy, or popular strategies to solve the word problems.

# Multiple-Choice Corners

This simple and efficient strategy gives you a snapshot of student thinking on a specific multiple-choice question. Students are shown a question or presented with a scenario. Then they place a shape, such as a star, in the box of the answer they choose. Because their names are not displayed on the shape, this strategy allows students to display even a wrong answer in a low-stakes environment. Even young learners can be successful with this strategy because the multiple-choice responses can easily be visual in nature, and moving a shape on the screen is a very simple skill for them to master.

While multiple-choice questions are frequent in a face-to-face classroom, the added benefit of this strategy is that it harnesses the visualization of all classmates. Students can view their peers' responses in real time, which triggers them to consider their reasoning and the thoughts of others as they decide how they want to respond. This reasoning and proof mindset is only accessed when the students can view their peers' thoughts. And, since every student has the opportunity to move the star, every student has a voice.

Consider using Multiple-Choice Corners whenever reviewing a multiple-choice scenario, especially when there are multiple correct answers.

Let's take a look at how Mrs. Norris, a third-grade teacher, used Multiple-Choice Corners in her class.

## Mrs. Norris: Multiple-Choice Corners

Mrs. Norris chose for students to anonymously identify their selection on a multiple-choice question. Using the Multiple-Choice Corners strategy, she asked her students which image best depicts the following problem: I have 12 pieces of candy. I want to share that candy with some friends so that we all get the same amount. How much would each person get? Students moved a star to their selection corner simultaneously. Mrs. Norris was able to view their responses in real time. She then used this

*(Continued)*

(Continued)

activity to launch a whole-group conversation about how different models can be used to visualize problems.

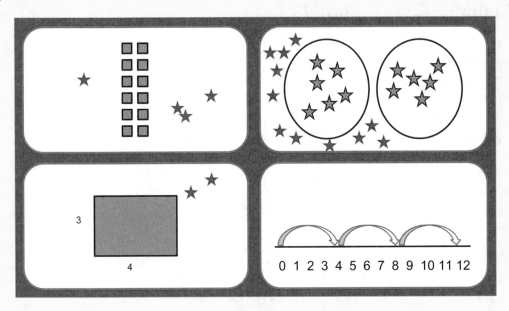

This vignette showcased the strategy in third grade, but it can be applied across other grades as well. For example, in secondary, students often struggle with the multiplicative and additive ideas behind proportional reasoning and rate of change. There are often several mathematical models that are used to show the constant growth and overall proportionality of equivalent ratios. But regardless of the grade level, whenever your aim is to have students visualize mathematics through models, this activity values more than one representation.

## Defend Your Choice

This systematic strategy organizes student rationales in both anonymous and public formats. In response to a multiple-choice question or scenario, students first write a rationale for their particular response anonymously. This allows students to give a rationale and defend it while considering the rationales of other choices. After additional discussion of the responses, students solidify their thinking and take a final stance. This final response includes their name and can be used as an assessment or for reteaching purposes.

Some educators argue that multiple-choice questions only reveal what students don't know, but when students defend their choice, either anonymously or publicly, teachers are able to gain this qualitative insight into their understanding.

Consider using Defend Your Choice whenever you want students to verbalize their thinking through reasoning and proof.

Let's revisit Mrs. Norris's third-grade class to see how she uses Defend Your Choice as an extension of the Multiple-Choice Corners strategy. In that scenario, she presented the following question: I have 12 pieces of candy. I want to share that candy with some friends so that we all get the same amount. How much would each person get?

## Mrs. Norris: Defend Your Choice

After all of her students anonymously posted their responses to the multiple-choice question, Mrs. Norris now wants her students to defend their thinking using a rationale. First, all students posted their rationale anonymously. This is shown in the first slide. This allowed students to read similar rationales because they were grouped together. Then, she asked students from each corner to elaborate on their rationale over the microphone as she engaged the whole class in conversation about mathematical models. Finally, she asked her students to commit to a selection and type their final rationale on the second slide. She used these results as an assessment.

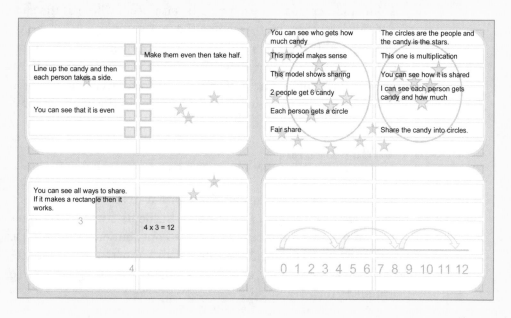

(Continued)

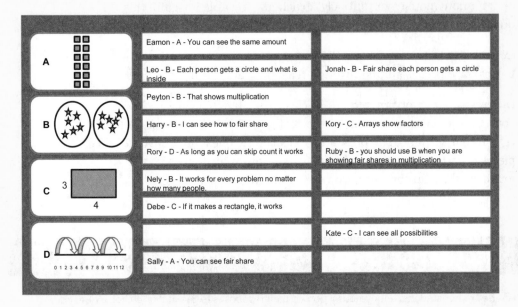

| | | |
|---|---|---|
| **A** | Eamon - A - You can see the same amount | |
| | Leo - B - Each person gets a circle and what is inside | Jonah - B - Fair share each person gets a circle |
| | Peyton - B - That shows multiplication | |
| **B** | Harry - B - I can see how to fair share | Kory - C - Arrays show factors |
| | Rory - D - As long as you can skip count it works | Ruby - B - you should use B when you are showing fair shares in multiplication |
| **C** | Nely - B - It works for every problem no matter how many people. | |
| | Debe - C - If it makes a rectangle, it works | |
| **D** | | Kate - C - I can see all possibilities |
| | Sally - A - You can see fair share | |

This vignette showcased the strategy in third grade, but it can be applied in other grades as well. For example, when using the suggestion in the strategy above about equivalent ratios and proportions, secondary students will find the use of both of these progressive models for justifying answers. The first model allows students to organize their thoughts with peers who had the same response. As they are developing the summary, you can ask purposeful questions to ensure that students understand the various arguments. Finally, when students use the last template, they are signing their name to a justification. This new level of accountability increases the motivation for engagement in the entire activity.

## Tweet Board

This simple strategy uses an open format to allow all students to make contributions. In this strategy, students respond to a question, topic, or scenario with a short contribution. Students can also include images, gifs, or clip art to support their responses. This can be done anonymously or students can add their name or initials to their response.

To the untrained eye, Tweet Board can appear messy and unstructured, but the lack of structure allows for student creativity in length of statement and media used. In a face-to-face class, this strategy is usually implemented by a teacher calling on students as they share their thinking, but doesn't value duplicate contributions. Furthermore, the teacher is usually the one to write down these contributions. By using this strategy in a digital environment, students are the creators of the knowledge and the way that knowledge is displayed. It is also okay that duplicate or highly similar responses are shared.

Consider using Tweet Board whenever you need a quick check or student opinion, or to field prior knowledge whenever there are a plethora of correct answers. Here, sixth-grade math teacher Ms. Henry uses Tweet Board to elicit collective student knowledge at the midpoint of a unit.

## Ms. Henry: Tweet Board

Ms. Henry began with a blank slide and a very open question: What is everything you know about triangles? Students interacted by inserting a text box anywhere on the slide and typing information that they knew about triangles. Students must summarize their thinking into a small box because Ms. Henry used the norm to keep it "short and sweet, like a tweet." Sometimes students typed duplicate copies of the same idea. Her students developed a norm to first change the duplicate to bold font, and then delete the second copy. This way, there were fewer text boxes while acknowledging every student's contribution. Ms. Henry used this knowledge to plan her math learning stations.

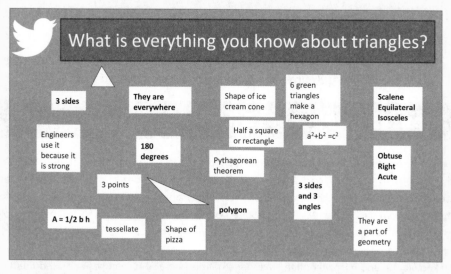

*Source:* TWITTER, TWEET, RETWEET and the Twitter logo are trademarks of Twitter, Inc. or its affiliates.

This vignette showcased the strategy in sixth grade, but it can be applied in other grades as well anytime you want students to respond to a question, topic, or scenario with a short contribution. When using this strategy with early elementary students, special considerations should be made for early literacy and keyboarding skills. While it may take a bit of practice for younger learners, the purpose of this strategy is to display all ideas efficiently and visually.

## Tweet Board Sort

This collaborative strategy requires students to read, interpret, and categorize student-elicited information. It can be completed in an open sort, which allows for creativity as students compare the different entries and interact through the drag-and-drop capability. Or, you can make this into a closed sort by predetermining the titles of the classifications.

This strategy is similar to sorts done in face-to-face settings where students read index cards with predetermined terms, but the striking advantage is the speed at which students can engage in the initial contribution and then immediately sort those collaborative contributions.

Consider using a Tweet Board Sort after the Tweet Board strategy or whenever you want your students to read, analyze, and classify ideas as they discuss similarities and differences. Further, Tweet Board Sorts can be used to develop generalizations or reason to develop proofs.

Let's revisit how Ms. Henry extends the Tweet Board strategy with her sixth graders to complete a Tweet Board Sort.

## Ms. Henry: Tweet Board Sort

Ms. Henry divided students into multiple breakout groups and assigned a copy of the Tweet Board to each group. Then, students read, analyzed, discussed, and categorized each entry. As students discussed the similarities and differences of each box, they simultaneously moved the boxes closer or further away from each other. Ms. Henry rotated between the groups, observing their groupings. While many of the groups' sorts were similar, Ms. Henry used the subtle differences to probe students about the rules governing their classifications. These purposeful questions helped Ms. Henry uncover knowledge and misconceptions that her students had about triangles and used them to create homogeneous reteaching groups during her math learning stations.

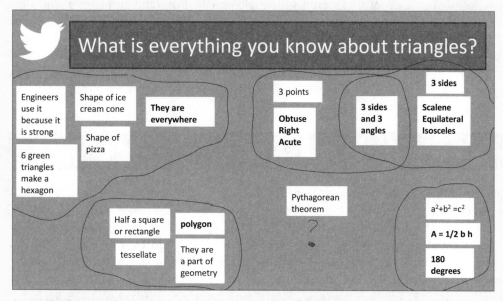

This vignette showcased the strategy in sixth grade, but it can be applied in other grades as well whenever you want students to read, interpret, and categorize student-elicited information. When young students work in groups to make order of the initial Tweet Board, they will likely have terms and images that are unfamiliar. Encourage them to sort the ones that they know while allowing for a "not sure" pile. If you are conducting a whole-group conversation, the "not sure" pile is a great starting point for student explanations and participation.

# Dump and Develop

This collaborative strategy incorporates teamwork in small groups and as a whole class. Students receive a prompt, question, scenario, or topic, and interact by *dumping* their initial ideas on the group space while viewing the *dumps* from other groups to *develop* a more comprehensive list. This allows for different perspectives and interpretations. As the strategy continues, these lists develop into sophisticated sentences. When the teacher values diverse opinions, students strive to not only include peers' ideas but also develop a unique perspective on the prompt.

Consider using Dump and Develop whenever you are eliciting student ideas on a vast topic or when opinions and prior knowledge are diverse.

Let's take a look at how Mr. Davis, an eighth-grade math teacher, used the Dump and Develop strategy to discuss prior knowledge about graphing.

## Mr. Davis: Dump and Develop

Mr. Davis decided to use this strategy instead of conducting a brain dump as an entire class because he wanted more students to speak, listen, and read what other students typed on their slide. He split his class into four groups, and while each group only had audio access within their group, they could visually read what other groups were typing as their ideas developed. Whenever a group was stumped or ran out of ideas, they gathered new ideas from their peers' lists. As Mr. Davis rotated through the breakout rooms, he heard students ask each other questions such as "What is the origin again?" or "Is it the *x*- or *y*-axis that goes up and down?" and even "Did you have Ms. Baker last year? Remember how we had to label *everything*?" He used this information to plan his upcoming lessons, but also to personalize his lessons with comments from his students.

**Group 1**
- Label the x and y axis
- Give it a title
- Make sure the intervals are even
- Line up your points
- Make sure your first point is on the x axis and the second is on the y axis

**Group 2**
- (x,y) the x is horizontal and the y is vertical
- Label everything

**Group 3**
- (0,0) is the origin
- Slope is rise over run
- Intervals should go by 1's or 5's or another number but be the same

**Group 4**
- Pick x and y axis that makes sense for your information
- First move in the x direction, then up and down for y
- Slope is rise over run
- Label things so people know what you are talking about

This vignette showcased the strategy in eighth grade, but it can be applied across other grade levels as well. Consider asking students questions about prior knowledge of addition, multiplication, money, temperature, or measurement. Not only will the students think of their own ideas, but the small-group conversation will be easier for students who are not typically self-starters because they have access to other groups' responses.

# Mine, Yours, Ours

This is a more complex strategy that uses the classroom routine of carousels. In the face-to-face classroom, students would move in groups to different areas of the room, read the prompt or question on the sheet of chart paper located there, add a new piece of information, and continue to rotate. In the virtual classroom, students follow the same procedure, but they rotate around to the different available slides that they are collectively working on instead of actual sheets of chart paper.

It is important to first divide students into purposeful groups (I prefer three to four). Groups begin on their own slide (mine), then add to another group's slide (yours) until they return to their original slide with the contributions from all the other groups (ours). The strategy utilizes a space for each group to contribute as the choices within the slide become reduced. This provides more access as there is more choice in the beginning, while keeping students accountable for learning and contributing to the more difficult concepts.

Consider using Mine, Yours, Ours whenever students are making connections to an overall concept (e.g., five representations of a function, as shown in the vignette) while finding similarities and differences among unique situations (e.g., each problem).

Here, Ms. Miller used the Mine, Yours, Ours strategy with her Algebra 1 students to explore the five different representations of a function—real-life situation, pictures, graph, table, and symbolic function—in order to strengthen students' ability to solve problems and understand computations (Lesh et al., 2003).

## Ms. Miller: Mine, Yours, Ours

Ms. Miller used the Mine, Yours, Ours strategy to create a space for students to record each of the representations of a function and had students rotate to each slide, adding one representation to each slide. Each slide used an identical format but included a different problem. Group A began on

*(Continued)*

(Continued)

slide 1 and chose to insert a table, group B began on slide 2 and chose to insert a table, and group C began on slide 3 and inserted a story problem. Once a group finished their contribution, they rotated to the next slide. As group A moved to slide 2, they were disappointed that the table was already taken, but quickly chose the graph because the table was already done. When they moved to the third slide, they had only two choices left and chose the story problem. Finally when they rotated back to slide 1, their only choice was to complete the equation. Ms. Miller noticed that as students applied their understanding of these five representations to different functions, they had obvious favorites and struggled to connect the story problems. She used that information to focus her next lesson on contextual problem solving.

## Slide 1

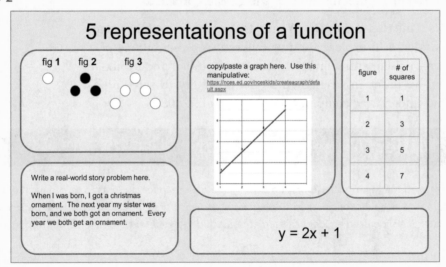

## Slide 2

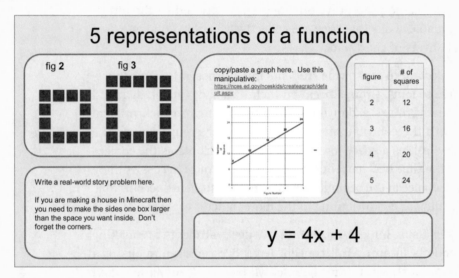

Slide 3

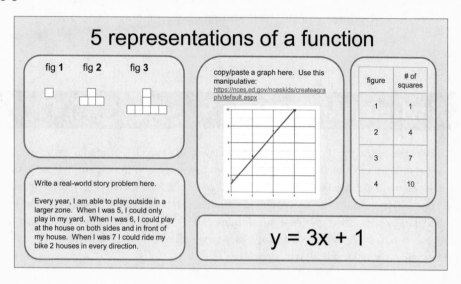

This vignette showcased the strategy in algebra, but it can be applied across other grades as well. Consider the multiple models for multiplication or visualizing fractions. No matter the concept, if it is important for students to use multiple representations, and not simply use the representation that they like the most, then all of the representations should be modeled together in a shared space so that students can visualize the similarities and differences between each model.

# Blank Slides

This strategy is both simple and complex. It's simple in that all it takes to set up is a shared deck of blank slides, one per student. But it's complex because it requires students to have a strong knowledge of the tools available to edit the slides. The slides can be created by an individual student or a small group in a breakout room. Because each student or group is assigned their own slide, they all have a place to make their thinking visible.

Consider using Blank Slides in accessing prior knowledge, as an alternative for summative assessments, as an icebreaker, as an introduction routine at the beginning of the year or semester, or as a way to complete student or star of the week. When students have the unstructured environment of a blank slide, they are not limited in the modality to tell their story.

Here, Ms. Kaytrell, a sixth-grade math teacher, used Blank Slides for students to share their knowledge of fractions both at the beginning of the unit and again at the end of the unit.

## Ms. Kaytrell: Blank Slides

Ms. Kaytrell wanted to use the Blank Slide strategy as a way to assess her students' knowledge. She used the initial slide as a formative assessment of prior knowledge and the end-of-the-unit slide as a summative assessment showcasing students' personal growth of new knowledge. In both instances, she gave the students a blank slide within a class slideshow deck. Her students were empowered through this strategy and added many elements to their slides: images, text, word art, clip art, virtual manipulatives, animated gifs, drawings, and selfies. At the end of the unit, Ms. Kaytrell shared each student's before-and-after slide in a class slideshow.

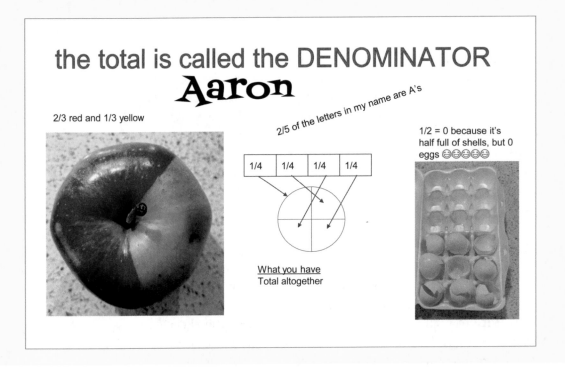

This vignette showcased the strategy in sixth grade, but it can be applied across other grades as well. Special considerations should be made for students who are learning a variety of technology tools as they will need support in learning the clicks needed to upload pictures, take screenshots, and create digital drawings.

# ●●● REFLECT AND REIMAGINE

This chapter encouraged you to look at a variety of strategies, from simple to complex, from individualized to group, to whole class. Some strategies gave students a large space or a very small space to make their thinking visible. Other strategies allowed students to interact with peers and groups. However, each strategy gave every student access to making their thinking visible on the slide. When deciding on which strategy to use, consider the following questions:

- What is the "answer" that I want my students to provide? Which strategy gives purpose and space for students to answer appropriately?

- How much time is available for implementing the activity? How will I account for additional wait time and slower responses for keyboarding skills?

- Do I want individual or collaborative responses?

- When and why do I want anonymous responses?

For more practice, tutorials, and templates, visit www.theresawills.com.

+ chapter

# 7

# STRATEGIES TO FACILITATE COMMON ROUTINES ONLINE

This chapter is all about implementing quick routines and warm-ups. These activities are efficient ways of practicing reasoning, uncovering prior knowledge, and engaging students to participate with open-ended questions and many possible answers. It is the perfect place to begin trying out some different modalities. If you are familiar with the math routine, consider how the technology replaces important face-to-face elements such as individual student voice, recording space, pointers, and discussion. Figure 7.1 shows a variety of routines, modalities, and advantages for how students engage, interact, and have a voice in their learning.

## Figure 7.1

# Math Routine Strategies at a Glance

| STRATEGY | COMPLEXITY LEVEL | DELIVERY METHOD | STUDENT TECHNOLOGY MODALITIES USED | INTERACTIVE SLIDE FEATURES | ADVANTAGES |
|---|---|---|---|---|---|
| Choral Counting | Intermediate | Synchronous | Microphone<br><br>Raise hand | Visual notation<br><br>Typing text<br><br>Students use pointer | This strategy values students' words while including content vocabulary.<br><br>Every student practices with the microphone. |
| Same But Different | Intermediate | Synchronous | Microphone<br><br>Chat box | Copy student text from the chat box into the slide | This strategy values students' words while comparing and contrasting through discussion. |
| Estimation | Basic | Synchronous | Microphone<br><br>Raise hand | Typing text | This strategy efficiently polls all students with options for low-stakes estimates. |
| Which One Doesn't Belong? | Basic | Synchronous | Raise hand<br><br>Emojis<br><br>Microphone | Drag and drop | Every student participates in the anonymous selection. |
| Slow Reveal Graphs | Advanced | Synchronous | Chat box<br><br>Microphone | Ability to view all previous slides | Every student's idea is valued, and students can choose to type in the chat box or use audio.<br><br>Some students practice with chat box before audio to increase confidence with using the microphone. |

# Choral Counting

Choral Counting (Franke et al., 2018) is a math routine that incorporates both rhythm and repetition as well as identifying and extending numerical patterns. The numbers are displayed to visually support students as they count, and you can pause the count at strategic places to help students understand the patterns that emerge in the number sequences. The goal is not only to practice rote counting, but also to help students realize the patterns, build their reasoning skills, and help them justify their predictions for what comes next in the pattern.

Let's see how Mrs. Garcia, a kindergarten teacher, uses skip counting by 2s to reveal patterns while teaching her remote class synchronously.

## Mrs. Garcia: Choral Counting

Mrs. Garcia began by displaying an empty grid on her screen and revealed the first row. With their microphones muted, her students said the numbers as Mrs. Garcia said them aloud.

**Mrs. Garcia:** Say the numbers out loud as I say them. 2, 4, 6, 8, 10. Let's do that again: 2, 4, 6, 8, 10. Now, I'm going to pat and clap when I say the numbers. First, I will pat my legs, then I will clap my hands and say 2.

*<Mrs. Garcia models patting as a silent place holder for the odd numbers and clapping while saying the even numbers.>*

**Mrs. Garcia:** Now, let's turn on our microphones and make some music. Ready?

*<Mrs. Garcia waits for microphones to turn on.>*

**Mrs. Garcia and class *<while patting and clapping>*:** 2, 4, 6, 8, 10.

*<Mrs. Garcia mutes her whole class.>*

**Mrs. Garcia:** I'm going to show another row. But before I do, try to guess the next number.

*<Mrs. Garcia gives wait time, then reveals the next row.>*

**Mrs. Garcia:** Let's say the numbers out loud while clapping. 2, 4, 6, 8, 10, 12, 14, 16, 18, 20. Now turn on your microphones and we will do it together.

*<Mrs. Garcia waits for all microphones to turn on.>*

*(Continued)*

(Continued)

**Mrs. Garcia:** Clap and say it with me.

**Mrs. Garcia and class:** 2, 4, 6, 8, 10, 12, 14, 16, 18, 20.

Mrs. Garcia continued to reveal more of the grid as her students practiced counting out loud. Since she only spends five to seven minutes each day on the routine, she paused here and returned to the same grid the next day. Following is the discussion from day 2.

| 2 | 4 | 6 | 8 | 10 |
|----|----|----|----|----|
| 12 | 14 | 16 | 18 | 20 |
| 22 | 24 | 26 | 28 | 30 |
| 32 | 34 | 36 | 38 | 40 |
| 42 | 44 | 46 | 48 | 50 |
| 52 | 54 | 56 | 58 | 60 |

**Mrs. Garcia:** Let's look at our numbers again and count them one more time, then we will find some interesting patterns. Go ahead and turn on your microphones.

*<Mrs. Garcia waits for all microphones to turn on.>*

**Mrs. Garcia and class:** 2, 4, 6, 8, 10, 12, 14, 16, 18, 20, 22, 24, 26, 28, 30, 32, 34, 36, 38, 40, 42, 44, 46, 48, 50, 52, 54, 56, 58, 60.

**Mrs. Garcia:** Well done. Now, who sees an interesting pattern? Kia?

**Kia:** There are 2s in that first line.

*<Kia moves the pointer to the 2 and drags it down the first column.>*

*<Mrs. Garcia covers the first column with a red box (see image on facing page).>*

**Mrs. Garcia:** Is this where you see the 2s?

**Kia:** Yes.

**Mrs. Garcia:** Kia, I'm going to type that in the comment box. It says, "I see 2s in each number," is that correct?

**Kia:** Yes, well, there are other numbers, like 12 is a 1 and a 2, but they all have a 2.

**Mrs. Garcia:** Kia, you did a great job of clarifying your thinking. Jay, go ahead.

**Jay:** I know to count by 10s. 10, 20, 30, 40, 50, 60.

*<Mrs. Garcia circles the numbers in the right-hand column with a blue circle and types his thinking in the comment box.>*

**Mrs. Garcia:** Jay, that reminds me of last week's pattern. Go ahead, Leo.

**Leo:** There is a 2, 4, 6, 8, 0 every time.

**Mrs. Garcia:** Where do you see the 2, 4, 6, 8, 0?

**Leo:** In the second row there is a 12, but it has a 2 and the 14 has a 4 and 16 has a 6.

| | | | | |
|---|---|---|---|---|
| **Mrs. Garcia:** | | That reminds me of what Kia said, but Kia noticed a 2 in a column and Leo noticed that 2, 4, 6, 8, 0 are in each row. Peter? | | |

**Mrs. Garcia:** That reminds me of what Kia said, but Kia noticed a 2 in a column and Leo noticed that 2, 4, 6, 8, 0 are in each row. Peter?

**Peter:** That's diagonal too.

**Mrs. Garcia:** What is diagonal?

**Abdiel:** 2, 4, 6, 8, 0 is diagonal.

**Mrs. Garcia:** I want to note this on our grid. What number should I start with?

**Abdiel:** 2, then go diagonal.

*<Abdiel uses the pointer to show the 2, and then the 14.>*

*<Mrs. Garcia notes the diagonal that Abdiel described and writes his comments in the box.>*

**Mrs. Garcia:** Abdiel, is that correct?

**Abdiel:** Yes, but it is in every diagonal. Can you make another one but start below 2 at 12?

**Mrs. Garcia:** Oh wow, that is cool that it appears again. I'll make a second diagonal. Jenny?

**Jenny:** When you go across, every number has the same number except for the last box.

**Mrs. Garcia:** Can you show us where you mean by "across"?

*<Jenny uses the pointer to move from 42 to 50.>*

**Jenny:** See, there is a 4 in each number except the last one, it becomes a 5.

*<Mrs. Garcia notes it with green circles and writes her comment in the box.>*

**Kayla:** I also see the blue circles are the way that you know what the next row will be.

*<Mrs. Garcia notes this new wondering but is ready to close the routine for the day.>*

**Mrs. Garcia:** Kayla has an interesting comment, and I want us to think about it more. We will find even more patterns tomorrow.

Mrs. Garcia used a similar format of Choral Counting in her face-to-face class. There were several elements that she had to reimagine in the online class, such as the notation both on the numbers and in the comment boxes, and a visual pointer for students to use in explaining where they see the pattern. In both of these situations, her students experienced two additional challenges because of their age and development. Kindergartners are still developing literacy and hand–eye coordination, but this activity allows Mrs. Garcia to use numbers and sight words in her comments as well as visual cues.

This vignette showcased the strategy in kindergarten, but it can be applied in any grade where number sense is developed. Students often struggle with the idea of equivalent fractions, and the value of the numerator and denominator in different forms. Consider using Choral Counting pattern-finding routines with fractions and decimals in simplified forms, common denominators, improper fractions, or common numerators, and explore the many patterns throughout as a way to build stronger fractional number sense.

# Same But Different

Same But Different (Looney, 2017) is a math routine that prompts students to compare two images and determine the similarities and differences between the images. Responses can be visual or numerical, or found in patterns, and they can both relate to the mathematics as well as simply be observational.

Let's take a look at how Ms. Quinn, a calculus teacher, used Same But Different remotely as her students analyzed two related graphs.

## Ms. Quinn: Same But Different

Ms. Quinn began by revealing the two graphs, and students used the norm of typing Same But Different before their observation in the chat box (not the interactive slide). Students have practiced this norm and are familiar with the requirement that every student uses the chat box to type their observations. Ms. Quinn purposefully selected some chat responses and pasted them on the slide as she asked her students to elaborate on those specific comments. This routine allows all students voice, but specific selection for audio based on lesson goals.

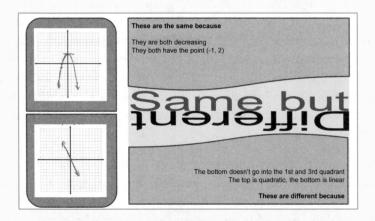

These are the same because

They are both decreasing
They both have the point (-1, 2)

Same but Different

The bottom doesn't go into the 1st and 3rd quadrant
The top is quadratic, the bottom is linear

These are different because

<Everyone types in the chat box. Ms. Quinn reads the comments and purposefully selects only a few, but related, comments to copy and paste onto the interactive slide.>

**Ms. Quinn:** Darren, you said that they are the same because they are both decreasing. How do you see that?

**Darren:** Well the top graph is kinda doing both, increasing and decreasing, but there are many more solutions that are negative than positive.

**Ms. Quinn:** How does that relate to the second graph?

**Darren:** Well that one is just decreasing. So they are kinda both negative.

**Ms. Quinn:** Hal, that might be connected to your thinking. Why did you post the difference that the bottom graph doesn't go into the 1st and 3rd quadrant?

**Hal:** So the bottom graph only goes through the 2nd and 4th quadrant, and the top goes through all four.

**Ms. Quinn:** Is that connected to Darren's idea in any way?

**Hal:** If it is decreasing, it will go through those quadrants, well, if it goes through the origin.

**Ms. Quinn:** Ah, so that is a generalization about decreasing slopes. That is going to be really important later in our lesson.

**Ms. Quinn:** Martina, you said that they both have the point (–1, 2), do they have any other points in common?

**Martina:** They probably do, way down in the 4th quadrant, but you can see (–1, 2) on the graph.

**Ms. Quinn:** Indeed, they probably used a table of values or an equation to make the graph. Kate also noticed a difference that the top graph was quadratic and the bottom graph is linear. This is the very essence of what we will talk about today.

In this example, Ms. Quinn used Same But Different to set the stage about the visual aspects of derivatives. Ms. Quinn used a feature of online learning that made her discussion time efficient and purposeful: She asked all of her students to type in the chat box, but then carefully selected just a few comments to lead the discussion. That allowed her to fill the audio space with targeted discussion while encouraging all students to have a voice in the chat box.

This vignette showcased the strategy in calculus, but it can be applied across other grades as well. For example, from early grades, students are learning about fractions using set models, area models, and number line models. When these models are compared directly through this routine, students can identify similarities and differences in both a visual model and the abstract number form.

## Estimation

Estimation is an important mathematics concept and can be addressed quickly yet thoughtfully through math routines (Stadel, 2012). In the Estimation routine, an image is used to have students create an estimate. Since students need to learn how to estimate, and how to establish better estimates, it is important to consider estimates that are too low and too high. Then, when students rationalize their estimates, they can ensure that their estimate makes sense within the range that they established as their minimum and maximum.

Mr. Drake's third-grade class uses the Estimation strategy regularly. Mr. Drake uses the routine to not only hold his students accountable for purposeful estimates, but also build confidence in using the microphone.

## Mr. Drake: Estimation

**Mr. Drake:** Here is a big bowl of marshmallows for the big bonfire this weekend. I'm hoping that we have enough marshmallows for every kid to get a s'more. Everyone knows the drill, go ahead and type an estimate that is too low, an estimate that is too high, as well your actual estimate on our interactive slide.

| Estimate that is too LOW | | | | | Estimate that is too HIGH | |
|---|---|---|---|---|---|---|
|  | 1 | | | | 60 | 100 |
| 1 | 17 | | | | 100 | 50 |
| 1 | 1 | | | | | 100 |
|  | 10 | 32 | 52 | 49 | | 75 |
| 16 | 3 | 56 | 45 | 40 | 70 | 90 |
| 11 | 10 | 39 | 60 | 47 | 100 | 90 |
| 11 |  | 48 | 42 | 35 | 86 | |
|  | 15 | 35 | 45 | 40 | | 82 |

*<Students type in their assigned cells.>*

**Mr. Drake:** I see several people wrote a number 1. Who can tell me why 1 is a correct answer?

*<Mr. Drake waits 10 seconds as seven hands are raised.>*

**Mr. Drake:** Go ahead, Morise.

**Morise:** Well, you said a number that is too low. You can't get much lower than 1. Well, you can't if you still want marshmallows.

**Mr. Drake:** Good point, Morise. I also noticed several that are 10–11. Why might that number be a good choice for too low?

*<Mr. Drake waits 10 purposeful seconds of wait time.>*

**Mr. Drake:** Yes, Camila.

**Camila:** Eleven makes sense to be too low because I can count 11 that I see and I know there are some that I can't see, so there are at least 11.

**Mr. Drake:** That's some good reasoning thinking about the ones you can see and the ones you can't. What about the too-high estimates? Who wants to defend an answer?

*<Mr. Drake waits 10 purposeful seconds of wait time.>*

**Mr. Drake:** Kenny, tell us first the number and then defend it.

*(Continued)*

> ## Wait Time
>
> Wait time is important online, and it is important to give even more wait time for students to process information and then find, click, or type the response.

(Continued)

**Kenny:** Camila said there were 11 that we can see, right? So there aren't going to be 100 that you can't see, maybe only 50 or so, but not 100.

**Mr. Drake:** Nice job using Camila's method. Jamie, go ahead.

**Jamie:** Most of us picked 90 or 100 because we aren't sure if there are like 70 in the bowl. Well, 70's probably too high also, but it gets kinda close.

**Mr. Drake:** It does get kinda close, doesn't it? In fact, there are some matches in the middle section, which is our actual estimate, to the too-high section. Who thinks they can tell us why there might be an overlap?

*<He waits 10 seconds, but that produces only two hands, so he waits another eight seconds and more hands are raised.>*

**Mr. Drake:** Go ahead, Chin.

**Chin:** I'm not sure if this is right, but most of us picked things in the 40s but some got 30s and 50s. There aren't many 50s in the too-high section, but there is one.

**Mr. Drake:** Chin noticed most were in the 40s. Great noticing. Lara, why do you think they overlap?

**Lara:** If we are trying to get a too-high estimate that is just a little bit high, like you usually ask us to, then it is going to be just a little bit more than the actual estimate.

**Mr. Drake:** You are right, Lara, and I do like it when the too-high estimate is pretty close to the real estimate. Now is everyone's favorite time. Who can defend their real estimate?

*<Almost all hands go up in three seconds.>*

**Mr. Drake:** Tamika.

**Tamika:** I saw four layers of marshmallows and I think there are 10 in each layer.

**Mr. Drake:** Great idea with layers. That can help us visualize the pieces we can't see. Thomas?

**Thomas:** You see that there are . . . um . . . I forgot.

**Mr. Drake:** It's okay, Thomas, that happens to everyone. Raise your hand again when you remember and I'll be sure to call on you. James?

**James:** The bowl isn't the same at the top and the bottom, so I looked at the ones I could see and thought of a front, middle, and back. I thought of 12, 12, and 12.

*<Thomas raises his hand.>*

**Mr. Drake:** I'm hearing now two ways of thinking about multiplication. Excellent. Thomas, I can't wait to hear your idea.

**Thomas:** I was thinking about Tamika's way but I didn't use 10 for the layers, I used 11.

| **Mr. Drake:** | How many layers did you see? |
| **Thomas:** | I kinda saw three and four. |
| **Mr. Drake:** | Sometimes I see different amounts and use that information in my estimate too. Let's take one more person. Go ahead, Tavian. |
| **Tavian:** | There are more marshmallows that overflow the bowl than are inside, so I took about 15 inside and 20 outside and added them together to make 35. |
| **Mr. Drake:** | Partitioning the space is a great way to think about how many are inside. Well done, everyone. |

In addition to discussing the process for making reasonable estimates, Mr. Drake was able to discuss misconceptions by identifying the number, but not the student. As students continue to practice this routine, their estimates become more thoughtful and their minimum and maximums become closer to their actual estimate.

This vignette showcased the strategy in third grade, but it can be applied in other grade levels as well. Measurement, specifically very small and very large numbers, such as the distance from Earth to the sun, or the width of a strand of hair, can be difficult for students to estimate. If you are trying to develop a sense for these numbers, regular estimation will help students relate these numbers to lived experiences.

# Which One Doesn't Belong?

Which One Doesn't Belong? (Danielson, 2016) is a math routine that gives four choices, but each answer is correct. Since students know that their answer is correct regardless of the choice, they are at ease to consider the *why* behind their choice. This rationale is at the heart of the mathematics discussion.

Let's take a look at how Ms. Sweeney used Which One Doesn't Belong? in her first-grade synchronous online class as a launch into their math lesson, while building classroom community.

Okay, class, place a "No" symbol over which one doesn't belong. Be ready to share your answer.

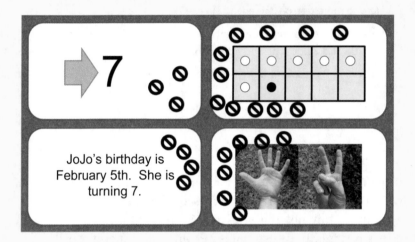

This week was JoJo's seventh birthday, and Ms. Sweeney used this in her routine.

**Ms. Sweeney:** Okay, class, place a "No" symbol over which one doesn't belong. Be ready to share your answer.

<"No" symbols are moved anonymously to all four corners.>

**Ms. Sweeney:** We will start with everyone raising their hand, and you will share your idea for why that corner doesn't belong. I will move the red arrow to the one we are talking about. If someone explains your idea, you may put your hand down and make a connection with a smiley emoji in the chat box. Joshua, you are first, and then we will go in order of hands up.

**Joshua:** The 7 doesn't belong because it is the only one with just a number.

<Four hands go down and four smiley emojis are entered in the chat box.>

**Marcella:** The 7 doesn't belong because it is the only one with just one number.

**Ms. Sweeney:** Can you explain more, Marcella? How can the others have more than one number?

**Marcella:** Because this one <Ms. Sweeney moves the arrow to the upper-right ten frame.> has a 7, but it also has a 6 if you look at the white circles and a 1 for black circles. JoJo's birthday is on February 5th, so there is a 5, and the hands show 5 and 2.

**Brenna:** JoJo's corner is the only one with words.

<Eight hands go down, emojis are inputted in the chat, and a hand goes up.>

**Kelem:** The hands doesn't belong because they are the only picture.

<Four hands go down and emojis are inputted.>

**Oscar:** JoJo's birthday doesn't belong because it said she's turning 7. Her birthday is on Friday, so she is still 6.

*<Two hands go up.>*

**Abram:** The second one doesn't belong *<Ms. Sweeney moves the arrow to the ten frame model.>* because it shows three numbers. It shows 6, 7, and 3.

**Ms. Sweeney:** Abram, where do you see 3?

**Abram:** The boxes without any circles.

*<Two hands go up.>*

**Ms. Sweeney:** What do you think that means?

**Abram:** That she will be 10 in 3 years.

**Ms. Sweeney:** Wow, that will be an exciting birthday.

**Jade:** The 7 doesn't belong *<Ms. Sweeney moves the arrow to the upper left corner with the numeral 7.>* because the rest have a 5 in them.

*<Ten hands go down and many emojis emerge.>*

**Ms. Sweeney:** Wow Jade, lots of friends agree with you. Where do you see the 5s?

**Jade:** The top of the ten frame is 5, JoJo was born on February 5th, and there are 5 fingers on a hand.

**Ms. Sweeney:** Did you know that today we are going to talk more about the number 5? The number 5 can be really useful when counting.

Ms. Sweeney was purposeful in establishing the Which One Doesn't Belong? routine and student expectations. She reviewed the expectations as the routine began. She kept her students engaged by ensuring that each student could place their choice on the board and then state their justification. She also valued each student, even if their idea had already been shared, by using emojis to make connections. Her students loved using the emojis, and it was a great way for Ms. Sweeney to ensure that her students were engaged in the lesson. She used the arrow pointer to maintain clear communication as students discussed the four corners.

This vignette showcased the strategy in first grade, but it can be applied across other grades as well. For example, algebra and calculus are filled with important elements that are visualized on graphs such as intercepts, slope, solutions, minimums, maximums, asymptotes, and more. It is important to be purposeful in the four graphs that you choose, but when four are displayed, students can often use logical reasoning to find similarities and differences between each, leaving one graph different from the rest. Other ideas that you can use for this strategy are fractional representations or 2-D and 3-D shapes.

## Slow Reveal Graphs

Slow Reveal Graphs (Laib, 2020) is a math routine where the teacher removes important characteristics of a graph and purposefully selects when to reveal these pieces. Important characteristics include axis labels and intervals, points or bars, and titles. The purpose of Slow Reveal Graphs is for students to interpret the shape of the graph before becoming overwhelmed with data specific to the situation. These interpretations become increasingly more sophisticated when more of the graph is revealed.

In this example, Mx. Andretta used Slow Reveal Graphs in their sixth-grade synchronous online class because they wanted students to develop a need and purpose for labeling the axis and creating equal intervals on the $x$- and $y$-axes. Mx. Andretta purposefully used both chat and audio features to ensure that every student had a voice. The routine began with one slide, and Mx. Andretta continued to add a new slide with additional information, increasing the length of the slide deck over time.

## Mx. Andretta: Slow Reveal Graphs

**Vera:** It is going up.

**Parvit:** It's getting faster.

**Justin (via chat):** Increasing.

**Helen (via chat):** Going higher and higher.

**Mx. Andretta:** Helen, what do you mean by "higher and higher"?

**Helen:** You read it starting at the left, like a book, and as you read it your eyes move higher and higher.

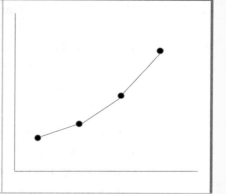

**Mx. Andretta:** Was there a reason that you wrote higher twice?

**Helen:** Well, it's never going low.

**Quisha (via chat):** It's going higher but then higher than higher.

**Mx. Andretta:** Quisha, can you elaborate?

**Quisha:** It goes higher a little, then more higher, then a big jump higher.

**Mx. Andretta:** Those are great observations. I'm going to keep thinking about that big jump higher.

---

*<Mx. Andretta adds this slide.>*

**Mx. Andretta:** How does this information help you to think about the graph?

**Quisha (via chat):** The big jump is from 3–6.

**Jacob:** One to Two isn't a big jump, but 3–6 is.

**Lathum:** Nothing is bigger than 6, so whatever this is is small.

**Mx. Andretta:** Lathum said "whatever this is is small." Who can give us ideas of what this graph could be about?

**Yara (via chat):** Cookies.

**Tim (via chat):** Number of days in a week.

**Christina (via chat):** How fast you run.

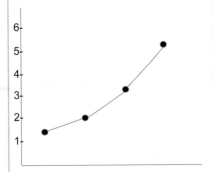

---

*<Mx. Andretta adds this slide.>*

**Mx. Andretta:** What can you interpret now?

**Quisha:** 2020 has the most.

**Jacob:** The big jump happened this year.

**Parvit (via chat):** 2020 has 6.

**Mx. Andretta:** Jacob, can you tell us more about the big jump?

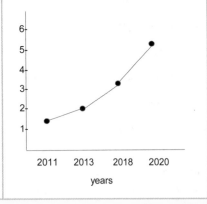

*(Continued)*

(Continued)

| | |
|---|---|
| **Jacob:** Something little happened in 2011, but something bigger happened in 2020.<br><br>**Mx. Andretta:** What is 2011 and 2020?<br><br>**Jacob:** Years.<br><br>**Mx. Andretta:** How do you know?<br><br>**Jacob:** Well, it just makes sense, but it also tells you.<br><br>**Samir (via chat):** The years aren't right.<br><br>**Mx. Andretta:** Samir, what isn't right about the years?<br><br>**Samir:** You are missing 2012, 2014, 2015, 2016, 2017, and 2019.<br><br>**Mx. Andretta:** Have you ever seen a graph where they skip numbers?<br><br>**Tim:** I agree with Samir. You can skip count, but that's not skip counting.<br><br>**Mx. Andretta:** Why isn't it skip counting?<br><br>**Tim:** Cause you need to skip the same amount.<br><br>**Mx. Andretta:** Will everyone write in the chat box, how could we skip count the years?<br><br>**Tim (via chat):** 2010, 2012, 2014, 2016, 2018, 2020<br><br>**Christina (via chat):** 2010, 2015, 2020<br><br>**Jacob (via chat):** Just put every year.<br><br>**Yara (via chat):** Skip count by 2s.<br><br>**Samir (via chat):** Any way as long as they are equal. | |
| *<Mx. Andretta adds this slide.>*<br><br>**Mx. Andretta:** What do you know now?<br><br>**Parvit:** People do more screen time in 2020.<br><br>**Lathum (via chat):** The big jump is because we use more screens in 2020.<br><br>**Mx. Andretta:** Lathum, why do you think we use more screens in 2020?<br><br>**Lathum:** Because the graph is highest there. | 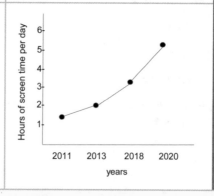 |

**Mx. Andretta:** What about the big jump?

**Lathum:** So it's higher there, but the next highest jump was in 2018 and 2018 to 2020 is two years and 2013 and 2018 is 5 years, so the middle jump isn't that big.

<Mx. Andretta adds this slide.>

**Mx. Andretta:** What new information do we have?

**Parvit:** It says we watch too much TV.

**Mx. Andretta:** Do you agree?

**Parvit:** No, I use my phone more than TV.

**Samir (via chat):** Is it TV or all screen time?

**Jacob:** They are trying to say that kids watch too much TV, but we might be on our phone or playing a video game.

**Dustin:** Does it double count if I'm playing a game on my phone while watching TV?

**Mx. Andretta:** You all have explained some really important elements of graphs. It really matters what we put as our title, the labels on the x- and y-axes, and the intervals for the years. Remember this during our unit.

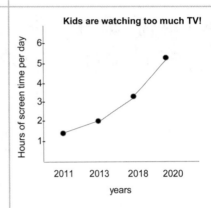

Mx. Andretta implemented Slow Reveal Graphs while incorporating several online pedagogies. A benefit of using interactive slides is that the students can scroll back to view previous slides. Mx. Andretta did not delete slides, but simply added more information to the slide deck. Since all the previous images were still there, students had more agency to compare and contrast the images. Further, Mx. Andretta used both the chat box and audio to receive ideas from students. This showed students that their voice is important, regardless of the modality of chat or audio. By valuing chat, students could increase their confidence by first typing their ideas before Mx. Andretta asked them to elaborate over the microphone.

This vignette showcased the strategy in sixth grade, but it can be applied in other grades as well. Often, young students learn about graphs and are reminded to label the x- and y-axes, title, and key, but don't always identify these as relevant pieces—rather as annoying things that their teacher requires. This activity builds upon the purpose of these important labels and the considerations for mislabeled graphs.

## ••• REFLECT AND REIMAGINE

Math routines and warm-ups are commonplace in the math classroom, and it is important to continue implementing these in remote learning. As you reimagine how you will use them in your classroom, begin with a familiar routine that you have implemented previously in the face-to-face classroom.

- What is the purpose of the routine? Did I maintain the same purpose when transitioning online?

- What NCTM process standards (problem solving, communication, connections, representations, reasoning and proof) were evident in the routine? How can I modify the online routine to include or enhance those process standards?

- How will students view and interact with the math routine?

- What classroom management norms encouraged collaboration and structure, and how are those transitioned online?

For more practice, tutorials, and templates, visit www.theresawills.com.

# FACILITATING MATHEMATICAL DISCOURSE ONLINE THROUGH RICH TASKS

Rich mathematics discussions include a great task, multiple student strategies and representations, purposeful questions, student voices debating, laughter and joy, and connections to the mathematical objective. Many educators have embraced the simple and predictable structure of Smith and Stein's (2011) 5 Practices for Orchestrating Productive Mathematics Discussions (anticipating, monitoring, selecting, sequencing, and connecting) when teaching in a face-to-face environment, but how do we offer the same experience in an online class? How do you monitor student work in the moment and facilitate the discussion? In many ways, the online math discussion looks and sounds much like the discussion in the face-to-face class, and with practice, you can leverage the benefits of remote learning that give more students a voice in the virtual class.

Based on my experience as an online math educator, here is how I use the 5 Practices framework (Smith & Stein, 2011) when facilitating math discourse in a virtual setting using a rich task for investigation:

1. Select the objective and identify the task.
2. Anticipate student strategies and technology use.
3. Launch the task synchronously.
4. Allow for small-group work time.
5. Select and sequence student work.
6. Design questions for discussion.
7. Connect student work to the math goal.
8. Summarize the task.

In this chapter, we will dive into each of the steps for effective rich-task investigation. The purpose of this chapter is not to change the purposeful 5 Practices, but rather to show how they can be adapted and implemented in the online setting to maintain the original intent. Alongside each step we will experience how Ms. Wall, a fourth-grade teacher, used a rich task in her classroom. Ms. Wall has a few months of distance teaching experience and enjoys implementing rich tasks so that she can engage students in debate as they understand connections between mathematical representations. Her pedagogy remains the same from her face-to-face class. She uses only the technology that supports her students in exploration and communication as they dive into the problem.

## Select the Objective and Identify the Task

A rich task will look exactly the same, regardless of whether it is shared in a face-to-face or online class. According to Wolf (2015), rich tasks include the following six characteristics:

- Is accessible to all learners
- Depicts real-life scenarios
- Allows for multiple approaches and representation

- Allows for collaboration and discussion
- Promotes engagement, curiosity, and creativity
- Offers opportunities for extension

These characteristics are based on the initial design of the task or problem, so it can be helpful to imagine the task in a familiar setting, like a face-to-face classroom. Some characteristics lend themselves more to online learning—especially opportunities for extension since there are an abundance of additional websites and interactive games to explore online. Rich tasks are only the vehicle for great mathematics. The driver is the discussion that develops as students engage and connect with the mathematical goal of the rich task.

Many structures, norms, and routines should be considered in the implementation of a rich task so that students can interact, collaborate, and share their representations and ideas. I make these norms available for my students through a problem-solving oath (Figure 8.1). I read the oath out loud to my students before beginning the task, and I offer them an opportunity to pledge the oath by typing their name in the chat box. This serves two purposes: it lets me see who is ready for the problem-solving experience and also lets me know who is actively at their computer, which can make launching the task and reading the directions smoother.

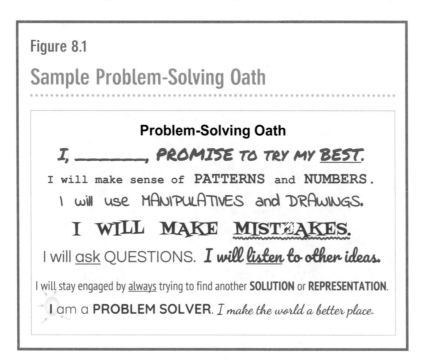

Figure 8.1

## Sample Problem-Solving Oath

**Problem-Solving Oath**

I, _____, PROMISE TO TRY MY BEST.

I will make sense of PATTERNS and NUMBERS.

I will use MANIPULATIVES and DRAWINGS.

I WILL MAKE MISTAKES.

I will ask QUESTIONS. I will listen to other ideas.

I will stay engaged by always trying to find another SOLUTION or REPRESENTATION.

I am a PROBLEM SOLVER. I make the world a better place.

As we go through the steps of the rich task, we will follow Ms. Wall's class as she implements this one task during the entire math block. This allows us to see how the task unfolds over time throughout the process.

## Ms. Wall: Rich-Task Identification

Ms. Wall has identified a task that met all of the rich-task criteria and provided her students with an exploration that connected with the mathematical objective: students will generalize visual patterns and students will use multiplication and division to determine factors and multiples. Ms. Wall selected the following task:

**The Problem:** Your school wants to unveil a hopscotch course on the 100th day of school. If this pattern continued to 100 boxes, what is the placement of the 100th box? Does it make sense to end at 100?

**Optional: The Follow-Up Business**

Infinity Hopscotch wants to create a pricing template for the hopscotch business. For every foot of blacktop, they can paint one row of the hopscotch course. How much should each row cost? What is your reasoning?

Your local park asked for a quote to paint a hopscotch course on their blacktop. Estimate the length and determine the cost.

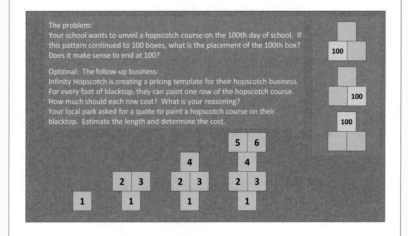

# Anticipate Student Strategies and Technology Use

The next step is to predict how students might interact with this problem, and how they might meet the goals of the lesson. It is important to investigate a variety of tools that you want to offer students for use in demonstrating their thinking so that you can understand how they work, as well as anticipate any mathematical misconceptions or technical issues that students may have.

With younger students, it is important to provide them with a choice of tools but to limit the choices to two or three tools. This gives them freedom to select a tool that makes sense for them, but doesn't give them so many choices that they get overwhelmed in how to proceed.

## Ms. Wall: Rich-Task Anticipation of Student Strategies

Before implementing the task with her students, Ms. Wall used Smith and Stein's (2011) 5 Practices and anticipated student work. She anticipated seven different models using a variety of virtual manipulatives and shapes the students might select. She even anticipated what mathematical misconceptions and technical problems might arise. Here are her considerations with each tool:

| APPLET | MS. WALL'S CONSIDERATIONS |
|---|---|
| | The applet allows students to color code the repeating section and align squares like a hopscotch pattern. |

*(Continued)*

(Continued)

| APPLET | MS. WALL'S CONSIDERATIONS |
|---|---|
| 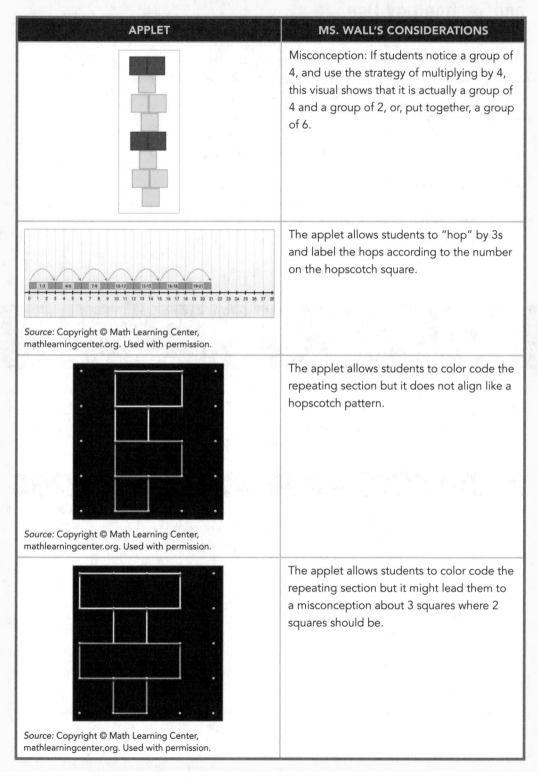 | Misconception: If students notice a group of 4, and use the strategy of multiplying by 4, this visual shows that it is actually a group of 4 and a group of 2, or, put together, a group of 6. |
| *Source:* Copyright © Math Learning Center, mathlearningcenter.org. Used with permission. | The applet allows students to "hop" by 3s and label the hops according to the number on the hopscotch square. |
| *Source:* Copyright © Math Learning Center, mathlearningcenter.org. Used with permission. | The applet allows students to color code the repeating section but it does not align like a hopscotch pattern. |
| *Source:* Copyright © Math Learning Center, mathlearningcenter.org. Used with permission. | The applet allows students to color code the repeating section but it might lead them to a misconception about 3 squares where 2 squares should be. |

| APPLET | MS. WALL'S CONSIDERATIONS |
|---|---|
| *Source:* Copyright © Math Playground LLC, mathplayground.com. Used with permission. | Students are already familiar with this applet. The visual keeps the single and double boxes separated. It does not align the hopscotch pattern. |
| *Source:* Unifix® is a registered trademark of Findel Education, Limited. Used with permission of Didax, Inc., Rowley, MA, USA. | Students are already familiar with this applet. They can color code the single and double boxes and rotate it to match a number line model. |

Ms. Wall was careful to consider the type of representation that each tool offered, knowing that some tools would not line up the hopscotch game as shown in the problem, some tools would snap together, and others would break the model apart into a linear representation. Since she hoped to showcase a variety of representations, she ensured that she offered students a variety of tools that led them to diverse models. She used these diverse models to ensure that she selected specific student examples that showcased the goal of the mathematics, as students thought flexibly between familiar and unfamiliar models. Of the five tools, three of them were used in previous problem solving, and students were familiar with the applet. Ms. Wall usually incorporated at least one new manipulative because she acknowledged that there are a few students in her class that thrive on tinkering with the new tool in the hope that they will be selected to unveil it to the entire class. Here is the slide that she shared with her students, letting them know their options for tools to use to solve the problem.

*(Continued)*

(Continued)

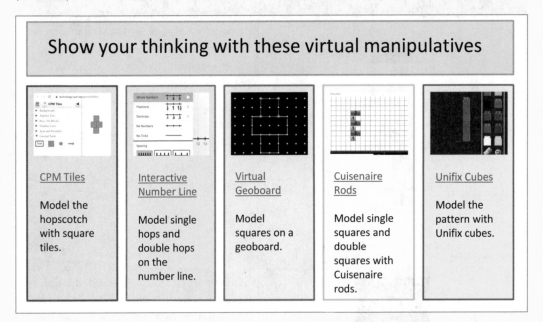

## Show your thinking with these virtual manipulatives

**CPM Tiles**

Model the hopscotch with square tiles.

**Interactive Number Line**

Model single hops and double hops on the number line.

**Virtual Geoboard**

Model squares on a geoboard.

**Cuisenaire Rods**

Model single squares and double squares with Cuisenaire rods.

**Unifix Cubes**

Model the pattern with Unifix cubes.

*Image sources:* CPM Educational Program; Math Learning Center; Math Learning Center; Math Playground; Unifix® is a registered trademark of Findel Education, Limited. Used with permission of Didax, Inc., Rowley, MA, USA.

## Launch the Task

A rich task should be launched using a hook or a story that relates to the students' prior knowledge and interests. This is important to motivate students to solve the problem and to support their connection to mathematics in the world around them.

In order to best support your students, you can decide how much scaffolding or support you provide to them at this phase of the task. For example, you can dissect the vocabulary in the task and discuss the meaning of key words. Or, you can launch a questioning routine such as Notice and Wonder, where students share things they notice about the task and things that they wonder or aren't sure about before diving in to solving.

Let's continue with Ms. Wall's fourth-grade class.

Ms. Wall launched the task by relating the problem to her students and asking them to consider a Notice and Wonder routine.

**Ms. Wall:**     Infinity Hopscotch is a company that paints hopscotch templates on blacktops around schools and parks. They have become popular for their incredibly long hopscotch courses. Some are hundreds of numbers long. What do you notice? What do you wonder?

*<Ms. Wall gives about two minutes of wait time for her students to type.>*

---

Infinity Hopscotch is a company that paints hopscotch templates on blacktops around schools and parks. They have become popular for their incredibly long hopscotch courses. Some are hundreds of numbers long.

What do you notice? What do you wonder?

Type the following into the chat box:
I notice _____, I wonder _____.

---

**Gabrielle (via chat):**   I notice it is a really long hopscotch, I wonder how far it goes.

**Josie (via chat):**   I notice it looks fun and I want to do it, I wonder if we can get a hopscotch like this.

**Mark (via chat):**   I notice that it starts at 1 and keeps going, I wonder when it ends.

**Janelle (via chat):**   I notice that it is long, I wonder how many people can go on it.

**Shantel (via chat):**   I notice there is a curb next to it, I wonder if people use it for taking breaks.

*<The chat contains many more notice/wonder statements.>*

*(Continued)*

(Continued)

**Ms. Wall:** Mark and several other students wonder when it will end. That is actually what we will solve today. Our problem states that your school wants to unveil a hopscotch course on the 100th day of school. If this pattern continued to 100 boxes, what is the placement of the 100th box? Does it make sense to end at 100?

Ms. Wall posted a slide with the question, a visual, and an optional extension for students who finish early. The task is also linked to Google Translate so that students can listen to it again because Google Translate will read it to them in English or another home language.

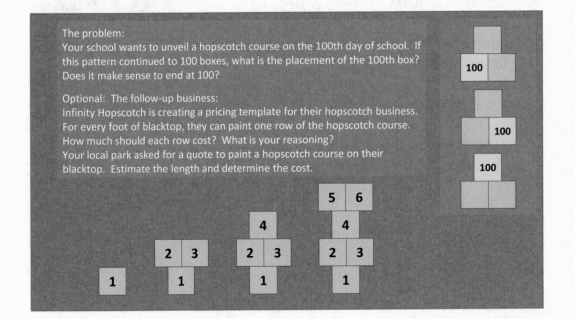

## Allow for Work Time

It is common in face-to-face classrooms for teachers to give students five minutes of independent think time followed by small-group collaboration time. During this first five minutes, students think individually about drawings, models, numbers, and patterns they see in the problem. This time allows for students to have a starting point when transitioning into their small groups for discussion. In the face-to-face classroom, some students are quick to jump into the conversation. There are visual cues such as eye contact and looking at another student's work that help the conversation, which is not always available online. For that reason, it is important to set up specific norms for how students show that they want independent think time or they want to begin a conversation.

Let's revisit Ms. Wall's class to see how she broke up students into groups for work on this task.

## Ms. Wall: Rich-Task Work Time

Ms. Wall purposefully places her students in breakout rooms based on a variety of considerations: mathematical development, mixed abilities, ability to use the technology, confidence using the microphone, and creative representations of the math task. Their class norm is to self-differentiate the first five minutes of think time. Some students want some independent think time, so they notify team members by posting an away message, muting their computer, and setting a five-minute timer (either using a clock or embedded digital timer). They are responsible for their independent work time and are not interrupted by group members until they decide to unmute their computer and remove their away message. Ms. Wall practiced these norms early and often so that students could implement them efficiently. Some students prefer to talk it out and discuss the problem with their group members immediately. These students implement the norm of turning on their microphones and keeping them on as the group discusses the problem. They begin talking about the problem immediately. Ms. Wall has learned a little bit about her students' preferences and sometimes groups students by who enjoys talking it out with a partner or group versus who likes to work independently at first. She maintained a master list of class groupings according to classification so that she could purposefully alter groups based on her classroom needs.

## Monitor Group Time

In face-to-face classrooms, teachers monitor group time by walking around the class and observing conversations, models, and drawings. They ask questions to probe or extend the group's thinking.

These elements are present in the remote classroom too, but in different ways. Rather than walk around the classroom, you can view the different groups' slides and enter their breakout rooms. Once in the breakout rooms, you can listen in on the conversations and pose purposeful questions.

# Ms. Wall: Rich-Task Group Time

Ms. Wall is very busy during the monitoring time. She is virtually moving in and out of each breakout room. She is also scrolling through the slides as she visually records the various representations that are emerging on the screen. She is noting each strategy that she predicted and using her time checking in with students who have blank screens or a group without microphones on.

She notices a group who still has their away messages up after the five-minute independent time norm; however, their slides already contain three representations. She enters the room.

**Ms. Wall:**    Hello, group 3. I notice that your slides are filling up but that your away messages are still up.

*<Three of the four students immediately remove their away messages and turn on their microphones.>*

**Randy:**    Oops, I was just having too much fun with the number line.

**Ms. Wall:**    Oh, is that your model on the slide?

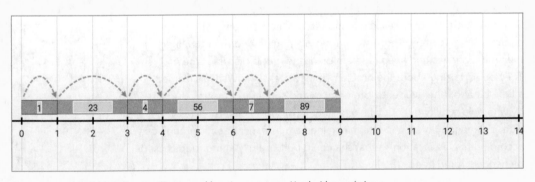

*Source:* Copyright © Math Learning Center, mathlearningcenter.org. Used with permission.

**Randy:**    No, I'm still making mine, but it doesn't look the same.

**Ms. Wall:**    Who here posted the number line representation? I love it and want to know what you were thinking.

*<Sabin, the fourth student with the away message, removes it and turns on his microphone.>*

| | |
|---|---|
| **Sabin:** | That was mine, and I just did exactly what the problem said to do. |
| **Ms. Wall:** | Oh, so you used the problem to decide how far to make the jumps? |
| **Sabin:** | Yeah. |
| **Ms. Wall:** | Why do they jump different amounts? |
| **Sabin:** | It's like your feet. You jump on one leg for #1, then two legs for #2 and #3, then one leg for #4, then two legs for #5 and #6. |
| **Ms. Wall:** | That makes sense to me. Randy, you said that your number line looks different. Could you take a screenshot and paste it next to Sabin's so that we can see the difference? |
| **Randy:** | Yeah, but it's not right. |
| **Ms. Wall:** | Sometimes math looks different, and it is still right. I'd love to see what you were thinking. |
| **Randy:** | Okay, here it is. |

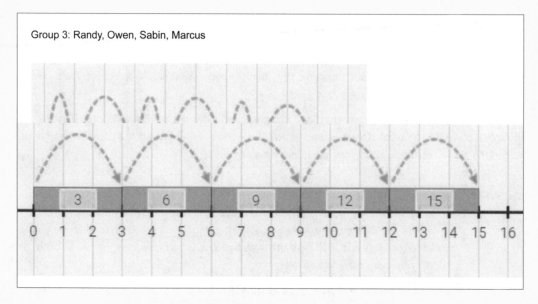

Group 3: Randy, Owen, Sabin, Marcus

| | |
|---|---|
| **Ms. Wall:** | Oh Randy, that really helps me see the problem differently. Why did you do jumps like that? |
| **Randy:** | Well, you don't have 3 feet, so it's not right. |
| **Sabin:** | Yeah it is. You just put together my 1 foot and 2 foot. |

*\<Sabin moves Randy's model directly below his model so that it was clearer how the jumps aligned.\>*

*(Continued)*

(Continued)

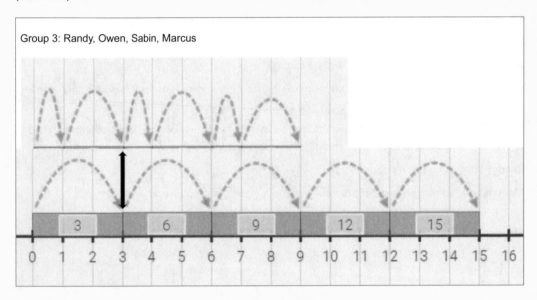

Group 3: Randy, Owen, Sabin, Marcus

*Source:* Copyright © Math Learning Center, mathlearningcenter.org. Used with permission.

**Randy:**    Yeah, they are almost the same, but I think I need to split my 3 hops apart. We should just use Sabin's.

A norm was already established and practiced that students would not delete work, even if they thought it contained an error. If they wanted to edit the work, they simply made a copy of it and then edited the copy. Therefore, Randy does not delete his work.

**Ms. Wall:**    Randy, not only is your work correct, it is one of the representations that I was looking for today. I was even more surprised when I see how you and Sabin have so many similarities and differences in your models. I'm going to ask you both to describe your model to the class and then have the class figure out the similarities. Try to use both models when you solve the problem.

Because Ms. Wall could easily view all other groups' slides simultaneously as they were developed, she knew when to move to another breakout room because she identified the unifix cube strategy from her anticipated strategies and wanted to give that group a heads-up that she will call on them.

**Ms. Wall:**    Hello group 1. Who created the unifix cube model?

**Laurie:**    Me, do you like it?

**Ms. Wall:**    You know how much I love mathematical representations! Why did you use two colors?

**Laurie:**    The white is for one square, the blue is for two squares that are next to each other.

**Ms. Wall:**    I noticed that you put some numbers on top of the picture.

Group 1: Tammy, Tania, Rachel and Laurie

*Source:* Unifix® is a registered trademark of Findel Education, Limited. Used with permission of Didax, Inc., Rowley, MA, USA.

**Laurie:**    That's because Rachel said that she saw a pattern in the white numbers, and we think it goes odd, even, odd, even, odd.

**Ms. Wall:**    How could that pattern help you to find out where the 100th block is placed?

**Laurie:**    Because 100 is even.

**Rachel:**    Yeah, and it is times three.

**Ms. Wall:**    Hmm, how do those two go together?

**Tammy:**    Can you just multiply them? 3 × 100 = 300 and that is an even number.

**Laurie:**    But that is too long, we need 100.

**Ms. Wall:**    Tania, I noticed that you have a table and I'm wondering if that could help your group make sense of the even-and-odd pattern.

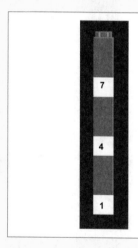

Group 1: Tammy, Tania, Rachel and Laurie

| 1 |
|---|
| 23 |
| 4 |
| 56 |
| 7 |
| 89 |
| 10 |

*Source:* Unifix® is a registered trademark of Findel Education, Limited. Used with permission of Didax, Inc., Rowley, MA, USA.

*(Continued)*

(Continued)

**Tania:** We could just change the color of the box for even and odd.

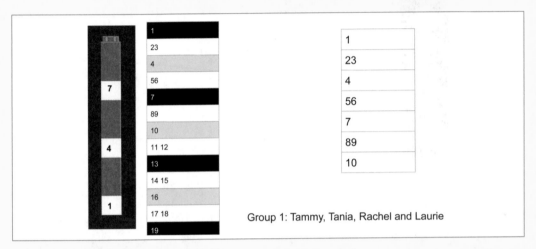

Group 1: Tammy, Tania, Rachel and Laurie

*Source:* Unifix® is a registered trademark of Findel Education, Limited. Used with permission of Didax, Inc., Rowley, MA, USA.

The group abides by the norm to make a copy of the table and edit the copy while preserving Tania's original work. Ms. Wall is careful not to lead the group too far off their original thought about evens and odds. Even though Ms. Wall did not predict that pattern, she knows that it is important for students to identify patterns and then explore the patterns to see if they make sense in the context of the problem. She plans to revisit that group.

Group 5 noticed a grouping of 4, much like Ms. Wall predicted. She entered their group and asked them to explain their thinking as a way to unveil the misconception.

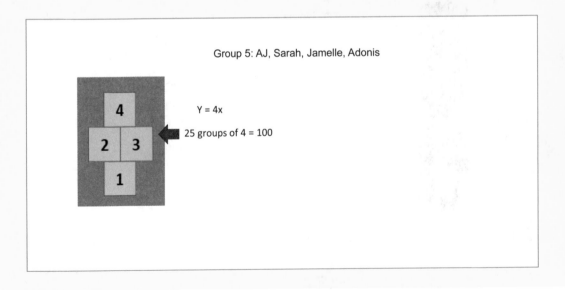

Group 5: AJ, Sarah, Jamelle, Adonis

$Y = 4x$

25 groups of 4 = 100

| | |
|---|---|
| **Ms. Wall:** | Hi group 5. I see that you are hard at work. What did you notice? |
| **AJ:** | 100 will be on the top of the pattern because 4 is on the top and $25 \times 4 = 100$. |
| **Sarah:** | Yeah, and we remembered how to write an equation, it is $y = 4x$. |
| **Ms. Wall:** | Wow, I like that you are thinking about equations and variables. What does the $x$ mean? |
| **Sarah:** | $x$ is 25. |
| **Ms. Wall:** | What does the $y$ mean? |
| **Sarah:** | 100. |
| **Ms. Wall:** | Does $x$ always equal 25? |
| **Sarah:** | Yes, that is the only number that makes 100. |
| **Ms. Wall:** | Does $y$ always equal 100? |
| **Sarah:** | I think so. |
| **Ms. Wall:** | Does anyone else have ideas about $x$ and $y$? |
| **Adonis:** | It is just 100 because that is what we are trying to figure out. You could make it 50 if you wanted. |
| **Ms. Wall:** | Adonis, you just showed some great understanding of the variables. Let's use that. If $y = 50$, what is $x$? |
| **Sarah:** | It doesn't work. |
| **Ms. Wall:** | What do you mean, Sarah? |
| **Sarah:** | Well, if we make $y = 48$, then it works because $x = 12$. |
| **Ms. Wall:** | Interesting. What other numbers work for $x$ and $y$? |
| **Sarah:** | I think that's a factor or a multiple? |
| **Ms. Wall:** | What do you think, group? Is this a factor or multiple? |
| **AJ:** | I think it's a factor, but I always get them mixed up. |
| **Ms. Wall:** | Tell me your thinking, AJ. |
| **AJ:** | So it's like 4, 8, 12, 16, 20, and then anything else that is plus 4. |
| **Ms. Wall:** | Your thinking is correct. Those are called multiples of 4. |
| **Jamelle:** | I think factors are the reverse, right? |
| **Ms. Wall:** | Tell me more, I think you might be right. |
| **Jamelle:** | So 48 works because 4 is one of its factors. But 50 didn't work because 4 isn't a factor. |
| **Ms. Wall:** | That is some great thinking, group! I'm curious—what if $y = 8$? Would it work? |
| **Jamelle:** | Yes, because 4 is a factor of 8. |
| **Ms. Wall:** | Could you draw that out for me? I'll come back in a few minutes. |

Ms. Wall saw that group 2 was making many duplicates of the interactive squares from the initial problem and wanted to probe the group to make generalizations, rather than any more copies.

(Continued)

(Continued)

**Ms. Wall:** Wow, group 2, you have a lot of squares on your slide, what is your thinking?

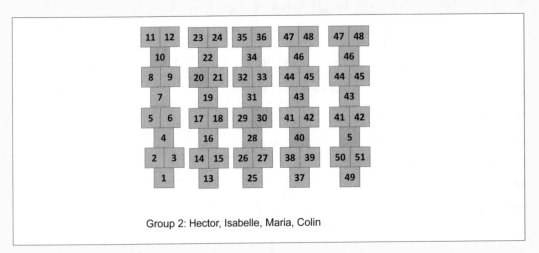

Group 2: Hector, Isabelle, Maria, Colin

**Hector:** We are just gonna make the whole hopscotch.

**Ms. Wall:** That might take a long time.

**Hector:** No, we are just taking turns writing in the numbers. Once the first row was made, we just copied it.

**Ms. Wall:** Great job sharing jobs and being efficient. I wonder if you are noticing any patterns in your hopscotch.

**Ms. Wall:** Go ahead and finish up the column that you are working on, but then try to find patterns. I'll come back in a few minutes to check in.

Ms. Wall joined group 4 to talk about their table.

**Ms. Wall:** Hi group 4. Is that a table that you are making?

Group 4: Jay, Steve, Marta, Greg

| Only one square | 22 | 46 | 70 | 94 |
|---|---|---|---|---|
| 1 | 25 | 49 | 73 | 97 |
| 4 | 28 | 52 | 76 | 100 |
| 7 | 31 | 55 | 79 | |
| 10 | 24 | 58 | 82 | |
| 13 | 27 | 61 | 85 | |
| 16 | 40 | 64 | 88 | |
| 19 | 43 | 67 | 91 | |

| Greg: | Yep. |
| Ms. Wall: | What kind of numbers do you have on this table? |
| Greg: | We did all the numbers, like for the squares that are just one, not the double-up squares. |
| Ms. Wall: | Interesting, why did you decide to use those numbers? |
| Greg: | I don't know, that was already like that. Jay, didn't you start it? |
| Jay: | Yeah, we didn't need the double squares because we wanted to see if 100 ended on a single square. |
| Ms. Wall: | But what if it ended on a double square? |
| Jay: | Then we wouldn't see it on the table. But we do, so it works. |
| Ms. Wall: | What do the missing numbers mean? |
| Greg: | That it doesn't work. |
| Ms. Wall: | What doesn't work? |
| Greg: | Ah, I'm confused now. |
| Ms. Wall: | That's okay. Mathematicians often feel confused when they find patterns and try to explain them. Let's see if your group members see it. Marta and Steve, do you know what the missing numbers mean? |
| Marta: | Those are the doubled up ones. |
| Steve: | I agree. It's like when both feet touch the ground. |
| Ms. Wall: | Greg, is that helping you at all? |
| Greg: | Yeah, it's because we are just showing the single squares. |
| Ms. Wall: | So this table tells us a lot about the numbers we see on it and the missing numbers. How does the table help us to figure out where #99 is placed? |
| Greg: | It's not a single because it's not on the table. |
| Jay: | Well, it is going to be on the left, no, right side of the double because it is right before 100. |
| Ms. Wall: | Great discussion, group. |

Ms. Wall returned to group 5. They have expanded their drawing but don't have much more on their slide.

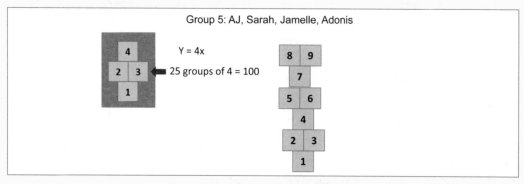

Group 5: AJ, Sarah, Jamelle, Adonis

(Continued)

(Continued)

**Ms. Wall:** Hi group 5. I see that you have more numbers on your hopscotch board. What did you notice?

**Jamelle:** It's not working. 8 should work because 4 is a factor, but it's in a double block.

**Ms. Wall:** Do you notice any other patterns?

**Adonis:** I keep telling them about 3, 6, 9.

**Ms. Wall:** What do you mean by that?

**Adonis:** I see multiples of three in the right-hand side of the doubles.

**Ms. Wall:** What do you think of that group?

**Sarah:** Yes, that is a pattern, but we don't really care about the right side of the doubles, we care about the single boxes. That's why we need to look at those numbers and not 3, 6, 9.

**Ms. Wall:** You are both bringing up really important points. Adonis, can you explain more about the 3, 6, 9?

**Adonis:** Okay, so there are three squares and they end on a 3.

*<Adonis color codes these.>*

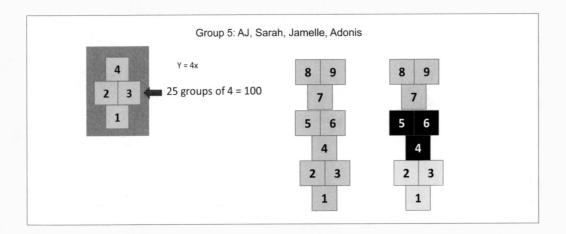

Group 5: AJ, Sarah, Jamelle, Adonis

Y = 4x

25 groups of 4 = 100

**Adonis:** Then there are three more squares and they end on a 6. Then three more that end on a 9. So it is like 3 + 3 + 3 = 9.

**Sarah:** Ohhhhhhhhhh, wait, it's not 4, it's 3.

**Ms. Wall:** I'm going to check in with another group. Be sure to listen to everyone's ideas as you think about this 3.

Ms. Wall notices that group 2 has color coded a pattern that they found using 10s and how they extrapolated the pattern for 50–100. She has run out of time during the monitoring stage, and notes this as she considers how to use it during the math discussion.

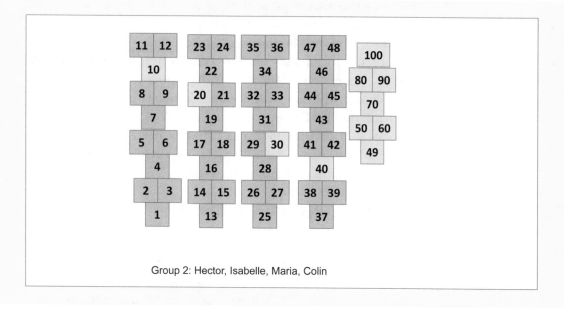

Group 2: Hector, Isabelle, Maria, Colin

Students engage with the problem during the group time while effortlessly implementing many of the practiced norms. They share their work on the interactive slides by copying and pasting images and screen captures from web-based virtual manipulatives and online sources. Their unstructured slides become cluttered quickly with a variety of representations, and students use the norm of rearranging the slide for reading clarity. They also create additional slides whenever they need additional room. Students duplicate others' work whenever they are inspired to change it or continue a representation in a unique way.

## Select and Sequence Student Work and Design Discussion Questions

Preparing for the whole-group discussion is a thoughtful and purposeful process that begins with selecting and sequencing students' work. It is not necessary to select every student's work, and in fact your conversation will become more focused if you select only the pieces of work that connect to the mathematics objective. Once the selections are made, consider how you will order them. Some teachers prefer to order student work beginning with a very concrete (manipulatives) example and moving toward

### Confidence in Messiness

Problem solving often includes many rough drafts and messiness. While it might be tempting to organize student thinking, recognize the purpose of the unstructured spaces and show students that you value the messiness. That will give them the confidence to continue to post their rough-draft thinking as they problem solve.

abstract (equations) representations so that students can see how the math models relate to formulas. Similarly, some teachers use rich tasks to teach their students where familiar formulas originate. If your students are familiar with a formula, but do not show a strong understanding of how to manipulate the formula, you might choose to begin with abstract formulas and then move to the connection to concrete models. Regardless of the sequence, be sure that it is purposeful to meet student needs and paired with thoughtful questions that will guide the students to making the connections during the math discussion.

## USING MANY REPRESENTATIONS

Because online learning has the ability to copy and paste so efficiently, there are often an abundance of representations. Teachers moving from the face-to-face classroom might initially be excited that students are able to make so many representations, but then quickly become overwhelmed by trying to give each student a turn to explain their work. Smith and Stein (2011) address this by purposefully selecting only a few pieces that relate to the mathematics goal. However, there are several ways that you can use the abundance of representations to your advantage. Since they are all visible to the other students, students often browse the different representations as they try to make connections. A simple homework assignment is to have students copy a peer's strategy and apply it to a different situation. That way the students are browsing a variety of strategies, evaluating each strategy, and choosing the one for the homework problem.

## CREATING A CONNECTIONS MAP

A Connections Map is a visual guide for you to consider the sequence, questions, and important mathematical concepts that you want your students to discover in the discussion. Wills (2015) found that when teachers actually create the Connections Map, they are more likely to ask open-ended questions until students are able to verbalize the math connection, rather than explicitly stating the connection for the students.

Ms. Wall selected a few models to discuss during the math discourse time. She considered the big idea that she wanted her students to gain from this problem, and then she set out to create questions that would lead them to this big idea. The mathematics goal of the lesson was to identify and continue algebraic patterns, and use multiples to determine the placement of the 100th square. She created a Connections Map (Figure 8.2) to remember her questions, the selected representations, and important connections that she wanted her students to make during the discussion.

## Figure 8.2

## Connections Map From Ms. Wall's Hopscotch Problem

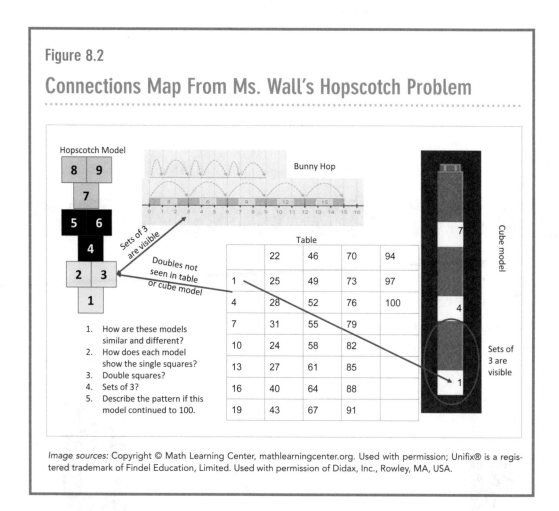

*Image sources:* Copyright © Math Learning Center, mathlearningcenter.org. Used with permission; Unifix® is a registered trademark of Findel Education, Limited. Used with permission of Didax, Inc., Rowley, MA, USA.

## Connect Student Work to the Math Goal

The final step in the 5 Practices is connecting students' work to each other and to the overall math goal. "Connecting may in fact be the most challenging of all of the five practices because it calls on the teacher to craft questions that will make the mathematics visible and understandable" (Smith & Stein, 2011, p. 49). The strategies presented in this section use questioning to encourage whole-group participation by allowing not just one or two responses, but the visual responses of all class members simultaneously.

## DYNAMIC MATH TALK

If there is one advantage to online learning, it can be found during the discussion. Since all students have the ability to duplicate and draw on the slides, more students can make their thinking about connections visible. Dynamic Math Talk (Wills, 2019) uses interactive slides and allows students to add arrows, text boxes, and color to identify connections in real time. You can ask questions that connect algorithms or graphs to table representations, and students can respond directly on the slide to where they can visually see the similarities. This dynamic math talk is showcased when students interact with peers' work on the discussion slide.

Let's see how the discussion unfolded in Ms. Wall's classroom.

# Ms. Wall: Rich-Task Math Talk

Ms. Wall returned her students to the main room. She knew that some of her students were not yet comfortable with the microphone and others had great tech skills. She used all of this knowledge during the math talk.

**Ms. Wall:** You all did a fantastic job on this problem today. I saw so many patterns and listened to so many great generalizations. I have selected four models that we will compare in order to find patterns and then extend those patterns. The four models are called

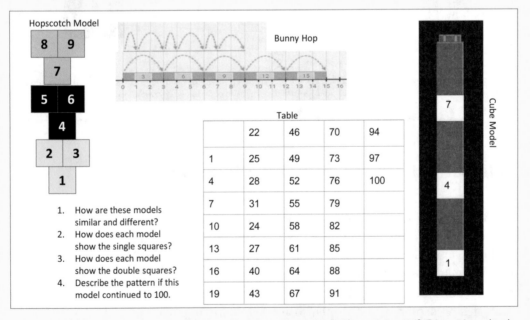

Image sources: Copyright © Math Learning Center, mathlearningcenter.org. Used with permission; Unifix® is a registered trademark of Findel Education, Limited. Used with permission of Didax, Inc., Rowley, MA, USA.

hopscotch model, bunny hop, cube model, and table. Be sure to say which model you are talking about. How are these models similar and different? If you see a similarity or difference, raise your hand and keep it up. If someone says your answer, you may put your hand down and make your connection in the chat box.

**Randy:** The 1, 2, and 3 in the hopscotch model are the same as my jump of three in the bunny hop.

**Ms. Wall:** Raise your hand if you see that and I'll ask you to show it on the slide.

**Ms. Wall:** Owen, can you mark it for us?

**Ms. Wall:** Very nice. Does anyone else see this set of three numbers in the other models?

**Jamelle:** Yeah, in the cubes, it's like if you snap them apart so that each tower is one white and two blue.

**Ms. Wall:** Owen, can you mark that too? *<Ms. Wall looks at the list of students with hands raised.>* Tiana, what pattern do you see?

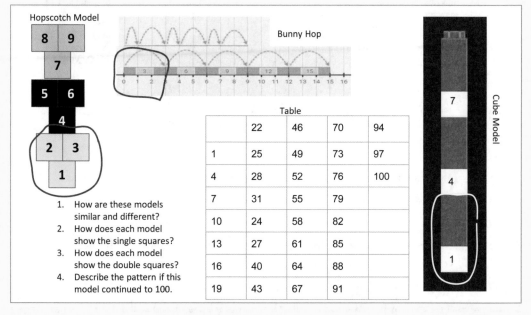

Hopscotch Model

Bunny Hop

Cube Model

Table

|   | 22 | 46 | 70 | 94 |
|---|----|----|----|-----|
| 1 | 25 | 49 | 73 | 97 |
| 4 | 28 | 52 | 76 | 100 |
| 7 | 31 | 55 | 79 |   |
| 10 | 24 | 58 | 82 |   |
| 13 | 27 | 61 | 85 |   |
| 16 | 40 | 64 | 88 |   |
| 19 | 43 | 67 | 91 |   |

1. How are these models similar and different?
2. How does each model show the single squares?
3. How does each model show the double squares?
4. Describe the pattern if this model continued to 100.

**Tiana:** I saw that the table and cube model are exactly the same numbers.

**Ms. Wall:** Tell us more, Tiana. Let's mark those numbers. Rachel, would you use shapes to mark them for us?

**Tiana:** You see the 1. There is a 1 in the table and on the cube model. Next is a 4 and you see it on both again, then a 7.

*<Rachel draws stars, hearts, and circles on those three numbers.>*

*(Continued)*

(Continued)

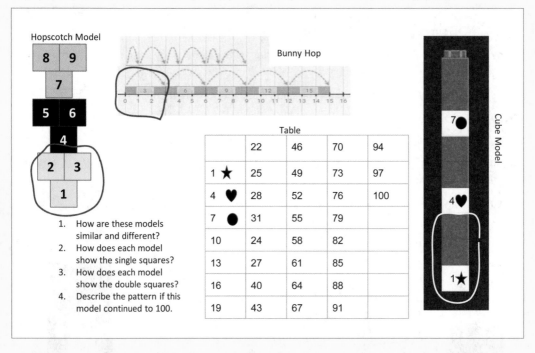

1. How are these models similar and different?
2. How does each model show the single squares?
3. How does each model show the double squares?
4. Describe the pattern if this model continued to 100.

*Image sources: Copyright © Math Learning Center, mathlearningcenter.org. Used with permission; Unifix® is a registered trademark of Findel Education, Limited. Used with permission of Didax, Inc., Rowley, MA, USA.*

**Ms. Wall:** Tiana, what do you think the blue cubes represent?

**Tiana:** Those are the double squares. So, like 2 and 3 and 5 and 6.

**Sabin:** It is like my double jump in the bunny hop.

**Ms. Wall:** Tell us more, Sabin.

**Sabin:** I did the top bunny hop. Each hop is 1, then 2, then 1, then 2. The 1s are the white cubes and the 2s are the blue cubes.

**Ms. Wall:** Isabelle, you can be the recorder for Sabin's work.

**Sabin:** It's my bunny hop, the top one that is turned. *(See the image at the top of the next page.)*

**Ms. Wall:** Wow, Isabelle, you made that really clear for me to understand. Did that help anyone else?

*<Chat messages from several students roll in.>*

**Ms. Wall:** So far, we have found sets of 3s that Owen marked with circles and single squares that Rachel marked with shapes. Are there any other similarities that we see?

**AJ:** Sometimes you see the double squares and sometimes you don't.

**Ms. Wall:** AJ, can you explain where you see them, and Marta, can you record for us using arrows?

**AJ:** The doubles are in the hopscotch model because they are next to each other, and they are in the top bunny hop with bigger hops and the blue cubes, but they aren't in the table.

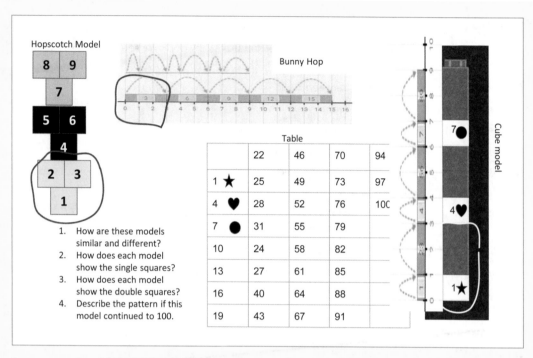

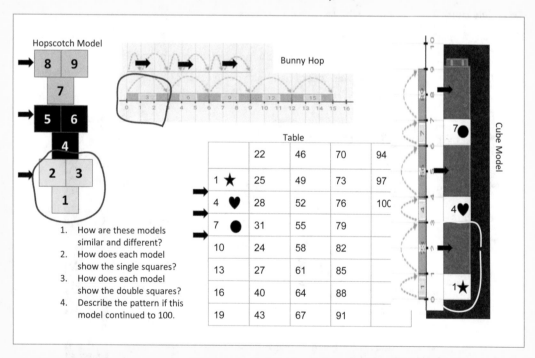

*(Continued)*

(Continued)

| | |
|---|---|
| **Ms. Wall:** | Would everyone type in the chat box? Why don't we see the doubles in the table? Where did they go? |
| **Marta (via chat):** | They are in between 1 and 4. |
| **Gabrielle (via chat):** | You don't need to see them. |
| **Colin (via chat):** | They didn't write them because they aren't a single. |
| **Jay (via chat):** | Singles are what we are looking for. |
| **Ms. Wall:** | Adonis, your group talked a lot about factors and multiples. How did you use those ideas to solve the problem? |
| **Adonis:** | Okay, so you gotta look at the ones with 3s. If your number has a factor of 3, then it is going to be in the right side of the double. |
| **Ms. Wall:** | What if the number was 30? Where would that go? |
| **Adonis:** | It has a factor of 3, so it goes in the right side. |
| **Ms. Wall:** | What about 31? If you think you know where 31 goes, type your reasoning in the chat box. |
| **Adonis (via chat):** | It is a single because it comes after 30. |
| **Jay (via chat):** | Single 30 + 1 = 31. |
| **Sarah (via chat):** | It either goes on the left or is a single, but not on the right. |
| **Sarah (via chat):** | It goes on the top, a single square. |
| **Ms. Wall:** | Sarah, noticed that you typed that it would be a single square, can you tell us why? |
| **Sarah:** | 3 times 10 is 30 and that is on the right, then one more is on top. |
| **Ms. Wall:** | Hector, can you record Sarah's thinking for us? |

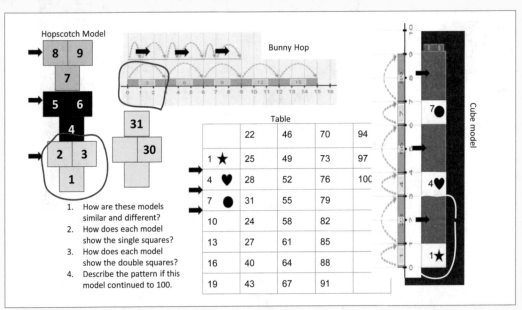

1. How are these models similar and different?
2. How does each model show the single squares?
3. How does each model show the double squares?
4. Describe the pattern if this model continued to 100.

*Image sources:* Copyright © Math Learning Center, mathlearningcenter.org. Used with permission; Unifix® is a registered trademark of Findel Education, Limited. Used with permission of Didax, Inc., Rowley, MA, USA.

# Summarize the Task

Summarization—sometimes called consolidation—at the end of every lesson is an important skill for students to develop to give meaning to the lesson and to contribute to long-term retention (Wormeli, 2005). Summarization strategies can include a variety of explanations, connections, and rationales, but the important thing is that *all* students have the opportunity to summarize. In the remote classroom this means that *all* students need a place to type or verbalize their summary. It is common for teachers to eliminate the summarization exercise in the name of time management, but there are affordances to online learning that make summarization routines quick and useful while giving every student a space to summarize. Chapter 6 includes strategies to support summarization of learning.

## Ms. Wall: Rich-Task Summarization

At the end of the discussion, Ms. Wall implemented a whole-class exit ticket. She was curious if her students could make the connection to the overall math goal and modify any strategy discussed for a slightly different situation. This was a quick routine and required students to summarize using only words. She displayed a new hopscotch situation and asked students what strategy they would use and what they would need to change in the strategy to make it work for this new situation.

What strategy would you use and what would you need to change in the strategy to make it work for this new situation?

Rich Tasks are an effective way to use real-world situations to connect prior knowledge to mathematical procedures and algorithms. As you reflect on how you used rich tasks in the face-to-face classroom, consider the elements that were most effective.

- What are the mathematical solutions and misconceptions that my students may encounter during the task?

- What technology challenges are prominent in this task?

- What structures will I create to encourage participation during small-group work?

- How will I monitor the breakout groups?

- How will I encourage multiple representations (concrete, virtual manipulatives, and abstract notation) and students' confidence in finding appropriate virtual manipulatives?

- Where will my students record their group work? Is that recording space accessible to the individual recorder, whole group, and/or whole class?

- How will I select and sequence the student slides? Will I add markings on slides to give students notification that they will present?

- What is the mathematical goal of the lesson? What questions will I ask so that students can connect the multiple representations to that goal?

For more practice, tutorials, and templates, visit www.theresawills.com.

+ chapter

9

# LEARNING STATIONS

This chapter is inspired by the work of Jennifer Lempp (2017), the author of *Math Workshop: Five Steps to Implementing Guided Math, Learning Stations, Reflection and More, Grades K–5,* and our collaboration to reimagine learning stations in the virtual setting. When students are placed in learning teams to play, explore, and discuss mathematics, it gives them ownership of the learning while providing a structure for you to have the freedom to move around the various groups as they listen in on the conversations and ask purposeful questions. This chapter will describe six different types of math learning stations, and then give a vignette about how classroom co-teachers used this model.

## Preparing for Breakout Groups

A fundamental structure in math learning stations is the ability to group students, and for the students to work together, without teacher assistance, to complete the station. In the online environment, this will mean that you will need to set up breakout group structures.

## START SLOW AND ADD ON RESPONSIBILITY

Begin slow. Before you can implement breakout groups of four to five students for 30 minutes, you need to create collaborative, safe learning norms for two students in two minutes. To do this, give your students opportunities to create the rules and norms that they want in their breakout groups. Give them practice and experience by implementing "pair-share" routines with two students for two minutes, and then four students for two minutes, and then four students for four minutes. Teach them roles such as "Timekeeper" to ensure equitable talk time or "Mayor" to ensure that all voices are heard. (See Chapter 2 for information on roles and responsibilities within breakout rooms.) As you increase the time and responsibilities for students in breakout rooms, and increase their confidence in using the microphone and interactive tools, students of all ages will gradually accept longer group times until the times meet the needs of your learning stations.

## GROUP SLIDES

It is integral to consider how and where your students will type their solutions, show their work, and transition or rotate to new activities. You might have each group show their thinking on a slide within the main slide deck, or you might give each group their own slide deck to work within. It is important to use clear directions, visual cues, color codes, and more so that each student knows exactly where to post their work. Posting a clear directions slide can be especially useful if done consistently so that students know where to go if they are confused. When working in a whole-group slide deck, color coding slides by changing the background color or having a colored bar at the top can be an effective way of identifying group-specific slides. If you are giving each group their own slide deck, be sure that everyone in the group has access to it, and so do any teachers in the class. I like to have five different tabs open; one for each of my five groups. That way, I can click on the group's slide to view the activity that they are completing and any work that they have shown. This helps me to consider questions that I might ask the group to help expand their thinking.

Younger students will need additional practice with routines and scaffolds when working in small groups. Before sending them to breakout rooms to play a game, practice with a more simplistic slide that uses drag and drop, and discuss the exciting moments and challenges of using group slides. Encourage students to make mistakes and learn how to use the undo button. Give them sentence starters to use when a peer makes a mistake so that they can use calm and kind words in the moment. Once they have these basics mastered, then gradually release them into breakout rooms for longer and with more challenging tasks.

## NAMING CONVENTIONS

If you are creating group slides, this could quickly result in an overwhelming number of slide decks. Therefore, it is important to consider naming conventions so that you can keep all of their files organized. You will want to be able to go back and reference them for formative assessment or as evidence of student learning to support grading or for conferences with families/IEPs. For example, I like to use the group number first in my naming convention. That way, even if I have 10 tabs open and can only view a few characters of the title, I can still see the group number and navigate easily as I meet with each group during rotations (Figure 9.1). I also use the date, unit numbers, standards, and any other searchable feature before using words to describe the slide deck. One advantage to online learning is that you can create incredibly long file names, full of searchable terms that will help you find your materials easily.

### Figure 9.1

### Sample Screen With Tabs Displayed

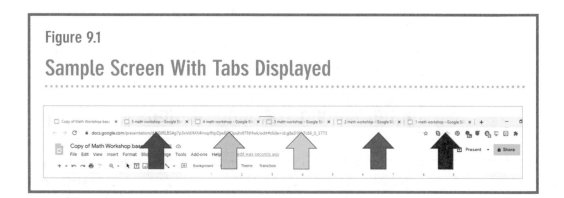

## TITLE SCREENS

Each time my students get access to learning station group slides, I begin with a title screen (Figure 9.2) that shows them all the activities within the slide deck. This includes the required activities (must do's) and the optional activities (can do's), sometimes assigned using color. The color coding is especially helpful for young students.

---

**Figure 9.2**

## Sample Title Screen

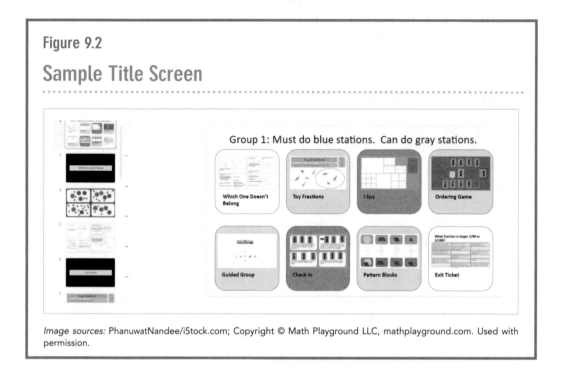

*Image sources:* PhanuwatNandee/iStock.com; Copyright © Math Playground LLC, mathplayground.com. Used with permission.

---

I also include activity title screens so that they can easily navigate throughout the slide deck to locate the different activities. These are easily viewed on the left-column slide preview as black slides. Some teachers may prefer to hyperlink the activities on the main title screen with the starting page of each activity.

## Implementing Learning Stations

Learning stations, a common routine in face-to-face classes, are implemented by placing students in small groups and having them physically move around the room to access each station. Stations often include games, partner work, independent work, and even small-group mini-lessons directed by the teacher. Implementing learning stations can be accomplished in a virtual environment, but the technique is a bit different. The important thing about preparing for learning stations is that your directions are clear and that you have practiced small groups enough to ensure that students are self-starting and self-directed while working away from the teacher.

## BEGIN WITH WHOLE-CLASS NUMBER ROUTINES

When beginning learning stations, start with a whole-class launch such as a Number Routine. This primes the students in two ways: it gets them in math mode by stimulating connections to numbers and patterns, and it gets them in discussion mode through typing and using audio. Try to select Number Routines that give every student a voice (speaking, typing, dragging, etc.) so that every student is active as that sets the stage to remain active in the rest of the activities. There are suggestions for Number Routines in Chapter 7, but you can also use your own ideas or routines that you already know or have used with your students. The important element of this activity is to keep it short—about seven minutes—so that there is time to engage in the small-group activities.

## TYPES OF LEARNING STATIONS

It is important to consider the various goals (pedagogical, social, technological, and mathematical) of each station. The station ideas that follow showcase some unique characteristics about how to leverage group work and independent contributions for accountability and cooperation.

### Independent-to-Partner/Group Activities

Activities that include an independent element first are useful when you want to include all students. There is added accountability, as each student must first do their part before they can interact with their partner. Consider activities such as "Guess My Rule," which can be used in multiple grade levels. With this strategy, the independent component consists of a student developing a rule and some possible clues to the rule. Then, when the setup is complete, the partner can participate in the guessing portion. Here is an example:

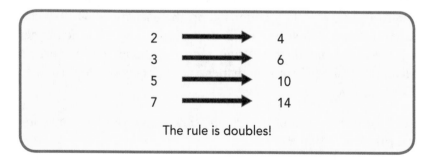

When creating Independent-to-Partner Activities, give students a clear space and direction for their independent work. This can be accomplished by assigning each student their own slide, or multiple students can work on the same slide that is divided into independent sections. If partners are going to type on another student's slide, the directions should clearly state this so that feelings are not hurt and shared learning occurs. Regardless of the activities you choose for this learning station, the important element of Independent-to-Partner Activities is that every student is accountable for their portion before collaboration begins.

Here are a few examples that you can modify to help reimagine your math class online:

- **Solve and Switch:** Each person solves a part of the same problem and then exchanges information to solve the overall problem.

- **Collaboration Clues:** Each person gets one private clue to solve and that clue is used in the bigger group.

- **Make and Guess:** Make a figure using shapes (e.g., a simple circle or square or a complex shape such as an equilateral triangle with a base twice the length of the square) and then describe it to your partner using math terms as they guess what it is.

- **Guess My Rule:** Each person creates a slide that shows numbers/shapes/graphs that fit the rule and don't fit the rule and the partner guesses the rule.

## Small-Group Activities

Small-Group Activities value collaboration and multiple perspectives. In this learning station, choose activities that have a wide variety of possible solutions so that students can not only share their own solution, but also become inspired by new solutions that they otherwise might not have considered. The idea here is that students will do a better job on the assignment if they collaborate with their group, because it is only through unique peer perspectives that they will find more solutions. The important element of Small-Group Activities is that collaboration leads to more solutions.

Here are a few examples that you can modify to help reimagine your math class online:

- **How Many Ways Can You . . . :** Each group lists as many ways as they can that fit the rule made at the end of the sentence (e.g., make 26 cents with coins, skip count on this chart, create an equivalent ratio of 2:3, or graph an integral function to show variations of *c*).

- **Modify the Problem:** Each group begins with an original problem; modifies one portion of the problem (a number, variable, or word to change the problem); and solves it together.

- **Multiple Representations:** The group must provide multiple representations and each member of the group contributes a different way of modeling the math (e.g., representations in fraction units include set, area, and number line models, or representations in algebra include table, graph, rule, and function).

## Partner Games

Partner Games are an engaging way to incorporate practice of mathematical concepts that can lead to procedural fluency. Games often lead to strategy, and the strategies are often based off of mathematical generalizations, rules, and patterns. This strategy, paired with additional practice, helps students to make sense of their reasoning in order to develop a sense of proof. Strategy is often easier for students to summarize and voice than out-of-context mathematical proofs, and therefore it connects context to procedure. Additional accountability can be incorporated by requiring partners to check a peer's work before taking their turn. The important element of Partner Games is that through practice and reasoning, students can make mathematical generalizations and improve procedural fluency.

Here are a few examples that you can modify to help reimagine your math class online:

- **Compare (WAR):** Students compete by flipping a card and comparing numbers, fractions, slopes, areas, and so on.

- **Strategy Games:** Students move a game piece, solve the mathematics, and strategically place game pieces.

- **Other Games:** Any individual-competitive, group-competitive, and collaborative games work well in this format.

## Guided Group Exploration

This learning station is the perfect space to do small-group inter-vention, extension, or direct teaching to review previous lessons or to launch new lessons. Here, you guide a small group of students through understanding of a specific procedure or exploration of a new concept with purposeful questioning and guidance. This is often done with you directly, where you stay in the breakout room with the students and interact with the small group. As students gain independence or as the concept warrants, other variations of this learning station can include written notes or video clips where the group reviews the notes or video and collaborates to com-plete the requirements to show understanding. This can be done using group graphic organizers or by completing a notes slide. The important element of Guided Group Exploration is that the group is guided to collaborate and learn the content.

Here are a few examples that you can modify to help reimagine your math class online:

- Target a small group of students with a specific math topic to address a specific math misconception.

- Target a small group of students with similar interests to relate the mathematics to their hobby.

- Target a small group of students with similar modality preferences (e.g., likes to talk, learns through visuals, or tech-savvy) and use their strengths to teach the mathematics.

## Independent-to-Small-Group Check for Understanding

Check for Understandings are any type of quick assessments where students can show their thinking. Often, these assessments are used in teacher planning to determine the next learning objec-tives for individual students. In this learning station, students complete an independent check for understanding and are often viewing other peers' responses, since they are in the same break-out room. There are many benefits to structuring the Check for Understandings in this way. Students are able to

- access a starting point if they otherwise wouldn't know how to respond.

- begin immediately but then read other responses and modify their response if they choose.

- ask peers to elaborate and explain their response, which builds deeper understanding.

- apply a peer's idea to their own situation.

This collaboration might leave teachers wondering if each student was able to summarize their thinking independently, and that is why I recommend using different problems with similar solutions. For example, each student solves a different two-digit addition problem. This will incorporate honesty and integrity as no two solutions are the same. You can do this by assigning specific problems to students, or give a choice of several similar problems where each student can select their own and apply peers' strategies to their unique context. The important element of Independent-to-Small-Group Check for Understanding is that each student is able to summarize their own thinking while considering the thinking of peers simultaneously.

Here are a few examples that you can modify to help reimagine your math class online:

- **Explain How to . . . :** Students describe the steps to a particular algorithm.

- **Find the Mistake:** Students identify and describe a mistake in various problems.

- **Compare and Order:** Students compare and order numbers throughout the number system.

- **Show Another Way:** Students have to share another way to solve a problem, graph, or other representation of a math topic.

## Independent-to-Small-Group Exploration

When students explore a mathematical concept through models and manipulatives, inequities emerge as some students take an active role and others take a passive role. With structures that give a space for each student to independently respond to a group exploration, each student is accountable for their own contribution. This is more than a simple divide-and-conquer routine since all the independent portions are related to one another by a mathematical rule, pattern, or procedure and all members of the group are responsible for ensuring that the entire group exploration is correct. The important element of the

Independent-to-Small-Group Exploration learning station is that each student has an assigned space to complete independently, but they can see the relationship of their contribution to the overall collaboration of the exploration.

Here are a few examples that you can modify to help reimagine your math class online:

- Graphing four different functions with a similar feature (such as slope or $y$-intercept)
- Creating polygons with different numbers of sides but similar lengths or areas
- Finding sums that add to 10 but use different addends
- Showing a common ratio in various quantities

## END WITH WHOLE-CLASS CHECK FOR UNDERSTANDING

Learning stations, much like any other math class, should end in a whole-group summary. This closure activity gives teachers and students a place to summarize their learning in each of the learning stations during that day's math instruction. The Check for Understanding is geared toward the overall mathematical objective that can be found in each of the learning stations rather than one specific learning station. In addition, each student should feel valued in making a contribution to the class. This can be accomplished using multiple modalities such as typing on a whole-class slide, typing in the chat box, or using audio to elaborate and extend connections. The important element of the Whole-Class Check for Understanding is that the class closes with the overall mathematical concept in mind and that every student is able to summarize their learning of this concept.

Here are a few examples that you can modify to help reimagine your math class online:

- Short summaries to specific questions about generalizations such as "Why is a negative number times a positive number a negative product?" or "Why is the sum the same if the addends are in a different order?"

- What is an a-ha moment that you had today?

- Who helped you today, and how did they help you?

- What activity do you want to do again?

# Learning Stations in Action

Ms. Lee and Ms. Gordon co-teach a fourth-grade class of 20 students and are beginning their second year of online teaching. They taught together in face-to-face settings and know the importance of using learning stations for targeted instruction, practice, and collaboration.

In the vignette that follows, you will see how Ms. Lee skillfully chose activities for students to do interactively in a virtual learning station. Ms. Lee was purposeful in her selections of activities, and this is only after two months of prepping the students about expectations when in groups.

During their fractions unit, Ms. Lee and Ms. Gordon implemented eight activities with their students, including a Whole-Group Number Routine at the start of each class and a Whole-Group Exit Ticket at the end of each class. Ms. Lee, the general education teacher, monitored all five breakout groups by asking students probing and clarifying questions. Ms. Gordon, the special education teacher, spent 15 minutes working with group 1 on a Guided Group Exploration to ensure that accommodations were implemented for a student receiving special education services. Then, she spent 15 minutes working with group 2 on a different Guided Group Exploration designed to extend the lesson for the group who will need an additional challenge. Since one of her students who received special education services was recently identified in the gifted program, she used this Guided Group Exploration to also evaluate his current accommodations to ensure that they meet his needs for being twice exceptional. Together, the co-teachers implemented activities based on group needs. This means that each group got a different workshop experience, and no two groups looked the same.

## Welcome and Whole-Class Number Routine

**Ms. Lee:**   Today in math, we will think about all the ways we can use fractions. We will work in groups for almost the entire math time. But first, let's think about this Which One Doesn't Belong? slide. Move the no symbol to one of the four corners that you think doesn't belong.

*<Each student simultaneously moves the symbol that they think doesn't belong to the corner.>*

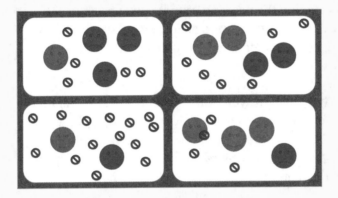

**Ms. Lee:**   Wow, I can see that we are going to have a great discussion. Please write your reasoning on the next slide.

*<Students type their rationale in the box provided. Ms. Lee highlights three of the statements to notify students that she will ask them to elaborate using their microphone.>*

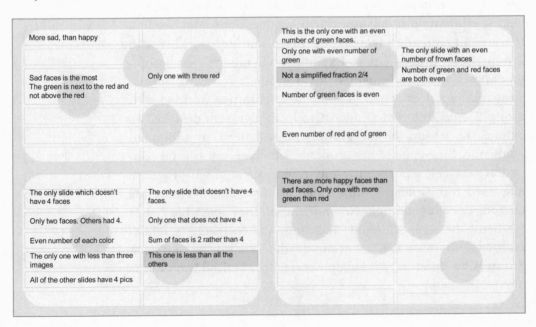

| **Ms. Lee:** | I want to hear more about the highlighted box that says, "There are more happy faces than sad faces." This is a great observation. What does this tell us about the others? |
|---|---|
| **Jordan:** | That was me. Because if you were taking a survey, more people would like that one. |
| **Ms. Lee:** | What a fun context, Jordan. Let's hear about the highlighted box that says, "This one is less than all the others." |
| **Bri:** | Well, it just has 2 faces, the rest have 4. |
| **Ms. Lee:** | Let's think about Jordan's survey example. How many people liked that one? |
| **Bri:** | 1 liked it and 1 hated it. |
| **Ms. Lee:** | Oh, I see. And how about the highlighted box that says "not simplified fraction $\frac{2}{4}$"? |
| **Nely:** | $\frac{2}{4}$ isn't simplified. It is the same as $\frac{1}{2}$. |
| **Ms. Lee:** | Interesting. Who else agrees with Nely and can restate it in your own words? |
| **Bruce:** | Nely is saying how it is half and half. |
| **Greyson:** | Yeah, so 2 people like it and 2 people hate it. It is still half of them like it. |
| **Ms. Lee:** | Who could tell us what fraction we should use for the lower left corner? |
| **Greyson:** | It's also $\frac{1}{2}$ because half of the people like it. |
| **Ms. Lee:** | But does that mean that the upper right and lower left are the same? |
| **Nely:** | Kinda, there were more people in the survey, but it is still half that like it. |
| **Ms. Lee:** | Does that mean that the other two diagonals are the same? |
| **Jillian:** | Yes. $\frac{1}{4}$ are happy and $\frac{1}{4}$ are sad. |
| **Greyson:** | I don't think so. It is $\frac{1}{4}$ happy and $\frac{3}{4}$ happy. |
| **Ms. Lee:** | Interesting, so it really matters how you label your work. We are going to explore some fraction activities today. Try to remember to use labels when you are describing your fractions. |

In this activity, students had to use reasoning and proof to create a rationale for their earlier decision. Since there were unlimited "no" symbols and space to write rationales, every student had a place to make their thinking visible.

## Small Groups Begin

Ms. Lee created breakout rooms and assigned students their group slides, which included an opening page of must-do and can-do stations. Ms. Lee used this choice board to motivate students to do more than the assigned (Must Do) activities. It also helped her with time management, as she could ensure that every group was learning during the entire group time even if they finished their must-do activities, because they could continue their learning through the optional (Can Do) activities.

*(Continued)*

(Continued)

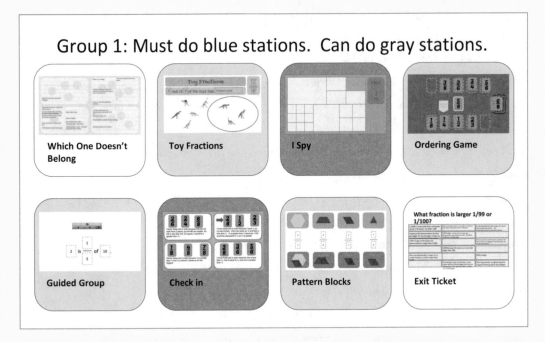

# Group 1: Must do blue stations.  Can do gray stations.

| | | | |
|---|---|---|---|
| **Which One Doesn't Belong** | **Toy Fractions** | **I Spy** | **Ordering Game** |
| **Guided Group** | **Check in** | **Pattern Blocks** | **Exit Ticket** |

*Image sources:* PhanuwatNandee/iStock.com; Copyright © Math Playground LLC, mathplayground.com. Used with permission.

## Guided Group Explorations

Ms. Gordon delivered a mini-lesson to group 1. She shared a video where she modeled fractions using a bar model. Since one of her students had a special accommodation to use both physical and virtual bar models, she ensured that both he, and the rest of her small group, knew how to manipulate the virtual model. Then they used the model to compare fractions with common denominators or common numerators.

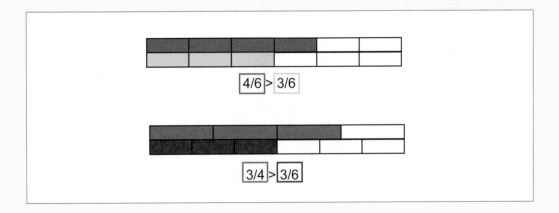

$$4/6 > 3/6$$

$$3/4 > 3/6$$

Ms. Gordon was able to give her full attention to the group of four students because she taught and practiced breakout room norms with students. Her students knew what to do if their microphone wasn't working, if they completed their slides early, or if a group member was not being nice. Further, Ms. Lee was spending her time listening to the mathematics and probing students with questions to help them analyze the math in their activities. She was not disciplining behaviors or fixing a computer because the students had practiced these routines and together, the teachers have a thoughtful classroom management plan.

After teaching group 1, Ms. Gordon moved to group 2 to have students explore fractional relationships.

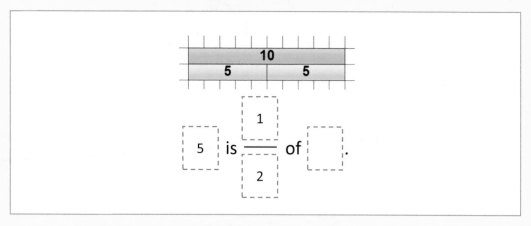

Source: Copyright © Math Playground LLC, mathplayground.com. Used with permission.

She began her mini-lesson with some specific examples, but then gave students access to a virtual version of a manipulative called Cuisenaire rods, a common physical manipulative in face-to-face classrooms. Students used that manipulative to create their own relationships and then define them using the open spaces below the model. Ms. Gordon specifically chose this open task because she knows that the students in this group often like to showcase their unique creativity as they grapple with challenging numbers and mathematical situations. Since they are the ones creating the content of their learning, Ms. Gordon used the guided group time to ask probing and extending questions to each of the students.

### Independent-to-Partner Learning Station

Group 3 began their slides with an Independent-to-Partner Activity. This activity included two components. First, the students worked independently on their own blank slide to create a rule by moving some toys into the oval. The example on page 196 shows how one student placed 3 green toys in the oval and the remaining 5 outside the oval. Once each child created their rule, they browsed the other three slides to try and guess each other's rules. All students turned on their microphones and shared their guesses as they collectively completed the missing blocks on each of

(Continued)

(Continued)

the slides. Ms. Lee was able to view the students' progress on this activity because she had access to each group's slides. She chose not to enter the breakout room and speak with the group because she had visual evidence of their thinking.

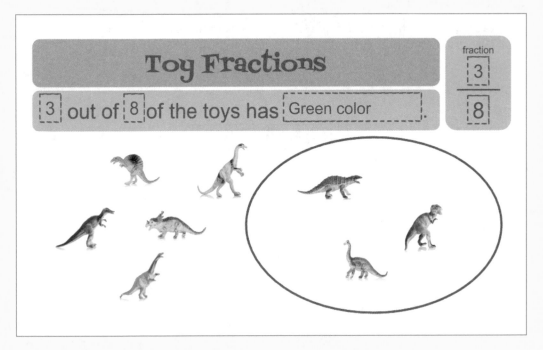

*Image source:* PhanuwatNandee/iStock.com

This group was able to work in harmony because there were a few norms and directions that ensured assigned space and roles. First, independent work was valued and students were motivated to complete their slide because of the group interaction to come. Each student had a space to interact before the group worked together. The format valued student independence while motivating students to discuss their ideas later as partners.

### Small-Group Activities

Small-group activities rely on the norms that all student microphones are on and students never delete or edit another student's work without making a duplicate copy. Because of these norms, students are quick to speak informally as they work together and use each other's ideas as they edit duplicate copies. In this activity, adapted from Lamon (2012), students worked to visualize various fractions using the entire picture as the whole. Since there were multiple ways of visualizing $\frac{1}{6}$, this group was quick to make duplicate slides as they moved the yellow box around to other representations of $\frac{1}{6}$.

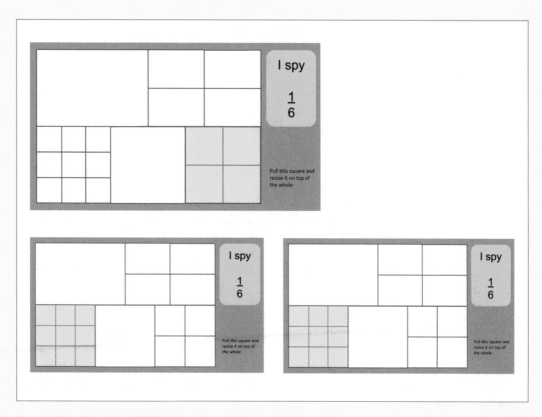

*Source:* Adapted from Lamon, 2012

Ms. Lee was monitoring the breakout rooms and joined group 2 just as they finished the three visualizations of $\frac{1}{6}$. She wanted to check for understanding before they moved to more complex fractions.

**Ms. Lee:**   Hi group 2, I noticed that you found three ways of visualizing $\frac{1}{6}$. How could you explain to someone that these are all equal to $\frac{1}{6}$?

**Mario:**   You could slide the yellow box.

*<Mario demonstrates this by moving the yellow box to all three sections while maintaining the size and shape of the box.>*

**Ms. Lee:**   Hrm, nice explanation. You convinced me that all three yellow sections are the same, but how could you convince me that they are all $\frac{1}{6}$?

**Luis:**   Because there are three on the bottom, so three doubled is six.

**Ms. Lee:**   And what does that six mean?

*(Continued)*

(Continued)

**Luis:** That's the whole. The picture is cut into six pieces. Each yellow box is $\frac{1}{6}$.

**Ms. Lee:** Does everyone agree with Luis?

*<All four students agree.>*

**Kayla:** It's the part that is one square and the whole is six, so $\frac{1}{6}$.

**Ms. Lee:** Luis mentioned something interesting. He said that three doubled is six. When you complete the other fraction visualization, make a note if you find any doubles or triples.

This group was able to work well together because the group activity encouraged discussion, all microphones were on, and student thinking was recorded and preserved. Ms. Lee used purposeful questioning to both check for understanding and probe the group to think about doubling and tripling as the group grapples with multiplication properties of fractions.

### Partner Game

Group 3 moved on to the Partner Game activity where they drew cards from the center deck and placed them in numerical order on their side of the game board. Their partner had to approve their placement before they could take their turn, and students could rearrange their cards when needed to accommodate the new card. By assigning the partner a role in approving the placement, both students were always thinking, and no one was waiting for their turn. Further, it gave the whole group accountability structure.

Students were familiar with this ordering game since they had used it in other lessons such as place value and multiplication, and had the agency to redefine the rules of the game to not allow a player to move cards once they are placed on the game board. This increased the rigor of the game. Ms. Lee's students understood the norm that all players must agree to the new rules before the game is modified.

Ms. Lee used a counterintuitive structure in her groupings for Partner Games. She assigned four students in every group, which means that there were two Partner Games taking place within the group, and four voices speaking about different games. This may appear chaotic to the untrained eye, but Ms. Lee was purposeful in creating these groups because she knew that two of these students were still becoming comfortable with the microphone. She wanted these students to hear more casual conversation from the more talkative students as they gained confidence in speaking within the group. The other reason for this double grouping is that one of the more talkative students needed support with verbalizing his thinking into mathematical generalizations. Ms. Lee knew that when there were more voices speaking in the breakout rooms, this helped her students to hear the conversational and mathematical language, which builds their confidence in speaking and verbalizing math.

### Independent-to-Small-Group Exploration

Group 4 engaged in a pattern block activity where they determined the relationship between four geometric shapes. This activity contained places for students to have an independent space while related to the whole-group space. Each student was responsible for a column and arranged the pattern blocks in the work space to make a visual proof of the situation. Then they typed the numerical representation into their assigned column. Each slide appeared similar in that there were four columns, but students grappled with different fractional situations on each slide. Each student in the group had to first complete their column and then check their column in comparison to the whole group. Since the fractions were all related to each other, the group was accountable for the entire slide, and not just their column. (Note: The gray box denotes the given information, and the given information changed on each slide.)

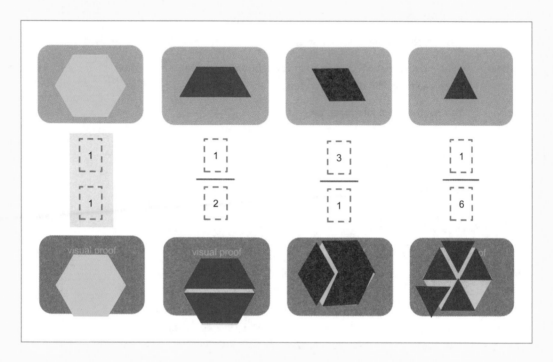

Ms. Lee noticed two different relationships on the group's slide and moved into their group to question them to consider the relationships between all four shapes.

**Ms. Lee:** Hi group 4, I'm enjoying seeing the visual proofs on your slide. Can you tell me how you are connecting the visual proof with the numbers in the fractions?

**José:** I had the hexagon, and since it is the starting piece, I knew that one over one is just one, so I put just one hexagon down.

**Kamila:** I'm the trapezoid and see how two trapezoids fit in the hexagon, that's how you know that it's one-half.

**Ms. Lee:** Kamila, I noticed that you said "two trapezoids fit in the hexagon" and also "one-half" but I'm curious how you thought about these different numbers. How did you see one-half?

**Kamila:** It's like if the hexagon was a pizza and you cut it in half, you get a trapezoid.

*(Continued)*

(Continued)

**Ms. Lee:**    And how did you see the number two in the pizza situation?

**Kamila:**    There are two pieces.

**Ms. Lee:**    Wonderful thinking. Who did the rhombus?

**Meg:**    Me. There are three rhombus pieces that fit inside a hexagon.

**Ms. Lee:**    How do you write that in the fraction space?

**Meg:**    $\frac{3}{1}$ because anything over 1 is itself.

**Ms. Lee:**    That is a rule that we discussed in class, but let's think about the rhombus as Kamila's pizza example. What could you tell me about this now?

**Meg:**    You cut the pizza into three pieces.

**Ms. Lee:**    Yes, and how big is each piece?

**Meg:**    Well, is it one-third?

**Ms. Lee:**    Tell me why?

**Meg:**    Because three pieces in the whole and each piece is $\frac{1}{3}$. So I should change my fraction.

**Ms. Lee:**    Meg, that was some big thinking you did there. Erin, can you explain the triangles?

**Erin:**    Yeah, the pizza is cut into 6 pieces so each slice is $\frac{1}{6}$.

In this exploration, each student had a place to make their thinking visible without any one student doing more work than their assigned portion. This helped Ms. Lee to understand each student's thinking and give them a similar topic to talk about as they justified their reasoning.

## Independent-to-Small-Group Check for Understanding

Ms. Gordon circled back to group 1 to assess their Check for Understanding slide. In this activity, each student independently selected three fraction cards and ordered them on their assigned corner space. Then they wrote an explanation for how they knew that this was the correct order. This activity involves choice as the students can select their three cards. Some students began with very complex choices but knew that they could swap out their selection at any time, a similar practice for students who initially selected choices that were too easy. As students summarized a strategy in the writing space, they also frequently traded cards to create a situation analogous to their written strategy. Because there are only a set number of cards, and once a card is selected it is removed from the collective pool, students could not copy each other's work—they all had unique situations. However, this activity did allow students to see connections between the work since the fraction cards and written explanations are modified in real time. Ms. Gordon used this slide as a formative assessment as she observed and checked off strategies that each student explained in their written summary.

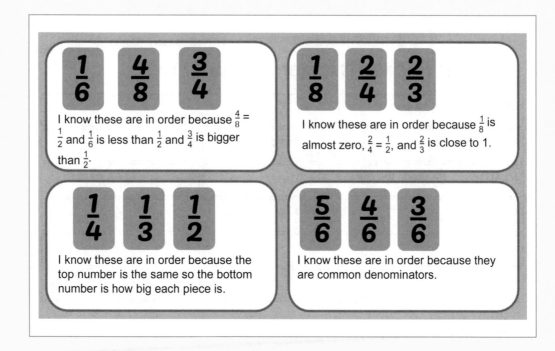

I know these are in order because $\frac{4}{8} = \frac{1}{2}$ and $\frac{1}{6}$ is less than $\frac{1}{2}$ and $\frac{3}{4}$ is bigger than $\frac{1}{2}$.

I know these are in order because $\frac{1}{8}$ is almost zero, $\frac{2}{4} = \frac{1}{2}$, and $\frac{2}{3}$ is close to 1.

I know these are in order because the top number is the same so the bottom number is how big each piece is.

I know these are in order because they are common denominators.

## Whole-Class Exit Ticket

Ms. Lee brought the class back together with only five minutes remaining and directed the students to the Whole-Class Exit Ticket. This routine required both Ms. Lee and Ms. Gordon to observe the real-time information as it displayed on the slide. Each cell of the slide was assigned to a particular student, and that information was shared only between that student and the teachers. This supported accountability, assessment, and anonymity, giving students the freedom to respond without peer judgment. As students typed their responses, Ms. Lee and Ms. Gordon noticed the following:

- Some students were quick to type $\frac{1}{99}$ or $\frac{1}{100}$ but paused before typing a response.
- Some students waited longer before typing.
- Some responses varied and some were similar.
- Some students changed their answers.
- Some students began to type their response and then changed their answer to match the response.
- Some students had duplicated responses.

Ms. Lee and Ms. Gordon found that since every student could anonymously read the collective thoughts of the class, more students were engaged in the exit ticket and felt the freedom to change their answer as they summarized their response. Following is an example of the exit ticket as it was being completed in real time.

*(Continued)*

(Continued)

## What fraction is larger 1/99 or 1/100?

| | | |
|---|---|---|
| 1/99 because 99 is smaller | 1/99 - 99 is s | 1/99 |
| 1/99 | 1/99 - 1/2 is bigger than 1/10000000000000000000000 | 1/99 - 100 is b |
| 1/100 but they are almost the same size | | |
| 1/99 | 1/100 - 100 is big | |
| 1/99 - same numerator so pick the small | | 1/99 the same num |
| 1/99 - because they both have 1 in | 1/99 | 1/99 smaller denominator is a bigger fract |

### ••• REFLECT AND REIMAGINE

As you reflect on the learning stations presented in this chapter, try to identify specific instances that would work for your teaching style and your classroom. Consider the activities that could be implemented early in the school year and which activities need additional practice of norms, rules, and routines, and thus would be better later in the year.

- What structures need to be established so that my students are self-starters in their breakout rooms?
- How will my students respond (typing, speaking, posting an image), and how will I provide the structure for the response?
- When do I want my students to collaborate, and which activities promote collaboration?
- When do I want to encourage individual accountability?

For more practice, tutorials, and templates, visit www.theresawills.com.

# CONSOLIDATING AND ASSESSING LEARNING

Part III is all about how to help students apply their knowledge of mathematics in more independent settings such as assessments and homework. It showcases a variety of ways to harness the technology to meet the needs of 21st century learners and provide them practice and models for using online resources with honesty and integrity.

# + chapter

# 10

# ASSESSMENT

Often, assessment is a big concern for math teachers who are just starting their journey into the remote teaching world. Efficiently and effectively utilizing both formative and summative assessment strategies will ensure that your students can show their thinking and that you can interpret that thinking as understanding and mastery of mathematical conception. The key component of this is making thinking visible.

## Formative Assessment

Formative assessment is defined as "all activities that provide information to be used as feedback to modify teaching and learning" (Fennell et al., 2017, p. 5). Different from summative assessments, which only give us a snapshot *of* the learning at the end of a unit or grade, formative assessments are sneak peeks that are used *for* learning. Fennell et al. (2017) offer several techniques, such as observations, interviews, Show Me, hinge questions, and exit tasks, and while each technique can be implemented in the remote classroom, observations might be the most difficult to reimagine in the remote classroom.

Observations will certainly look different online. Since you are not able to walk between desks, look over a student's shoulder, or see their whiteboard, you will need to consider other ways of observing. There are multiple modalities that can be used for online "observations," including the chat box, audio, video streaming, posting to an interactive slide, and comments and presenter's notes within an interactive slide. In addition to mathematical representations and problem solving, you can also observe technology competencies and how lack of competencies can restrict a student's ability to make their thinking visible. Figures 10.1 and 10.2 provide suggestions for how to observe and record student thinking. More information on making student thinking visible can be found in Chapter 6.

Figure 10.1

# How to Observe Student Thinking

| TOOL | OPTIONS FOR OBSERVATIONS |
|---|---|
| Teleconferencing Tool | • Chat box<br>• Audio<br>• Streaming video<br>• Interactive whiteboard<br>• Microphone icon when in small groups |
| Interactive Slides | • Streaming video of students manipulating concrete materials such as coins or LEGO bricks<br>• Photos or streaming video of handwritten drawings and algorithms<br>• Screenshots of virtual manipulatives<br>• Photos of students' physical manipulatives in organized groups<br>• Tables inserted on students' slides<br>• Text boxes to label images<br>• Student-created virtual manipulatives using the shape tool<br>• Arrows, circles, highlights, and lines to group, draw connections, or show emphasis<br>• Use of color for grouping and labeling<br>• Clip art images and gifs from the web<br>• Typed information in comments or presenter's notes |

## Figure 10.2

# Options to Record Student Thinking

- Create a Connections Map.

- Write directly on the interactive slide or in the presenter's notes.

- Use teacher symbols or color to add your notes and develop a norm that students don't delete those notes.

- Even if you are not in the virtual breakout room with group 2 because you are listening to group 3, you can use the comment feature and converse with group 2 through text.

- Record using a small-group tool that measures group engagement, mathematical noticings, and the next direction that their group has taken.

Figure 10.3 shows a planning organizer that can help you consider the kinds of observations as well as the ways in which you can record your observations or provide feedback in an online setting. A completed version is found in the vignette with Ms. Francis that follows. This organizer can then aid in your decisions about what in your lesson to use as formative assessment opportunities.

## Figure 10.3

# Observation Planning Organizer

1. What would you expect to observe online?

2. How would you know "it" if you saw it?

3. What mathematical challenges or misconceptions might you observe?

4. How will you record and provide feedback online of what you observed?

*Source:* Adapted from Fennell et al., 2017

Other formative assessment techniques—interviews, Show Me, hinge questions, and exit tasks—are transitioned into the remote classroom using purposeful planning and transitioning.

**Interviews** can consist of small-group or one-on-one meetings using a teleconferencing tool. They have "potential to yield cues regarding particular mathematical challenges, misconceptions, shallow understanding, and cues for next steps instructionally" (Fennell et al., 2017, p. 47). The interviews don't need to look much different from a face-to-face interview due to the opportunities available using cameras and image capturing. Students can simply hold their work up to the camera. However, sometimes the interview requires manipulation of virtual manipulatives. Again, the teleconferencing tools allow a seamless transition as the student can share their screen so that the interviewer can watch the physical movement.

**Show Me** is "a performance response by a student or group of students that extends and often deepens what was observed and what might have been asked within an interview" (Fennell et al., 2017, p. 63). When transitioning to the remote classroom, it is important to consider the shared collaborative Show Me space in which the student or group will display their thinking. While cameras can be used, they provide a static snapshot that cannot be manipulated by students or teachers. However, mathematical models created in shared slides offer the ability to dynamically change the representation.

**Hinge questions** require the teacher to consider student responses that relate to generalizable situations. Perhaps the toughest transition to remote learning when creating hinge questions is giving the appropriate wait time. It can be challenging to give wait time in a face-to-face classroom because silence is uncomfortable, but the silence without facial expressions that is experienced in remote learning can be even more uncomfortable. Fennell et al. (2017) suggest recording the anticipated student responses during the planning phase. In addition to this practice, you can also physically write the responses that they expect to hear from their students in real time as a tool to occupy the mind while giving wait time. Students need to not only formulate their response, but also type it or find the microphone button, so wait time needs to be increased.

**Exit tasks** are a "capstone problem or task that captures the major focus of the lesson for that day or perhaps the past several days and provides a sampling of student performances" (Fennell et al., 2017, p. 109). There is a seamless transition to remote learning when students understand the basic technology tools to make their thinking visible. Low-tech tools such as paper-and-pencil work uploaded as an image will provide a similar format to face-to-face, but students are also impressively creative with new technology tools to show their thinking.

Let's take a look at how Ms. Francis, a sixth-grade math teacher, uses formative assessment opportunities in her online class.

## Ms. Francis: Formative Assessment

Ms. Francis planned to present her students with the following problem:

> Grandma has a lot of Tupperware®. Sometimes a container or lid becomes cracked and she throws it away, but she usually forgets to throw away the matching lid or container. This means that her already unorganized Tupperware cabinet has several pieces that don't match.
>
> 2/3 of the lids match with a container.
> 3/5 of the containers match with a lid.
> What portion of grandma's
> Tupperware matches?

She used the planning organizer to consider how she would observe her sixth graders as they solved this problem. She decided to launch the problem in a whole-group setting and then move students to breakout rooms to problem-solve in small groups. Finally, she chose to engage the whole class in a discussion that used student-created representations to determine the solution.

*(Continued)*

(Continued)

Here is Ms. Francis's planning organizer.

---

**1. What would you expect to observe online?**

- Streaming video of students creating piles of lids and containers with actual Tupperware® or other manipulatives such as coins or LEGO bricks to make matching sets with some left over

- Handwritten drawings and algorithms of ratios ($\frac{2}{3}$ and $\frac{3}{5}$) as well as the other parts that didn't match ($\frac{1}{3}$ and $\frac{2}{5}$)

- Screenshots of virtual manipulatives that show area models and linear models of the two fractions

- Student-created virtual manipulatives of cubes and rectangles to represent the Tupperware pieces to show matching and unmatching sets alongside text boxes that label their manipulatives

- Clip art images of Tupperware lids and containers moving around the slide as students create matches

**2. How would you know "it" if you saw it?**

- When students double or triple the ratios (or sets of manipulatives that represent the ratio) to find equivalent numerators

- When their "matches" align with the given ratios

- When they say or type "common denominators don't work"

**3. What mathematical challenges or misconceptions might you observe?**

- Students trying to create common denominators to solve the problem

- Creating duplicate copies of the ratios equally and not matching the lids with containers

- Interchanging lids and containers with numerators and denominators

**4. How will you record and provide feedback online of what you observed?**

- I will write directly on the interactive slide using the norm of a blue text box so that students know it is from me.

- I will use the comment tool to pose my question and ask it verbally after students have replied.

- I will record using a small-group tool that measures group engagement, mathematical noticings, and the next direction that their group has taken.

---

Ms. Francis began with a whole-group launch where she read the problem to her students and checked to ensure that they understood the task. Then she divided her students into groups of four or five and placed them in breakout rooms. Since it was the beginning of the school year and students were still learning how to use the technology tools, she created her groups to include at least one student who had shown mastery of various technology competencies.

| MS. FRANCIS'S CLASS | HOW MS. FRANCIS OBSERVED, RECORDED, AND RESPONDED |
|---|---|
| Once in breakout rooms, students welcomed each other using their microphones for audio and began to unpack the task. Group 1 discussed virtual manipulatives and posted a screenshot of fraction circles that showed the initial fractions and equivalent fractions with common denominators. Ms. Francis left them a message in the chat box that stated, "How do these equivalent fractions answer the task?" | Ms. Francis observed group 1's screenshot and left a comment for the group. She recorded that the group was a fast starter, but potentially misinterpreting the problem.<br><br>Ms. Francis uses a probing thinking type of hinge question to encourage student explanation.<br><br>Group 1<br>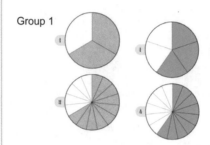<br><br>*Source:* Copyright © Math Learning Center, mathlearningcenter.org. Used with permission. |
| She was eager to hear group 1's answer, but noticed that group 4 did not have their microphones on and their slide was blank. She entered their breakout room.<br><br>**Ms. Francis:** Hi group 4, what are you thinking about?<br><br>**Kate:** I don't know what to do.<br><br>**Jay:** I know I need to match the tops and the bottoms, but you can't match them.<br><br>**Ms. Francis:** Why can't you match them?<br><br>**Jay:** Because 2 can't match evenly with 3.<br><br>**Ms. Francis:** Where did you get the numbers 2 and 3?<br><br>**Jay:** $\frac{2}{3}$ matches with $\frac{3}{5}$. That means 2 tops match with 3 bottoms.<br><br>**Kate:** It doesn't say 2 tops, it says $\frac{2}{3}$ tops. | Ms. Francis observed that group 4 was not yet collaborating. She entered the room and used some gathering information types of hinge questions to support the group collaboration.<br><br>Group 4<br>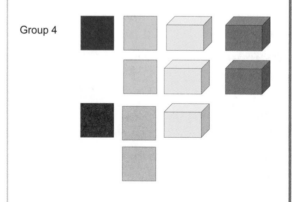 |

(Continued)

(Continued)

| MS. FRANCIS'S CLASS | HOW MS. FRANCIS OBSERVED, RECORDED, AND RESPONDED |
|---|---|
| **Jay:** Yeah, 2 tops out of 3 tops actually have a match.<br><br>**Kate:** Ms. Francis, can we make equivalent fractions? Like $\frac{4}{6}$ and $\frac{8}{12}$?<br><br>**Ms. Francis:** What do those equivalent fractions mean?<br><br>**Kate:** If we had 4 tops that match out of 6 tops altogether, that's the same as $\frac{2}{3}$.<br><br>**Ms. Francis:** I see that someone else in your group is using squares to make copies just like Kate said. Keep working on that idea and remember to label your work. | |
| Ms. Francis re-entered group 1's breakout room.<br><br>**Ms. Francis:** Hi group, I can see that you have answered the problem with 19. What does the 19 mean?<br><br>**Jazzmin:** That's how many matching pieces there are.<br><br>**Ms. Francis:** So we have 19 matching pieces. Does that mean 19 tops and 19 bottoms?<br><br>**Jazzmin:** No, 19 pieces all together. There's 10 tops and 9 bottoms equals 19.<br><br>**Clara:** Wait, that doesn't make sense.<br><br>**Jullian:** Yeah, we messed up.<br><br>**Ms. Francis:** Jullian, why do you think you messed up?<br><br>**Jullian:** Because if you have 10 lids and 9 containers, they don't match. You can only have an even number of pieces if they all match. | Ms. Francis observed that group 1 responded to her comment of "How do these equivalent fractions answer the task?" with "That's how you get the answer 19. You add 10 + 9 = 19."<br><br>Ms. Francis is thoughtful about this hinge question as she knows it will lead the students into a Show Me. |

| MS. FRANCIS'S CLASS | HOW MS. FRANCIS OBSERVED, RECORDED, AND RESPONDED |
|---|---|
| **Ms. Francis:** Ah, I see. What do you think you will do next?<br><br>**Jazzmin:** I don't think we should use the fraction circles, let's just get some lids and containers. | |
| **Ms. Francis:** Using manipulatives is a great way to think about this problem. You can use anything you have at your home. Just be sure to show it to each other.<br><br>**Jazzmin:** I'm going to use paper.<br><br>*<Jazzmin uses her video to show her groupmates how she was labeling the paper to represent lids and rectangles. Other students leave their computers to get materials.>* | Ms. Francis observed that a student left their computer and another moved their video camera to show work on paper. She could see that they were engaged and thinking collaboratively. |
| **Ms. Francis:** Hi group 2. Can you tell me what you are thinking about?<br><br>**Luis:** We got the answer. It's 6.<br><br>**Katrina:** No, it's 12.<br><br>**Luis:** How is it 12?<br><br>**Katrina:** You are seeing the 6 matching sets, but there are 12 pieces in the set.<br><br>**Luis:** Same thing.<br><br>**Ms. Francis:** Luis, can you explain the 6?<br><br>**Luis:** L is a lid and B is a bottom, we matched a lid with a bottom and made 6 matches.<br><br>**Ms. Francis:** By that logic, 6 is an answer, 6 matches. Katrina, you said it was 12. How could both 6 and 12 be correct?<br><br>**Katrina:** It's 6 matches which is 6 lids and 6 bottoms so 12 pieces. | Ms. Francis also viewed the slides of the other groups while she talked to this group. (This is an advantage to online learning as you can easily view what many students are doing while listening in on a particular group conversation.) She saw that group 2 had a model but their microphones were off, so she visited that group. She used hinge questions again to encourage the students to make the mathematics visible.<br><br> |

*(Continued)*

(Continued)

| MS. FRANCIS'S CLASS | HOW MS. FRANCIS OBSERVED, RECORDED, AND RESPONDED |
|---|---|
| **Ms. Francis:** I'm also curious about your model. Can you explain the colors and the $x$'s?<br><br>**Luis:** We started with 2 lids matching 2 bottoms, but knew that the other bottom needed a match, so we doubled the lids. Then we had an extra lid, so we doubled the bottoms, and then doubled the lids again.<br><br>**Ms. Francis:** How did you know that you could double the lids and bottoms?<br><br>**Luis:** Because we needed to make matches.<br><br>**Katrina:** The fractions are the same. $\frac{2}{3}$ is the same as $\frac{4}{6}$ and $\frac{8}{9}$. | |
| **Ms. Francis:** Great observation, Katrina. I heard from two group members, but I'd like to hear from everyone next time I come in here. Work together using a different model to ensure that everyone understands why 6 and 12 are correct answers. | Ms. Francis observed that only two of the four members of the group were talking, and instead of asking the two who showed mastery to explain, she asked them to work together in a new model to make sense of both 6 and 12. That way, Katrina and Luis are still making connections to the mathematical relationships and not simply teaching their method to the other group members. |

It is common for one or two students to dominate the small-group interview. The teacher can be specific in who they select to answer the interview question, or allow the group additional wait time to prepare. Either way, purposeful planning and facilitating can help the teacher learn information from an interview with all group members. And by planning and anticipating observations in the remote classroom, Ms. Francis was able to use these observations in the whole-group conversation and individually record the thinking and evidence of mastery of each of her students.

# Summative Assessment

Moving online means that we will need to reevaluate the purpose and products of our summative assessments, and whether the purpose is still relevant in our current and future age. Remember, students have access to the Internet, and all assignments are essentially "take home," so we need to reconsider norms for honesty and fairness.

For example, consider a multiplication assessment that uses a timed worksheet of problems. When done in the face-to-face classroom, students would have time to complete the entire sheet, or as much as they could, completely independently. I remember when I was a young student, my teacher telling me, "You won't always have a calculator with you, so you need to memorize these." Well, actually, now I do. I have a cell phone with me. And I don't even need to open the calculator app, I can just say, "Hey Google, what is $7 \times 8$?" But even before cell phones were prevalent, I received a bachelor's in mathematics while still using my fingers to add $3 + 8$ and multiply $6 \times 7$. I suppose I could train my brain to memorize these facts, but I just haven't found the need.

Consider the following modification of a summative assessment for the multiplication table. The goal is for students to use friendlier numbers to derive new products. The quiz includes the following directions:

1. Use a physical manipulative, such as cereal, beans, toys, or pebbles, to create a $6 \times 5$ array. Take a photo.

2. Add additional pieces to your array to create a $6 \times 7$ array. Take a photo.

3. Upload both photos to your recording space.

4. Explain how you can use the $6 \times 5$ array to help you solve the $6 \times 7$ array. You may use words, pictures, circles, arrows, and more in your explanation.

This summative assessment does more than simply test a student's ability to recall multiplication facts. It requires them to consider multiplication as a concept, and then manipulate that concept to help them to find other products. It gives ownership of the assessment to the student because they are the ones to find the manipulative in their real world. It emphasizes independence and fairness because the students need to take a picture of their work and the modification as well as give an explanation about their arrays.

As you consider summative assessments, give students more opportunity to take ownership and find the relationship to their world. Have them use images and video as evidence of both independent work ethic and creativity. In doing so, each student will develop a unique answer.

If you are concerned about student honesty and integrity, start from their perspective and ensure that you are teaching them how to use the resources at their disposal and how to be honest digital citizens. Figure 10.4 shows a sample overview sheet you can give to students before a summative assessment on the relationship between area and perimeter.

Figure 10.4

## Sample Area and Perimeter Assessment Overview Page

In this assessment, you may use

- Videos (e.g., YouTube, Khan Academy)
- Websites to research key terms such as area or perimeter

In this assessment, you may *not* use

- A parent, sibling, friend, neighbor, teacher, or other person
- An online tutor
- Online question-and-answer websites (e.g., Quora)
- Social media

The purpose of these rules is not to restrict student access to the Internet and informative websites that they will forever have at their fingertips, but rather to limit individual explanation of the actual question. Websites and videos will provide students with generalizations, but they will need to apply those general rules and theories to the specific problem. This is how we teach students to be honest and responsible digital citizens.

When giving a summative assessment, I allow students to upload their work in any modality that is easiest for them. This makes sense for the world in which they will grow up, as all of these modalities are easily accessible on the Internet. Figure 10.5 contains the sample directions for the same area and perimeter assessment.

Figure 10.5

## Sample Directions for Area and Perimeter Assessment

Complete this test and upload your responses in the easiest modality. For example:

1. **Solve digitally:** If it is easier to move squares around on a slide to explain area, then use the slide and then copy and paste it into the document.

2. **Upload a photo of your work:** If it is easier to print the image and draw squares to show area, then take a photo of your finished drawing and upload it to the document.

3. **Create a video:** If it is easier to take a short video to show how you accounted for squares that are halfway inside the image, then upload your video and link it on the document.

## ●●● REFLECT AND REIMAGINE

As you reimagine your remote classroom, remember to use the great pedagogies from your face-to-face class. This includes assessments. If you typically used observations as formative assessments, continue to use them in the online class. Rely on the same pedagogy, but just change the modality for how you observe it. If your summative assessments were simple recall questions, consider the world in which students are growing up and consider questions that require students to apply the rules and formulas in situations that cannot be found online. As technology improves, the responsibilities of

*(Continued)*

(Continued)

educators must also improve so that we teach students honesty and integrity in their digital world.

- What am I assessing, and how will my students show mastery?

- How will my students respond to the assessment (paper and pencil, images, text, voice, video, etc.), and will they have choice?

- When am I assessing (before, during, or after the unit), and how do I use this information to inform my teaching?

- How can I reimagine my assessments so that students are accountable and honest while accessing the plethora of information on the Internet?

For more practice, tutorials, and templates, visit www.theresawills.com.

+ chapter

11

# STRATEGIES FOR EFFECTIVE HOMEWORK

Homework has always been an integral part of mathematics lessons because it gives students an opportunity to practice and apply conceptual and procedural knowledge. While your homework assignments might be the same in both your face-to-face class and your online class, the modality in which students submit their assignments will look different in an online class. We can use that difference to reimagine how we assign, grade, and implement homework procedures. But before we reimagine the modality, take a moment to consider the purpose of homework, the benefits, and the drawbacks (see Figure 11.1).

## Figure 11.1

## The Benefits and Drawbacks of Homework

| BENEFITS OF HOMEWORK | DRAWBACKS OF HOMEWORK |
|---|---|
| • Projects will support students' organizational skills as they complete parts of the project.<br><br>• It provides formative assessment for teachers.<br><br>• It relates general lessons to personal experiences.<br><br>• Photomath can be used to check answers.<br><br>• It provides students with practice and procedural fluency. | • Students have additional screen time.<br><br>• If a student doesn't understand the procedure, they might practice it incorrectly many times.<br><br>• If homework is simply procedures, Photomath can be used and compromise accountability. |

### Homework Help

Photomath and similar apps will use a device to scan the problem, then provide not only the answer but also each step along the way, plus an accompanying video.

In this chapter, you will read about how five different teachers reimagined homework using the affordances of online learning—that is, how you make the best of the situation, and how to make it better. There are some things to consider when assigning homework:

- Students have access to the Internet.
- Students have access to a calculator, timers, and stopwatches.
- Students have access to crowdsource information.
- Students can watch videos of algorithms and procedures.
- Students have diverse manipulatives that change from home to home.
- Students can include families in games for togetherness.

## Multimedia Homework

Using multimedia as a hook for homework can automatically engage even the most reluctant students (Warren, Wakefield, & Mills, 2013). By opening up the possibilities of how you allow students to practice mathematical skills and show what they know,

Figure 11.2

# Homework Strategies at a Glance

| STRATEGY | COMPLEXITY LEVEL | DELIVERY METHOD | STUDENT TECHNOLOGY MODALITIES USED | INTERACTIVE SLIDE FEATURES | ADVANTAGES |
|---|---|---|---|---|---|
| 3-Act Video (multimedia homework) | Basic | Synchronous Asynchronous Blended | Video recording device Video uploading application | n/a | This strategy uses found items to create a video to show application of math standards. |
| Esti-Mysteries (multimedia homework) | Basic | Synchronous Asynchronous Blended | Camera | Varied | This strategy uses found items to show application of math standards and create puzzles for classmates. |
| Flipped Classroom | Basic | Synchronous Blended | View video Microphone Chat box Assignment dropbox | Insert images and text boxes | This strategy uses efficient structures for reviewing video and practicing procedural fluency. |
| Data as a Driver | Intermediate | Synchronous Blended | Stopwatch (or other data-gathering materials) Breakout rooms Microphone Chat box | Type text and insert text boxes Drag and drop Insert tables | This strategy uses real-world data to apply mathematical skills to students' lived experiences. |
| One Problem Before Many | Basic | Synchronous Asynchronous Blended | Assignment dropbox | Insert shapes, images, outlines, text boxes and change color | This strategy encourages multiple representations and connections to conceptual understanding. |
| Homework as a Checkpoint | Intermediate | Asynchronous | Video recording device Video uploading application | n/a | This strategy supports student collaboration and differentiation based on learning progressions. |

you provide a creative outlet and a real-world connection that many students who may otherwise struggle with mathematics often miss with traditional pencil-and-paper homework assignments. There are a variety of tutorials and videos online that can be used to support students, but teacher modeling and student practice in class will ensure that the mathematics stays in the forefront.

## 3-ACT VIDEO

This strategy is adapted from 3-Act Tasks (Fletcher, 2020; Meyer, 2011) in which students use mathematical reasoning and problem solving at three distinct moments (3 Acts) as they use creativity and meaning to arrive at a solution.

In this strategy, students must purposefully plan to make their own video. Before recording, they must do the following:

1. Determine the mathematical objective.

2. Determine a real-world application of the mathematical objective.

3. Identify the tools and resources that they have to create a video.

4. Determine the 3 Acts in the video.

   - **Act 1—Preview:** Give viewers an opening question and show the tools that you will use to answer the question. Give time for viewers to think about your question.

   - **Act 2—Give viewers partial information:** Be sure that the new information is valuable in solving the problem but that it is not too much or too little information. You want the viewer to use math problem solving to be able to give a reasonable answer to your question. Give time for viewers to think about your question.

   - **Act 3—Solution:** Give your viewers the solution by actually doing the problem. You might need to speed up the video if it takes a long time to complete the solution.

5. Film the video.

6. Upload the video to a specified location.

Let's look at how Ms. Amani, a sixth-grade math teacher, used the 3-Act Video strategy as a homework assignment to support her students' learning about measurement tools and conversions between imperial and metric units. This represents the first of two multimedia strategies that Ms. Amani allowed students to choose from to complete their homework assignment.

# Ms. Amani: 3-Act Video Homework

Mariko is a student in Ms. Amani's sixth-grade class. She chose to create her 3-Act Video using quarter cups to measure capacity. Her video emphasized estimation after revealing important pieces of information as the video progressed. She had her brother help record the video so that she could do the narration and the work of filling the container herself. Here is a recount of Mariko's 3-Act Video:

| | | |
|---|---|---|
| **Act 1** | **Mariko:** I am using a quarter-cup spoon and I am filling a glass. How many quarter cups do you think are in the glass?<br><br>*<Video is paused for viewer to estimate.>* | |
| **Act 2** | *<Mariko shows the quarter cup and the glass, then she begins filling the quarter cup with water. She counts the quarter cups as she fills the glass. After pouring two quarter cups into the glass, she zooms in to view the partially full glass.>*<br><br>**Mariko:** How many of these *<holds up the quarter-cup scoop>* will I need to finish filling the glass?<br><br>*<Video is paused for viewer to estimate.>* | |
| **Act 3** | *<Mariko patiently fills up each quarter cup and pours it into the glass until it is completely full. She used almost eight quarter cups.>*<br><br>**Mariko:** It takes almost eight quarter cups to fill the glass. | |

# ESTI-MYSTERIES

This strategy is adapted from the work of Steve Wyborney (2018), in which the student creates the task using clues to guide guessers to more accurate estimates. An Esti-Mystery slide includes an image and four clues, to be revealed in succession as the guess becomes more accurate. In this strategy, students must purposefully plan their slide. Before creating their interactive slide, they must do the following:

1. Determine the mathematical objective.

2. Determine a real-world application of the mathematical objective.

3. Identify the tools and resources that they have to create the slide.

4. Determine the clues. The clues must build on each other and be useful for the viewer to make a more accurate estimate after reviewing each clue. Clues can include the following:

   - **Range:** What is a number that is too large or too small?

   - **Multiples:** Is the number even, odd, or a multiple of another number?

   - **Units:** Is the number shown as inches, centimeters, or a mixture of units?

   - **Comparison:** Is the number in relation to another number in the image (e.g., half the height of the container)?

   - **Follow-Up Clues:** Does your clue need the viewer to solve the earlier clue to identify this clue?

   - **Equations:** Does the viewer need to solve an equation to find the number for the clue?

5. Create the slide with an image and clues.

6. Cover up the clues so that the viewer can reveal each clue after they have had time to think about the previous clue.

Let's revisit Ms. Amani's class to see how Michael used Esti-Mysteries to complete his homework assignment.

Michael is another student in Ms. Amani's class. He chose to use estimation of length measurement in his Esti-Mysteries to complete his homework assignment. His clues used both imperial and metric measurements, and he was careful to make sure that the clues got more specific as they progressed. Here is a snapshot of his slide with all of the clues revealed.

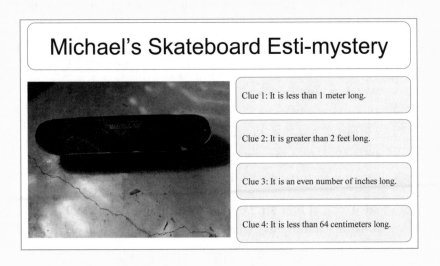

## Michael's Skateboard Esti-mystery

Clue 1: It is less than 1 meter long.

Clue 2: It is greater than 2 feet long.

Clue 3: It is an even number of inches long.

Clue 4: It is less than 64 centimeters long.

In this homework assignment, both Mariko and Michael had choice in the subject matter, measurement tools used, and modality to complete the assignment. By having choice in subject matter, Michael was able to showcase his interest in skateboarding, which connected to other students and created a stronger community. By having choice in measurement tools, Mariko and Michael were able to explore tools around their home. By having choice in submission modality, Mariko was able to include her brother in her homework assignment because he was in charge of recording the assignment. This sparked interest for her brother, and he created his own video filling a toy boat.

Since Ms. Amani's students modeled the routine in their homework assignment, they knew exactly how to participate and guess their peers' examples. Ms. Amani used this advantage to engage her whole class in each student's assignment.

# Flipped Classroom

In a Flipped Classroom, the teacher uses the synchronous class time for student-centered instruction instead of direct teaching (Cukurbasi & Kiyici, 2018). With a Flipped Classroom homework assignment, students experience the productive struggle piece in the synchronous part of instruction so that you can monitor their understanding and investigation of the mathematical concept(s). During asynchronous time, students are then expected to do some kind of independent work to further the investigation or complete a problem. Here are some ideas for the asynchronous assignments:

- Watch an instructional video.
- Complete a different problem similar to class work.
- Continue specific steps of an investigation started in class.
- Practice computations.
- Practice for procedural fluency.

Let's take a look at how Mr. Levy used the Flipped Classroom strategy to provide meaningful homework for his Algebra 1 class during a unit on systems of equations.

## Mr. Levy: Flipped Classroom Homework

Mr. Levy's class was studying systems of equations. In the unit, students needed to master both the elimination method and the substitution method. He wanted to spend the class time on investigations and not direct teaching, so he had the students watch the videos and apply new thinking as homework. Mr. Levy posed this problem to his students on Monday during his synchronous online class.

---

**Monday's Investigation Problem**

A video game store has two specials.

Buy 1 game device, 2 remote controls, and 2 games for $350.

Buy 1 game device, 6 remote controls, and 4 games for $550.

James is wondering if this is actually a money-saving deal, or if they just summed the prices of each piece and made it look like a deal.

---

His students tackled the problem through trial and error, and used friendly numbers to explore the problem. Students created organized lists and tables, and they uploaded pictures of work completed in their notebooks. During the discussion, four major ideas were discussed, as follows:

1. **Taylor explained:** As one item became more expensive, another item became less expensive (inverse relationships).

2. **Julian explained:** If the game device cost $350, then 2 remote controls and 2 games would be free. This didn't make sense because the second package would charge $200 for 6 remote controls and 4 games (substitution).

3. **May explained:** If you knew how much the game console was, then you could double or triple the packages to make the same amount of remote controls or the same amount of games (elimination).

4. **Said explained:** This problem was easy because of the friendly numbers, but the guess and check might be much harder if the numbers used dollars and cents and were not rounded (need for order and sophistication in a procedure that worked for all).

Because his students contextually explored both the elimination and substitution methods, and found a need for a more sophisticated procedure, Mr. Levy had a perfect opportunity for showcasing the elimination and substitution methods. That evening for homework, students watched a video that detailed the procedures of both methods.

**Tuesday's Investigation Problem**

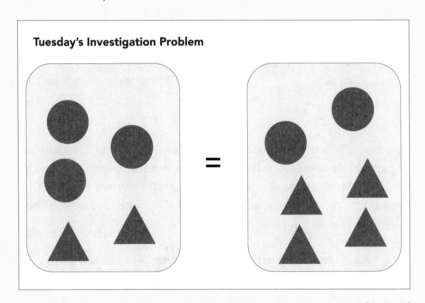

*(Continued)*

(Continued)

In Tuesday's synchronous class, Mr. Levy posted another investigation that contained no numbers, only images. The students were asked to use their knowledge of the videos of the substitution and elimination procedures to solve the riddles. He also asked them if they had a favorite procedure and to defend their thinking using the shape puzzles. While students were overwhelmingly successful at this fairly easy task, they grappled with why one procedure was more useful than another and when they should select a particular method. For homework that night, they were to create their own shape puzzle on an interactive slide. They uploaded their slides to the class slideshow and also to their assignment dropbox.

In Wednesday's synchronous class, Mr. Levy partnered students and sent them into breakout rooms with a copy of all 24 homework assignment puzzles. Students were assigned the role of either Substitution Expert or Elimination Expert, and they worked together to solve the problem with their assigned procedure. At the end of the class, Mr. Levy and his students discussed strategies for knowing when to use substitution and when to use elimination. His homework assignment was a revised video game problem, with not-so-friendly numbers. Students selected either the elimination or the substitution procedure and submitted their solution along with their work.

Since homework was due by midnight, Mr. Levy was able to quickly review the submissions Thursday morning and determine that six students could use additional teacher intervention, but the majority of his class showed mastery of the topic. In Thursday's class, he divided students into groups of four to six, while keeping the small group that he identified together. He provided a menu of tasks, games, and activities for the students to do in their groups, along with an exit ticket to summarize the group's understanding. During his one-hour block, he was able to reteach the small group of students and gradually release them into the other groups when they showed mastery.

Because of Mr. Levy's skillful homework assignments, he was able to provide differentiated instruction for each student during the week. His students were never sent home with a stack of problems, because he didn't want them practicing the procedure unless they fully understood it.

1. **He didn't start with the procedure.** He started with a context that demanded the procedure, which meant that students had motivation to want to learn it. Since learning the procedure can be done independently by watching a

video, he did not waste his precious synchronous time on the video.

2. **Tuesday's homework assignment could be self-differentiated.** Students could make their puzzles as complicated or as simple as they wanted. Mr. Levy didn't need to plan a lesson for the next day because his students did the work with their puzzles.

3. **Wednesday's homework was a bit more traditional**, but Mr. Levy had students complete only one problem, knowing that he would be able to see their understanding while being sure that they didn't practice incorrect procedures repeatedly. He used the homework submissions to form differentiated groups for the following day's class work. Since homework had a specific deadline time, he was able to use the results that next morning to create groups. While it may seem rather nontraditional to assign only one problem, the teacher is more purposeful with the assessment of this problem and the next steps to ensure that students only practice correct procedures. Mr. Levy also maintains a higher submission rate and higher effort in this one problem, which helps him to determine if students truly understand the information or are rushing through it.

# Data as a Driver

Anytime students can be in charge of their own learning and transition from passive attendees to active participants, it increases their motivation and deepens their investment in the concept(s) being studied (Nash, 2012). With this homework strategy, students are given a task to complete where they have to gather information or data on their own in order to fulfill the requirements of the work. This kind of independent investigation allows students to

- experience math in the world around them;
- choose the source(s) of the information they gather;
- apply real-world mathematics to solve a problem or complete a task;
- explore a variety of ways to collect data;

- use diverse problem-solving skills to explain unique strategies; and

- make sense of similar, different, or incomplete data to generalize meaning.

Let's take a look at the Data as a Driver homework assignment that Ms. Alvarez used with her fifth graders.

## Ms. Alvarez: Data as a Driver Homework

Ms. Alvarez created a unique homework assignment based on comparing, ordering, and rounding decimals with different place values. She knew that her students had a variety of tools at home, and that everyone would have a stopwatch tool to complete the assignment. She also knew that her students would have more fun if they could include their family and/or friends, so she created a competition. Here is the assignment:

---

1. How fast can you count to 50 (in any language)? Use a digital stopwatch to time your speed.

2. Time at least four other people (or time yourself four more times).

3. Order the five speeds from least to greatest and submit them on an interactive slide.

---

Ms. Alvarez purposefully designed the activity to take advantage of the wide range of stopwatches that students would have at their homes. Some students recorded speeds using seconds, tenths of a second, hundredths of a second, and thousandths of a second. Based on the responses to the homework assignment, during the next synchronous class she placed students in heterogeneous groups so that they would see the different place values. The groups then modeled a few decimals using three strategies: base-ten templates, coins, and aligning the decimal.

That evening, for the next homework assignment, the students modeled each of their decimals using different representations. The next day, Ms. Alvarez engaged her students in sharing their models and checking their work in groups. Because duplicating slides is quick and easy, they were able to share their recorded data and models with their peers. Once they determined that the models were correct, they ordered the collective slides (five numbers per person in the group) from least to greatest.

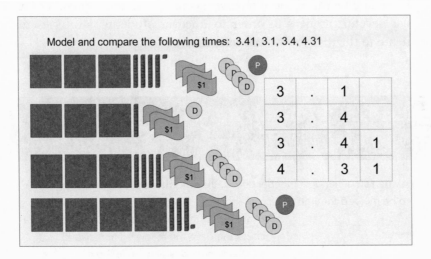

Model and compare the following times: 3.41, 3.1, 3.4, 4.31

| 3 | . | 1 | |
|---|---|---|---|
| 3 | . | 4 | |
| 3 | . | 4 | 1 |
| 4 | . | 3 | 1 |

For homework on the third night, the students used the ordered slides from all four groups to create a portfolio that explained how to compare and order decimals with different place values. Each portfolio contained many examples, models, and explanations.

Ms. Alvarez was purposeful in her delivery of synchronous group work and independent homework to support students with investigation time and practice time. Her students were motivated to complete the homework each night because of the role it played in the next day's activities.

## One Problem Before Many

With this homework strategy the teacher first assigns an open problem that has potential for multiple strategies and problem-solving approaches. Students have a defined deadline by which to complete the assignment so that the teacher can review the submissions and select the few to incorporate during the class time. It is critical that the selection focus on different strategies or misconceptions so that students can find connections between the problem-solving approaches. These differences will lead students into discussion and motivation for comparing the strategies. Once the single problem is discussed and students make connections, they can then apply those problem-solving approaches to a variety of problems as they build their procedural fluency.

Here, Ms. Vierheller used a single geometry task as homework for her seventh graders in order to uncover students' strategies to relate to the distributive property in her prealgebra class.

## Ms. Vierheller: One Problem Before Many Homework

Ms. Vierheller knows that when students work independently, they produce original ideas, but that those ideas often need to be molded through group collaboration. She used a geometry task to

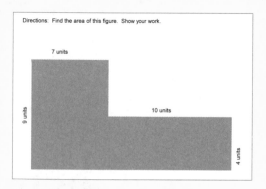

relate the distributive property in her prealgebra class. She gave the following homework problem and a deadline of 9:00 p.m.

The next morning, Ms. Vierheller opened the student submissions and quickly scrolled through noting each strategy. There were three general ways that the students solved the problem. They partitioned the shape vertically, they partitioned the shape horizontally, or they found the outer area and subtracted the missing piece. She chose three submissions, removed the student identification from the slides, and embedded them into her slide deck for that day's synchronous math class. During class, she facilitated a discussion on the similarities and differences of each method, both algebraically and geometrically.

The next homework assignment required students to apply all three strategies in similar situations while recording the algebraic equations.

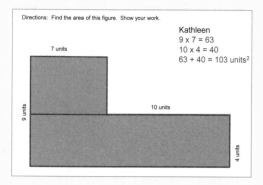

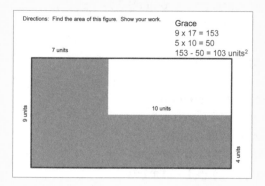

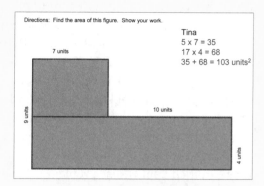

Because Ms. Vierheller assigned only one problem initially, she was able to view prior knowledge and intuitive student strategies. She used student work for her discussions and only assigned additional practice once she was sure that students could apply the three representations in different situations.

# Homework as a Checkpoint

Sometimes, especially in asynchronous classes, teachers want to feel connected to students through multiple checkpoints throughout the unit, rather than simply seeing a summative test of what students learned at their own pace. This strategy uses specific deadlines to inform the next lesson. There is still flexibility for the students to complete the assignment, but the deadline ensures that the teacher knows how the student is progressing through the learning of the unit.

Let's take a look at how Ms. Keyoh, a first-grade teacher, used specific checkpoints during asynchronous homework time to make sure her students were on track.

## Ms. Keyoh: Checkpoint Homework

Ms. Keyoh knows the importance of flexibility for families. Her goal is to provide regular homework check-ins during her asynchronous time. Families can still have the flexibility to complete the activities and submit them when their schedule allows, but it also gives Ms. Keyoh an opportunity to regularly formally assess the homework to differentiate the assignments for student learning.

Ms. Keyoh uses a collaborative video program so that she can post the assignment and students can upload their videos.

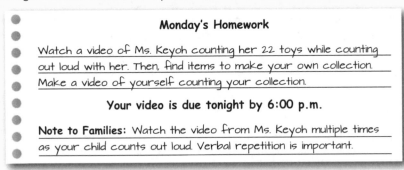

**Monday's Homework**

Watch a video of Ms. Keyoh counting her 22 toys while counting out loud with her. Then, find items to make your own collection. Make a video of yourself counting your collection.

**Your video is due tonight by 6:00 p.m.**

**Note to Families:** Watch the video from Ms. Keyoh multiple times as your child counts out loud. Verbal repetition is important.

*(Continued)*

(Continued)

> **Video Note to Families:** Counting mistakes are ok. They help us become more organized. You might notice your child counting the same item a few times because their collection is not organized. Resist the urge to organize this for them, as I need to see their rough-draft thinking. This is developmentally appropriate.

In her video, Ms. Keyoh modeled counting and the one-to-one touching of each toy as she said the number. She encouraged students to watch the video multiple times as they listened to the repetition of the counting. Ms. Keyoh wanted students to create their own videos to determine if students used one-to-one correspondence, rhythm when counting, and duplicate counting of the same item.

Tuesday morning, Ms. Keyoh watched all 22 videos and selected four students' videos to use for the next night's homework because of the way that they counted clearly and organized their toys into lines. Students in the videos did not double count or skip any items in their collection.

> ### Wednesday's Homework
>
> Watch four videos of other kids counting their collections.

By watching the four videos, students heard the repetition essential to learning at this grade. For Thursday's homework, Ms. Keyoh wanted students to analyze organizational strategies and verbalize them in a brief video.

> ### Thursday's Homework
>
> Rewatch the student videos. Choose one video to comment on. How did this student organize their collection? Make your own video to share your comment.
>
> **Your video is due tonight by 6:00 p.m.**
>
> **Note to Families:** You can use the following sentence frames to support your child: "I watched _____'s video." "I noticed that _____" or "I liked how _____ or "I saw that they _____"

Thursday evening, Ms. Keyoh viewed the comments and had enough observational information to extend the lesson for 6 of her 22 students, while incorporating additional practice for 16 of her students.

> ### Friday's Assignment
>
> **Group 1 (extension):** Create a collection of even more items (toys, beans, pasta, etc.) and create a video to show how high you can count. **Note to Families:** Children are learning how to group items efficiently. They might group items in 10s and skip count by 10s.

> **Group 2 (practice):** Create another collection of items. Practice organizing them into lines and counting them while playing the video of Ms. Keyoh counting her items. **Note to Families:** Children are learning how to organize and group items efficiently. They might line them up in rows, or make piles of 10.
>
> Make a video of your new collection. **This video is due Sunday evening by 6:00 p.m.**

While Ms. Keyoh assigned homework with specific due dates, those assignments could be done anytime before that due date. The deadlines were informative so that she could observe the progress of each of her students as they learned to count.

## ●●● REFLECT AND REIMAGINE

Homework in a math class has been a constant for generations, and there is still a purpose for homework in the remote classroom. In each of the examples shared throughout this chapter, the teacher used the homework time to complete independent assignments and then used those independent assignments to encourage collaboration and differentiation in their synchronous or asynchronous classroom settings. As you reimagine homework routines in your online class, consider the following questions:

- How can my students gain prior knowledge about a concept before we investigate it during the synchronous class time?
- How can I use homework as a checkpoint to ensure students are progressing in their learning?
- What videos or demonstrations was I planning to do in my synchronous class, and could they be watched as homework?
- What data am I using in the synchronous class and can my students collect those data rather than having the data provided to them?
- Can students create problem-solving scenarios that can be used during the synchronous class time?
- How can my students harness video and images to make mathematical meaning relevant to their world?

For more practice, tutorials, and templates, visit www.theresawills.com.

# GO AND MAKE A DIFFERENCE

## Start Slow

I am always reminded of how much my students have learned every time I begin teaching a new class—one that has never experienced or has limited experience with online learning. These students don't yet know the norms of a classroom community or how to use the microphone with confidence. They are quiet, nervous, and unsure how to jump in. I am reminded that I need to start slow. I need to ask them about themselves. I need to ask this while engaging them in the technology right from the beginning. I send them off with a scavenger hunt (Figure C.1) and I let them know that they will present their scavenger hunt to the class, but that I'm available for tech help and practice using the microphone for a time before this presentation. I model my presentation and record it for them to watch again if they need it.

## Figure C.1

## Sample All About Me Scavenger Hunt Slide

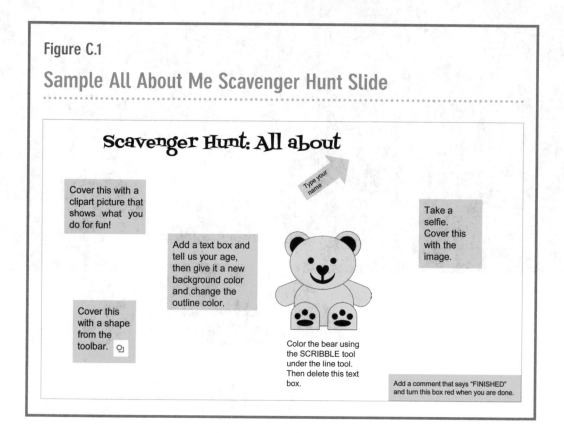

I also begin with small breakout rooms for a small amount of time. I send groups of pairs into rooms with microphones on and a script of what to say: "Hello, my name is _____. My favorite month is _____ because _____." Three minutes later, I return everyone to the main room. That's it. That's all the breakout room time they get the first class. But I know that I've got them hooked. I know they yearn for more.

Next up, we need to talk norms. I need to know what students want in terms of respect and safety in breakout rooms. I have a few non-negotiables myself. We make a class list. I include my class code of conduct, which includes protocol for consequences, just as in my face-to-face class (see Figure C.2).

Next are mistakes. I model them, and model them regularly. I model the language and tone to use when someone makes a mistake. In my first classes, I often restrict access to many of the amazing components described in this book (e.g., the ability to edit slides, write in the chat box, or use breakout rooms), and as my students show responsibility and have had time to practice

Figure C.2

## Sample Norms for Success Slide

# Norms for Success

Put away all distractions

Reduce background noise

Be prepared for class

All mics on in small groups

TEAM

Take turns and work together

Be a Ctrl-Z superhero

Don't drive while participating

Update your profile picture

*Image sources:* Tablet: robuart/iStock.com; Emoji: Iefym Turkin/iStock.com; Studying: Alina Kvaratskhelia/iStock.com; Microphone: DenPotisev/iStock.com; TEAM: Sudowoodo/iStock.com; Superhero: Tetiana Lazunova/iStock.com; Drive: OksanaOO/iStock.com; Selfie: Jesadaphorn/iStock.com

specific norms, I ease up on these restrictions. This gradual release method is a great way to show students the control that you can apply to the class, and the freedom and ownership that they can earn as they show responsibility.

## Use Technology to Keep the Lesson Student Centered

As teachers, we are often masters at creating the most beautiful lessons. We can write the script and enact a lesson worthy of a Tony award. However, this all takes time. It takes time to imagine the lesson, prepare videos and slides, enact the lesson, assess understanding, and extend and reteach. When considering all the time that we put into lessons, it can feel impossible to add one more thing. But teaching online doesn't need to be one more thing.

It can be an exchange of things. Remember the saying, "Never say anything a kid can say" (Reinhart, 2000)? This is the time to have the kids saying and doing the mathematics. If you are thinking of creating a video to show that there are 4 quarts in a gallon, 2 pints in a quart, and so on, pause and ask yourself if a kid can do it. Not convinced? Ask your students what they want to be when they grow up, and I guarantee at least one of them will say that they want to be a YouTube star. Students love to make videos, and you should harness that in your instruction. Whether it is reading the objectives out loud, summarizing the most important things to know about area and perimeter, or using the Pythagorean Theorem to determine how high they can hang a birdhouse, *they* want to be the ones to show *us*. They can use video to build classroom communities, show their mathematical thinking in a quick routine, or elaborate a rich task. They can use video in homework and assessments to give you a glimpse of their understanding. Give them the camera and the mathematical goals and they will spend more time on your video homework than on any worksheet.

## Keep the Slides Empty

It can be tempting to make a slide that offers step-by-step notes on how to solve a type of problem or a list of key content area vocabulary and their definitions. Resist the urge to do the summarization and note-taking for the students. Instead, ask them a question and let them create the summarization and notes. Give your students the space to show their thinking in multiple modalities such as images, text, and animated gifs. Let them own the slides and be the creators of the mathematics.

For younger students, consider making the summarization or note-taking slide a cloze activity where they fill in the missing words in the sentences. Or they could find images to visually support the information or definitions on the slide. The key is for them to do as much of the heavy lifting to synthesize their ideas as is developmentally appropriate.

## Make Once, Use Seven Times

Teachers are often inspired by lessons that require quite a bit of planning and creating. If you decide to create something from scratch, consider how you will use it in at least seven different ways. By purposefully planning the modifications of a tedious lesson creation, you can acknowledge the time it took to create and not feel so overwhelmed that every lesson will take that long. For example, if you make a slide with links to various virtual manipulatives to model fractions, you should use this slide as a recording space for students during group work, homework, an exit ticket, and even a game. Similarly, if you make a game (e.g., 4 in a Row), create it as a constant template and then allow the numbers on the mat to change for addition, subtraction, single digit, and double digit.

# Keep Pedagogy at the Forefront

Teaching in the remote classroom may be different from teaching in a face-to-face classroom but the pedagogy is the same. Pedagogy defines the art of teaching. It defines the way you teach math, the norms that maintain control, and the communities of learners that thrive in your classroom. Regardless of your setting, face-to-face or online, *what* you teach remains the same—it's just *how* you teach it that changes.

**Pedagogy is about teaching mathematics for understanding.** If you want students to explore a math concept, give them a problem that can be solved many different ways and with a variety of virtual manipulatives. Teach them that mathematics is about mistakes and understanding the generalizations that are found in patterns and mistakes by showcasing these on dedicated slides. *What* you teach about mathematics remains the same—it's just *how* you teach it that changes.

**Pedagogy is about teaching social norms.** If you want your remote classroom to run like a well-oiled machine, you will need to set norms, procedures, and routines early and often as your students learn how to interact. Furthermore, much like in a face-to-face classroom, students need opportunities to practice these procedures and understand the consequences of misbehaviors. *What* you teach about social norms remains the same—it's just *how* you teach it that changes.

**Pedagogy is about building communities of learners.** If you want students to collaborate, debate, laugh, and connect with each other, give them a place to share their unique personalities, hobbies, and interests. Integrate those interests into your lessons and give students a reason to connect with other students. *What you teach about classroom communities remains the same—it's just how you teach it that changes.*

## ••• REFLECT AND REIMAGINE

This book immersed you in the teaching practices through a variety of stories. Some of these stories will remind you of your classroom experiences, and some may seem difficult to replicate. I encourage you to start slow with lessons that you already know and love, use the technology to keep your lessons student-centered, and keep pedagogy at the center of all your purposeful planning and decision making. Finally, share your successes with the digital world as you become the inspiring online teacher who mentors others.

# References

Borup, J., Graham, C. R., & Velasquez, A. (2013). Technology-mediated caring: Building relationships between students and instructors in online K–12 learning environments. In M. Newberry, A. Gallant, & P. Riley (Eds.), *Emotion and school: Understanding how the hidden curriculum influences relationships, leadership, teaching, and learning* (pp. 183–202). Emerald Group. https://doi.org/10.1108/S1479-3687(2013)0000018014

Cameron, A. (2020). *Early childhood math routines empowering young minds to think.* Stenhouse.

Carpenter, T. P., Fennema, E., Franke, M. L., Levi, L., & Empson, S. B. (2014). *Children's mathematics: Cognitively guided instruction* (2nd ed.). Heinemann.

Cukurbasi, B., & Kiyici, M. (2018). High school students' views on the PBL activities supported via flipped classroom and LEGO practices. *Journal of Educational Technology & Society, 21*(2), 46–61.

Danielson, C. (2016). *Which one doesn't belong?* Stenhouse.

Davis, C., & Kriete, R. (2014). *The morning meeting book* (3rd ed.). Center for Responsive Schools.

Fennell, F., Kobett, B. M., & Wray, J. A. (2017). *The formative 5: Everyday assessment techniques for every math classroom.* Corwin.

Fletcher, G. (2020). *3-act tasks.* https://gfletchy.com/3-act-lessons/

Fosnot, C., & Dolk, M. (2002). *Young mathematicians at work: Constructing fractions, decimals, and percents.* Heinemann.

Franke, M. L., Kazemi, E., & Turrou, A. C. (2018). *Choral counting & counting collections: Transforming the preK–5 math classroom.* Stenhouse.

Huinker, D., Yeh, C., Rigelman, N., & Marshall, A. (2020, May) *Catalyzing change: An overview of the 4 key recommendations for early childhood and elementary mathematics*. Webinar series. https://www.nctm.org/change

International Society for Technology in Education (ISTE). (n.d.). Essential conditions: Equitable access. https://id.iste.org/connected/standards/essential-conditions/equitable-access

Laib, J. (2020). *Slow Reveal Graphs*. https://slowrevealgraphs.com/

Lamon, S. J. (2012). *Teaching fractions and ratios for understanding: Essential content knowledge and instructional strategies for teachers* (3rd ed.). Taylor Francis.

Lempp, J. (2017). *Math workshop: Five steps to implementing guided math, learning stations, reflection and more, Grades K–5*. Math Solutions.

Lesh, R. A., Cramer, K., Doerr, H., Post, T., & Zawojewski, J. (2003). Model development sequences. In R. A. Lesh & H. Doerr (Eds.), *Beyond constructivism: A models and modeling perspective on mathematics teaching, learning, and problem solving* (pp. 35–58). Erlbaum.

Looney, S. (2017). *Same But Different math*. https://www.samebutdifferentmath.com/

Meyer, D. (2011, May 11). *The three acts of a mathematical story*. https://blog.mrmeyer.com/2011/the-three-acts-of-a-mathematical-story/

Nash, R. (2012). *From seatwork to feetwork: Engaging students in their own learning*. Corwin.

National Council of Supervisors of Mathematics and TODOS: Mathematics for All. (2016). *Mathematics education through the lens of social justice: Acknowledgment, actions, and accountability*. Author. https://www.mathedleadership.org/docs/resources/positionpapers/NCSMPositionPaper16.pdf

National Council of Teachers of Mathematics. (2000). *Principles and standards for school mathematics*. Author.

National Council of Teachers of Mathematics. (2014a, November). *Access and equity in mathematics education: A position of the National Council of Teachers of Mathematics*. Author. https://www.nctm.org/uploadedFiles/Standards_and_Positions/Position_Statements/Access_and_Equity.pdf

National Council of Teachers of Mathematics. (2014b). *Principles to actions: Ensuring mathematical success for all*. Author.

National Council of Teachers of Mathematics. (2018). *Catalyzing change in high school mathematics: Initiating critical conversations*. Author.

National Council of Teachers of Mathematics. (2020a). *Catalyzing change in early childhood and elementary mathematics: Initiating critical conversations*. Author.

National Council of Teachers of Mathematics. (2020b). *Catalyzing change in middle school mathematics: Initiating critical conversations*. Author.

National Governors Association Center for Best Practices and Council of Chief State School Officers. (2010). *Common core state standards for mathematics*. Common Core Standards Initiative.

Parrish, S. (2014). *Number talks: Whole number computation, Grades K–5.* Math Solutions.

Polya, G. (1945). *How to solve it.* Princeton University Press.

Puentedura, R. R. (2013, May 29). SAMR: Moving from enhancement to transformation [Web log post]. Retrieved from http://www.hippasus .com/rrpweblog/archives/000095.html

Reinhart, S. C. (2000). Never say anything a kid can say! *Mathematics Teaching in the Middle School, 5*(8), 478–483.

Ritchhart, R., Church, M., & Morrison, K. (2011). *Making thinking visible: How to promote engagement, understanding and independence for all learners.* Wiley.

Shore, C. (2018). *Clothesline math: The master number sense maker.* Teacher Created Materials.

Smith, M. S., & Stein, M. K. (2011). *5 practices for orchestrating productive mathematics discussions.* Corwin.

Stadel, A. (2012). *Estimation 180.* http://www.meaningfulmathmoments .com/estimation-180.html

Suh, J. M. (2007). Tying it all together: Building mathematics proficiency for all students. *Teaching Children Mathematics, 14*(3), 163–169.

Warren, S., Wakefield, J., & Mills, L. (2013). Learning and teaching as communicative actions: Transmedia storytelling. In L. A. Wankel & P. Blessinger (Eds.), *Increasing student engagement and retention using multimedia technologies: Video annotation, multimedia applications, videoconferencing and transmedia storytelling* (Cutting-Edge Technologies in Higher Education, Vol. 6, Part F, pp. 67–94). Emerald Group. https://doi.org/10.1108/S2044-9968(2013)000006F006

Wills, T. (2015). *Use of strategy maps and virtual coaching: A case study of a teacher's development of connections in middle grades mathematics.* [Unpublished doctoral dissertation]. George Mason University.

Wills, T. (2019, November). *Analysis of mathematical representations in a synchronous online mathematics content course.* Paper presented at the 41st annual conference of the North American Chapter of the International Group for the Psychology of Mathematics Education, St. Louis, MO.

Wolf, N. B. (2015). *Modeling with mathematics: Authentic problem solving in middle school.* Heinemann.

Wormeli, R. (2005). *Summarization in any subject: 50 techniques to improve student learning.* ASCD.

Wyborney, S. (2018, September). *51 esti-mysteries.* https://stevewyborney .com/2019/09/51-esti-mysteries/

# Index

A SAGE Publishing Company

## Helping educators make the greatest impact

**CORWIN HAS ONE MISSION:** to enhance education through intentional professional learning.

We build long-term relationships with our authors, educators, clients, and associations who partner with us to develop and continuously improve the best evidence-based practices that establish and support lifelong learning.

The National Council of Teachers of Mathematics supports and advocates for the highest-quality mathematics teaching and learning for each and every student.